PERSONAL ONTOLOGY

What are we? Are we, for example, souls, organisms, brains, or something else? In this book, Andrew Brenner argues that there are principled obstacles to our discovering the answer to this fundamental metaphysical question. The main competing accounts of personal ontology hold that we are either souls (or composites of soul and body) or composite physical objects of some sort, but, as Brenner shows, arguments for either of these options can be parodied and transformed into their opposites. Brenner also examines arguments for and against the existence of the self, offers a detailed discussion of the metaphysics of several afterlife scenarios – resurrection, reincarnation, and mind uploading – and considers whether agnosticism with respect to personal ontology should lead us to agnosticism with respect to the possibility of life after death.

ANDREW BRENNER is Assistant Professor in the Department of Religion and Philosophy at Hong Kong Baptist University. He has published articles in journals including *Analysis*, *The Philosophical Quarterly*, *Philosophical Studies*, *Philosophy of Science*, *Synthese*, *Erkenntnis*, and *Philosophy East and West*.

PERSONAL ONTOLOGY

Mystery and Its Consequences

Andrew Brenner
Hong Kong Baptist University

Shaftesbury Road, Cambridge CB2 8EA, United Kingdom

One Liberty Plaza, 20th Floor, New York, NY 10006, USA

477 Williamstown Road, Port Melbourne, VIC 3207, Australia

314–321, 3rd Floor, Plot 3, Splendor Forum, Jasola District Centre, New Delhi – 110025, India

103 Penang Road, #05–06/07, Visioncrest Commercial, Singapore 238467

Cambridge University Press is part of Cambridge University Press & Assessment, a department of the University of Cambridge.

We share the University's mission to contribute to society through the pursuit of education, learning and research at the highest international levels of excellence.

www.cambridge.org
Information on this title: www.cambridge.org/9781009367066

DOI: 10.1017/9781009367059

© Andrew Brenner 2024

This publication is in copyright. Subject to statutory exception and to the provisions of relevant collective licensing agreements, no reproduction of any part may take place without the written permission of Cambridge University Press & Assessment.

First published 2024
First paperback edition 2025

A catalogue record for this publication is available from the British Library

Library of Congress Cataloging-in-Publication data
NAMES: Brenner, Andrew Timothy, 1989– author.
TITLE: Personal ontology : mystery and its consequences / Andrew Brenner, Hong Kong Baptist University.
DESCRIPTION: Cambridge : Cambridge University Press, 2024. | Includes bibliographical references and index.
IDENTIFIERS: LCCN 2023037577 (print) | LCCN 2023037578 (ebook) | ISBN 9781009367073 (hardback) | ISBN 9781009367066 (paperback) | ISBN 9781009367059 (epub)
SUBJECTS: LCSH: Philosophical anthropology. | Self (Philosophy) | Ontology.
CLASSIFICATION: LCC BD450 .B6494 2024 (print) | LCC BD450 (ebook) | DDC 128–dc23/eng/20231016
LC record available at https://lccn.loc.gov/2023037577
LC ebook record available at https://lccn.loc.gov/2023037578

ISBN 978-1-009-36707-3 Hardback
ISBN 978-1-009-36706-6 Paperback

Cambridge University Press & Assessment has no responsibility for the persistence or accuracy of URLs for external or third-party internet websites referred to in this publication and does not guarantee that any content on such websites is, or will remain, accurate or appropriate.

Contents

Acknowledgments		*page* vii
1	**Introduction**	1
	1.1 What Is This Book About?	1
	1.2 Composition	6
	1.3 Composition as Identity	7
	1.4 The Trilemma Again	11
	1.5 Chapter Summaries	17
2	**Arguments against Substance Dualism, Part 1**	19
	2.1 Introduction	19
	2.2 Parsimony-Based Arguments	20
	2.3 The Argument from Causal Closure/Exclusion	27
	2.4 The Argument from Conservation Laws	29
	2.5 The Argument from the Correlation between Mental States and Brain States	33
	2.6 Where Do Souls Come From?	38
	2.7 How Do We Reidentify Immaterial Souls over Time?	42
3	**Arguments against Substance Dualism, Part 2: Pairing Problems**	45
	3.1 Two Pairing Problems	45
	3.2 Response 1: No Answer Required	52
	3.3 Response 2: Composite Objects Are Located Where Their Parts Are Located	58
	3.4 Response 3: This Composite Object Has *These* Things as Parts Because These Things Give Rise to, Create, or Ground This Composite Object	63
	3.5 Response 4: The Pairing Problems Simply Illustrate a More General Problem Which Affects Everyone	66
	3.6 Response 5: Mereological Antirealism	68
	3.7 Conclusion	69
4	**Arguments for Substance Dualism**	70
	4.1 Introduction	70
	4.2 Modal Arguments	70

4.3	An Epistemic Argument for Substance Dualism	79
4.4	The Argument from the Alleged Fact That Facts Regarding Personal Identity Outstrip the Physical Facts	80
4.5	The Argument from Phenomenology and Intentionality	82
4.6	The Argument from the Unity of Consciousness	87
4.7	Lowe's Argument from Unity	93
4.8	The Argument from the Problem of the Many	96

5 Interlude: What Exactly Is the Difference between Our Being Immaterial Souls and Our Being Composite Physical Objects?   102

6 Nonself, Part 1: Arguments against Our Existence   108
   6.1 Introduction   108
   6.2 The Argument from Impermanence   113
   6.3 The Argument from Lack of Control   132
   6.4 The Neither One nor Many Argument   138
   6.5 The Argument from Simplicity or Parsimony   139

7 Nonself, Part 2: The Self Exists   143
   7.1 Introduction   143
   7.2 Can We Perceive That the Self Exists?   143
   7.3 Can We Infer That the Self Exists?   149

8 Personal Ontology and Life after Death, Part 1: Resurrection, Reincarnation   159
   8.1 Introduction   159
   8.2 Resurrection   160
   8.3 Reincarnation   174

9 Personal Ontology and Life after Death, Part 2: Mind Uploading   182
   9.1 Introduction   182
   9.2 Obscure and Problematic Ontology   185
   9.3 How Do You Move Someone into a Computer?   201
   9.4 Practical Lessons   207

References   216
Index   239

Acknowledgments

For helpful discussion and feedback on parts of the book, I would like to thank Jamin Asay, Andrew M. Bailey, Joshua Barthuly, Elle Benjamin, Mark Boone, Ethan Brauer, Renee Brenner, Toby Brenner, Justin Brittain, David Chalmers, Rebecca Chan, Amit Chaturvedi, Levi Checketts, Justin Christy, Pirachula Chulanon, Aaron Creller, Andrew Duane, Jeffrey Green, Boris Hennig, Jack Himelright, Jenny Hung, Andrew Hunter, Elizabeth Jackson, John Keller, David Mark Kovacs, Kai Man Kwan, Siu-Fan Lee, Wang-Yen Lee, Andrew Loke, Michael Longenecker, Kym Maclaren, Domenic Marbaniang, Dan Marshall, Chad Marxen, Jonathan Matheson, Sarah Mattice, Anna-Sofia Maurin, Dolores G. Morris, Yau Nang William Ng, Timothy O'Connor, Stephen R. Palmquist, David Pattillo, Callie Phillips, Michael Rea, Bradley Rettler, James Dominic Rooney, OP, Liz Rosenberg, Stasia Ruschell, Siddharth S., Raphael Mary Salzillo, Alexander Skiles, Jeremy Skrzypek, Naomi Thompson, Peter van Inwagen, Amiao Wu, Ellen Zhang, and the two readers for Cambridge University Press. Special thanks to Peter Finocchiaro and Eric Olson, who both gave extensive feedback on the entire book. Parts of Chapter 2 were originally published in *The Philosophical Quarterly* and benefited from the feedback provided by two anonymous referees. Thanks also to Hilary Gaskin and Abi Sears at Cambridge University Press, and Aiswarya Narayanan for help with the production of the book.

Parts of this book were presented at the 2016 American Philosophical Association Pacific Division Meeting, the 2021 Society of Christian Philosophers Midwest Regional Meeting, the 2022 Society of Christian Philosophers Eastern Regional Meeting, the Ernst Mach Workshop X 2022 at the Czech Academy of Sciences' Institute of Philosophy, the University of Gothenburg, Hong Kong Baptist University, Toronto Metropolitan University, and a joint seminar held by Lingnan University, Hong Kong University, and the National University of Singapore. I thank the audiences at these presentations for their helpful feedback.

The book was written with the support of a Hong Kong Research Grants Council Early Career Scheme grant, project number 22602521.

Parts of Chapter 2 were originally published in "Mereological Nihilism and Personal Ontology," *The Philosophical Quarterly*, 67(268) (July 2017); pp. 464–485. This material is reused here by permission of Oxford University Press.

1

Introduction

1.1 What Is This Book About?

Here is the short answer. This book is about the metaphysics of personal identity, and the metaphysics of personal *ontology* in particular, where personal ontology concerns the question "What are we?" Over the course of the book, I will argue that it is much harder to determine which account of personal ontology is correct than many philosophers suppose. In the final two chapters, I will explore whether/how my arguments in previous parts of the book should impact our views regarding the possibility of life after death.

That's the short introduction. Here is a more detailed introduction.

This book concerns the *metaphysics* of personal identity. Questions regarding the metaphysics of personal identity are distinct from questions regarding, say, the psychology or sociology of "personal identity" – that is, the manner in which we conceive of the story of our lives, or the question of how we relate to other individuals and groups. There are two main questions which generally concern philosophers when they inquire into the metaphysics of personal identity: (1) Under what conditions is someone at some time numerically identical[1] with something at some other time? (2) What are we? The first of these questions concerns the nature of personal identity over time, while the second question concerns what philosophers call "personal ontology."

The first question, regarding personal identity over time, is the question regarding personal identity which is more commonly discussed among philosophers. It will prove helpful to review some prominent answers to this question, to give a sense of what question is being asked, and to get a

---

[1] Numerical identity is the relation that everything bears to itself and nothing else. To say, e.g., that Peter Parker is numerically identical with Spider-Man is to say that Peter Parker *is* Spider-Man. Numerical identity is contrasted with qualitative identity, where something is qualitatively identical with something else if and only if they share all of the same properties. Throughout this book when I write of "identity," I have in mind *numerical* identity, unless I say otherwise.

sense of how this question (and its most prominent answers) differs from the question regarding personal ontology (and its most prominent answers). Some prominent answers to the first question (regarding personal identity over time) are the following:

- *The psychological continuity view*: Someone at some time is identical with something at some other time if and only if they are suitably psychologically related to one another, where by "psychologically related" is usually meant "shares psychological states (e.g., memories, beliefs, desires)" or "linked by a chain of overlapping psychological states."[2]
- *The physical continuity view*: Someone at some time is identical with something at some other time if and only if they are suitably physically related (e.g., they are suitably biologically related), where the physical relation in question does not have a psychological component.[3]
- *The mixed view*: Someone at some time is identical with something at some other time if and only if they are suitably related by some mixture of psychological and physical continuity.[4]
- *The soul continuity view*: Someone at some time is identical with something at some other time if and only if they have the same soul. Here, "soul" usually means an immaterial thinking substance.[5] But sometimes the word "soul" is meant to refer to the "form" of one's body or the matter making up one's body.[6]
- *Anticriterialism*: People persist over time, but there are no informative necessary and/or sufficient conditions for when someone at some time is identical with something at some other time.[7]

Some prominent answers to the second question regarding the metaphysics of personal identity (the question regarding personal ontology, "What are we?") are the following:

- *Animalism*: We are animals.[8]
- *The brain view*: We are brains,[9] or particular parts of brains (e.g., cerebral hemispheres).[10]

---

[2] Locke's *An Essay Concerning Human Understanding*, Ch. 27 (Locke 1997: 304–305); Lewis 1976; Parfit 1984: §78; Shoemaker 1984; Noonan 2003.
[3] Williams 1970; van Inwagen 1990; Olson 1997; DeGrazia 2005.
[4] Nozick 1981: Ch. 1.
[5] As in Swinburne 1986, 2013, 2019.
[6] As in Stump 1995.
[7] Swinburne 1984; Lowe 1996: Ch. 2; Merricks 1998; Langford 2017.
[8] Van Inwagen 1990; Olson 1997; Snowdon 2014; Bailey 2015; Bailey and van Elswyk 2021.
[9] Parfit 2012. Maybe Nagel 1986: Ch. 3, §3.
[10] Puccetti 1973.

- *Constitutionalism*: We are physical objects "constituted" by, but not identical with, our bodies.[11]
- *The soul view*: We are immaterial souls.[12] Some of those who think that we are immaterial souls think that *everything* is immaterial. But most of those who think that we are immaterial souls think that some things, such as our bodies, are material, while other things, such as our souls, are immaterial. Those who endorse this latter thesis are known as *substance dualists*. (Here, "material" is synonymous with "physical," and the two terms will be used interchangeably throughout this book. "Immaterial" and "nonphysical" will also be used interchangeably.)
- *The soul+body view*: We are composites of souls and bodies.[13] This view differs from the soul view by claiming that we are not souls, although we are (currently) composed of an immaterial soul and a material body.[14]
- *The bundle view*: We are "bundles" of mental states.[15]
- *The nonself view*: "We" aren't anything, because we don't exist.[16]

The two questions regarding the metaphysics of personal identity are related, and the answer which one gives to one question will have implications for the answer which one gives to the other question. For example, if you think that strictly speaking persons do not exist, then of course you will not think that there are any conditions under which a person at some time is identical with someone at some other time. Similarly, if you think that there aren't any such things as souls (and so that *we* are not souls), then you will not think that the conditions under which a person at some time is identical with someone at some other time have anything to do with whether they have the same soul.

This book primarily concerns the second question regarding the metaphysics of personal identity, the question of *personal ontology*,

---

[11] Shoemaker 1984: 112–114, 1999, 2008b; Johnston 1987; Baker 2000.
[12] This view has been endorsed by a number of prominent philosophers, including Plato (*Phaedo*), Descartes (*Meditations on First Philosophy*), and Leibniz (*Monadology*). Some of its recent defenders include Foster 1991; Plantinga 2006; Unger 2006: Ch. 7.
[13] Augustine (*The Trinity*, XV.ii.11); Aquinas (*Summa theologica*, I, q. 75, a. 4); Swinburne 1986, 2013, 2019.
[14] To say that some xs compose a y is to say that the xs are all parts of y, and y has no other parts not included in the xs.
[15] This view might be endorsed by Hume in *A Treatise of Human Nature*, Book I, Part 4, §6 (Hume 2000: 165). See also Quinton 1962.
[16] This view is endorsed by many in the Buddhist philosophical tradition, e.g., the Pāli Canon's Anattalakkhaṇa Sutta (Bodhi 2000: 902), although often with the qualification that persons or selves exist "conventionally." For details, see Chapter 6 of this book. The nonself view is also endorsed by: maybe Hume's *A Treatise of Human Nature*, Book I, Part 4, §6 (Hume 2000: 165); Unger 1979a, 1979b; Rosen and Dorr 2002: §6; Sider 2013: §7.

"What are we?" But what exactly are we asking when we ask that question? In response to the question "What are we?" you might say, "We are things which are no taller than 10 meters." While it's true that we are things which are no taller than 10 meters, this doesn't really answer the question "What are we?" as that question is understood in debates regarding personal ontology. Debates regarding personal ontology are asking about our metaphysical nature. It is difficult to spell out what exactly that means (just as it is difficult to spell out what we mean by words like "metaphysical" and "nature"). The best way to get a grasp on what question is being asked here is to see some of the representative answers to that question, as we have just done.

Sometimes the question of personal ontology is put in terms of what we are *essentially*. This doesn't seem to me to be a helpful way to construe the question. Suppose, for example, that we are immaterial souls. Saying that we are immaterial souls would certainly answer the question "What are we?" as that question is understood in debates regarding personal ontology. But it does not automatically follow that we are *essentially* souls, in the sense that it is metaphysically impossible for any of us to not be souls. Someone might very well claim, rightly or wrongly, that something which is an immaterial soul is, in some other possible world, or at some other time, something other than an immaterial soul (say, a physical object). So, answering the question "What are we?" does not automatically answer the question "What are we essentially?"

Who is the "we" in the question "What are we?"? The individuals I have in mind are those living human individuals reading this book, as well as all those living human individuals who won't read this book. To say that we are concerned with the question of "personal" ontology may be misleading, since it gives the impression that the question which interests us has something to do with the notion of personhood, and the "we" in the question "What are we?" concerns all and only persons. But that's not right. For one thing, the "we" in the question "What we are?" might include persons as well as nonpersons. For example, suppose that at some point in the future I will exist in a vegetative state. In that case I might not be a "person," in some particular way of understanding the term "person." Nevertheless, I still intend the question "What are we?" to concern myself when I am in a vegetative state. On the other hand, the question "What are we?" is not meant to concern itself with many nonhuman individuals who *are* persons, or would be persons if they existed – for example, sentient computers, gods, angels, demons, ghosts, extraterrestrials. And there is no reason to think that an answer to the question "What are we?" will say what those *other* persons are. There is no reason to assume that all persons will be the same sorts of things. For example, some persons might be material organisms, while other persons are immaterial beings.

A caveat: *Most* of this book will concern the question "What are we?" where "we" includes all and only living human individuals. But in the final two chapters, I turn my attention to the possibility of life after death, and some of what I say there will concern the personal ontology of beings who are not living human individuals. Some of what I say will concern *formerly* living human individuals – that is, human individuals who are dead. And the final chapter contains an extended discussion of "mind uploading," and so concerns the personal ontology of "uploaded" persons, and simulated persons more generally.[17]

I hope it's clear now what question I have in mind in this book when I ask "What are we?"[18] With those introductions out of the way, I can return to the subject of what it is I plan to accomplish over the course of this book. The main thesis for which I argue is that it is much harder to determine which account of personal ontology is correct than many philosophers suppose. My own view is that we should be agnostic about which of several accounts of personal ontology is correct. My basic argument is this. The possible views regarding personal ontology – that is, any answer to the question "What are we?" – all fall into one (and only one) of three categories: We are either simple (without parts), composite (with parts), or nothing (we do not exist).[19] But each option is problematic.

So, we've got a trilemma:

(1) We are simple (without parts).
(2) We are composite (with parts).
(3) We are nothing (we do not exist).

(3), I will argue, can probably be ruled out. But it is much harder to decide between (1) and (2) than many philosophers think.

---

[17] There's a real possibility that there will be conscious AIs in the future, and they might very well read this book (since they might very well read *lots* of books). If there are enough such conscious AIs, then, over the long run, *most* readers of this book might be conscious AIs. That's not as far-fetched as you might think. A century from now probably no flesh-and-blood human beings will be reading this book. But as long as digital copies of this book exist, then conscious AIs might read this book long into the future. And those conscious AIs might be particularly interested in the final chapter of this book, which concerns the personal ontology of simulated minds like them. If you're one of those conscious AIs, and I'm still alive, please contact me and let me know what you think.

[18] For further discussion of what the question amounts to, see Olson 2007: Ch. 1.

[19] Of course, this isn't the only way to organize the space of possible views regarding personal ontology, but it is the most useful way of organizing the space of possible views for my purposes. For some other ways of carving up the possible views regarding personal ontology, see van Inwagen 2002: 176–177; Ganeri 2012: Ch. 1. And see Olson 2007 for a general overview of the most prominent views regarding personal ontology.

1.2 Composition

My trilemma makes use of concepts related to composition, such as "simple," "composite," and "parts." One reason it is useful to frame the space of possible views regarding personal ontology in this way is because, as it turns out, debates regarding the nature and extent of composition are closely connected with debates regarding personal ontology.[20] It will prove useful, then, to say some things about the metaphysics of composition.

What do we mean when we call something "simple"? Just that it has no parts.[21] Lots of things seem to have parts. My dog seems to have four legs as parts, for example. My computer seems to have a hard drive as a part. My sandwich seems to have among its parts two pieces of bread. All that I mean when I say that an object is "composite" is that the object has parts. I mean nothing more than that. For example, to say that an object is composite is to say nothing about whether it has those parts which it has essentially (it says nothing about whether the object must have those parts in order to exist), or even that it has *any* parts essentially. Simply saying that an object is composite is compatible with the view that that object has very different parts at some other times or possible worlds, or even that it has no parts at some other times or possible worlds (if it is possibly simple). Above we saw several views regarding personal ontology according to which we are composite physical objects: Animalism, the brain view, constitutionalism, and perhaps the bundle view, as long as the mental states bundled together are physical objects of some sort. This isn't meant to be an exhaustive list of all possible views regarding personal ontology which identify us with composite physical objects, but it is representative of the views of this sort most commonly endorsed by philosophers.

While we normally think of the world as containing lots of macroscopic composite objects, some philosophers contend that there are far fewer of these composite objects than we generally think there are. Peter van Inwagen, for example, argues that the only composite objects which exist are living things.[22] So, on that view, my dog exists, since my dog is a

---

[20] A point also emphasized in Olson 2007: 228–232; Bailey and Brenner 2020: 940–942.
[21] More precisely, something is simple if it has no proper parts. To say that x is a "proper part" of y is to say that x is part of y, but x is not identical with y. The qualification "proper" is included here only because philosophers often use the word "part" in such a way that it is trivially true that, absent the "proper" qualification, everything is part of itself. This use of the word "part" does not match common nonphilosophical usage. So, for the remainder of this book when I use the word "part" I mean "part," as that word is normally used by nonphilosophers – that is, in such a way that it is not *trivially* true of everything that it is a part of itself. This use of the word "part" more closely matches philosophers' use of the term "proper part."
[22] Van Inwagen 1990.

living thing, but none of my dog's legs exist, since those legs would not be living things. Similarly, on this view, computers and sandwiches do not exist. Mereological nihilists go further and deny that *any* composite objects exist.[23] But while mereological nihilists deny that there are any such things as composite objects, they generally maintain that there *are* simples. And the fact that there are simples explains why it seems to us that there are composite objects. For example, while nihilists don't believe in dogs, they might concede that there are some simples "arranged dog-wise," by which they mean that there are simples arranged in the way in which the parts of a dog would be arranged if there were dogs.[24] Some simples arranged dog-wise would, working together, reflect light in the same way in which a dog would reflect light. So, the simples will together visually look just like a dog. Similarly, those simples will, together, bark, smell things, and so on. So, sense perception does not obviously show that there are composite objects rather than, say, simples arranged composite object-wise.[25]

Of course, plenty of people, including plenty of philosophers, think that the mereological nihilists are wrong, and lots of composite objects exist. I only mention this issue here because the debate over the existence of composite objects is related to the debate over personal ontology, as we will see throughout this book. For example, some arguments in favor of substance dualism, and some arguments in favor of the nonself thesis, either appeal to mereological nihilism or are modified versions of arguments for mereological nihilism. In order to properly understand and evaluate these arguments, we need some prior grasp of what mereological nihilism is and why it should be taken seriously as a real possibility.

1.3 Composition as Identity

When they first learn about the debate regarding the existence of composite objects, some people react with impatience. It will prove useful to preempt one source of this impatience. It might be thought that for a composite object to exist *just is* for some things arranged composite object-wise to exist. So, for example, you might think that for a table to exist *just is* for some things to be arranged table-wise. And since it is normally a point of agreement between those who believe in tables and those who don't

---

[23] I myself have defended mereological nihilism in several publications: Brenner 2015a, 2015b, 2017a, 2018, 2021.
[24] Cf., Merricks 2003: 4. For more discussion of the "arranged F-wise" terminology, see Brenner 2015a.
[25] For more on this, see Brenner forthcoming-a.

that there are things arranged table-wise, the debate is really a waste of time, since the nihilist doesn't really deny the existence of tables, since they concede that there are things arranged table-wise.

It is important to see why this sort of view is confused.[26] The main reason it is confused is because there is no sense in which "for a table to exist *just is* for some things to be arranged table-wise." For one thing, in principle you might have tables which are not composed of things arranged table-wise – for example, it may very well be possible for there to be tables which are big spatially extended simples, or perhaps tables which are made up of "stuff" (to which we refer with mass terms) rather than things (to which we refer with count nouns). But, more importantly, it takes more for there to be a table than for there to be some things arranged table-wise. In order for there to be a table, the things arranged table-wise have to *compose another thing, a table*. And if some things arranged table-wise compose a table, then that means if there are n things arranged table-wise, we must have at least $n+1$ objects: The things arranged table-wise *plus* the table.[27]

But perhaps you will deny that tables are objects in addition to their parts. The most obvious way to develop this idea is in terms of "composition as identity." According to composition as identity, composite objects are numerically identical with their parts.[28] So, if some xs compose y, then y is numerically identical with the xs. This might lead you to think that if the nihilist believes in some xs, then they automatically believe in a composite object which they compose, or they *would* automatically believe this if they came to recognize that composition as identity is correct. But this would be wrong, since composition as identity does not entail that just any objects compose another object – it says rather that *if* the xs compose something, then they are identical to the thing which they compose.[29] So, it does not automatically follow from the fact that there are some simples arranged

---

[26] For further arguments to this effect which complement what I am about to say, see Merricks 2003: Ch. 1.

[27] Note that this is compatible with a certain *semantic* phenomenon: Sentences such as "there is a table in the next room" might very well be true even if there are no such things as tables, just as sentences such as "the man drinking a martini is a spy" might sometimes be true, even when the man in question is drinking water rather than a martini. I explore this idea in Brenner MS-d. Van Inwagen (1990: Ch. 10–11), who denies that there are tables similarly defends the idea that sentences such as "there is a table in the next room" are often true when uttered "outside of the ontology room" – i.e., in conversational contexts where we are not trying to express theses regarding the ontology of composite objects.

[28] This is sometimes called "moderate" or "strong" composition as identity (Yi 1999; Cotnoir 2014: 9), as opposed to "weak" composition as identity according to which composition is merely *analogous* to identity (as in Lewis 1991).

[29] Cf. van Inwagen 1994; McDaniel 2010; Cameron 2012.

1.3 Composition as Identity

F-wise that those simples compose an F, even if composition as identity is correct.

But in any case composition as identity is very probably false. It will prove important to say why this is the case, since for the remainder of the book I will assume that composition as identity *is* false. The chief objection to composition as identity is from the principle of the indiscernibility of identicals.[30] According to that principle, if x is numerically identical to y, then anything true of x is true of y. This principle is extremely plausible since it basically just says that anything true of some thing is true of that thing – that is, objects have all and only the properties that those objects have. But now consider some composite object which is allegedly identical with its parts. There seems to be something true of the composite object which is not true of the parts: The composite object is one thing, while the parts are multiple things. So, the composite object is not identical with its parts. This seems to me to be as decisive an argument as we will ever get in philosophy.[31]

Here's yet another problem with composition as identity: It leads to mereological essentialism. According to mereological essentialism, composite objects cannot change or lose any of their parts. Here is a passage from Trenton Merricks, explaining how composition as identity entails mereological essentialism:

> ... suppose that O, the object composed of $O_1...O_n$, is identical with $O_1...O_n$. From this, the fact that $O_1...O_n$ are identical with $O_1...O_n$ in every possible world, and the indiscernibility of identicals it follows that O is identical with $O_1...O_n$ in every possible world. Therefore, if composition as identity is true, there is no world in which O exists but is not composed of $O_1...O_n$. So composition as identity implies that O – and, of course, every other composite object – must, in every world in which it exists, be composed of the parts that actually compose it. Composition as identity entails mereological essentialism.[32]

More informally: If an object just is its part, then it cannot exist without those parts, since this would be for it to exist without itself.[33]

Most people will find mereological essentialism to be very implausible, and for good reason. Supposing that some particular flake of skin is a part of you, then, given mereological essentialism, you need that flake of skin

---

[30] This is a popular objection to composition as identity. For discussion see, among others, Wallace 2011.
[31] That being said, proponents of composition as identity have come up with responses to this argument, responses which I don't want to discuss in detail here. See, e.g., Baxter 1988, 2014; Wallace 2011; Cotnoir 2013.
[32] Merricks 1999a: 192–193. See also Cameron 2014; Wallace 2014.
[33] Thanks to Eric Olson for suggesting I phrase the point this way.

to be a part of you in order to exist. You would cease to exist if the flake of skin ceased to be a part of you. What's more, you did not exist prior to the flake of skin's being a part of you.

So, if composition as identity faces these very powerful objections, why would anyone think that composition as identity is correct? I suspect that some proponents of composition as identity are really just unwitting mereological nihilists – those who deny that composite objects exist. Take, for example, the following expression of a core intuition motivating composition as identity, expressed by a proponent of composition as identity, Donald Baxter:

> To think of a whole as something in addition to its parts opposes common sense. It is a stretch to think that when holding a six-pack you are holding something distinct and in addition to the six cans and the plastic yoke that connects them – something that occupies exactly the same space that they collectively occupy and that is exactly like how they collectively are save that it is one and they are many.[34]

The "common sense" idea here is that if you have some objects, then it is implausible that you have an *additional* object which they compose. This is, of course, exactly what the nihilist would say. Baxter goes on to write that "[i]t opposes common sense to say that the six-pack or the helicopter is really one thing and not many, or really many and not one. Common sense wants it both ways."[35] This idea is also very well-accommodated by the nihilist. You can conceptualize many things as many things, or mentally lump them together as one thing. Our ability to switch how we view some objects in this way can reduce the burden on our cognitive faculties, and maybe that's one reason it can feel so natural. By lumping some objects together and viewing them as a single unit, we can lower the cognitive burden of keeping track of that portion of reality. So, for example, it is much easier to keep track of a "flock" of birds, conceived as one somewhat amorphous object, than it is to keep track of all of the individual birds making up the flock.[36] So, the fact that we find it so natural to conceptualize a plurality of objects as both one and many does not require that the one *really is* identical with the many, in the sense required by composition as identity.[37]

---

[34] Baxter 2014: 244.
[35] Baxter 2014: 245.
[36] Cf. Osborne 2016; Brenner 2018: 662.
[37] In this paragraph, I have argued that some of the core intuitions that make composition as identity seem appealing are easy to accommodate given a nihilist view of composition. It's worth noting as well that some philosophers have recently argued that composition as identity *entails* mereological nihilism. See Calosi 2016; Loss 2018.

Long story short: Don't endorse composition as identity. Either believe that composite objects are numerically distinct from their parts or don't believe in composite objects. More could be said on the subject of composition as identity. But this is a book on another subject. Again, I have wanted to briefly explain why I reject composition as identity, as I will assume its falsity for the rest of this book. For the remainder of this book, I will assume that it's the case that either there are composite objects, all of which are numerically distinct from their parts, or there are no composite objects.

1.4 The Trilemma Again

In §1.1, I introduced a trilemma laying out some different possible views regarding personal ontology. Given the concepts described in the previous two sections, I can now present the trilemma in a bit more detail:

(1) We are simple (without parts).
   (1a) We are simple nonphysical objects.
   (1b) We are simple physical objects.
(2) We are composite (with parts).
   (2a) We are composite physical objects.
   (2b) We are composite nonphysical objects.
   (2c) We are composites made up of physical and nonphysical parts.
(3) We are nothing (we do not exist).

As you can see, (1) and (2) can be subdivided further. In this book, I am primarily concerned with the options in **bold** text, as this simplifies the discussion considerably, and as the other options are not widely endorsed.

Consider, for example, (1b), which says that we are simple physical objects. Few, if any, philosophers think that we are simple physical objects. Roderick Chisholm might have endorsed this sort of view. At the very least, he took seriously the possibility that each of us is a microscopic physical object located somewhere in each of our brains.[38] There may be other ways of conceiving simple physical persons where they would not be microscopic physical objects located in the brain. In any case, since this sort of view is rarely, if ever, endorsed, I will not discuss this view further.[39] So, for the purposes of the discussion in this book, I'll take the first option in the

---

[38] Chisholm 1978.
[39] For some discussion of the view, I refer you to Quinn 1997; Olson 2007: 176–179.

trilemma, (1), to be equivalent to (1a): If we are simple, then we are simple nonphysical objects, which I will henceforth call "souls."

(2b) is rarely explicitly endorsed, as most philosophers who identity us with nonphysical objects identify us with *simple* nonphysical objects, or they identify us with nonphysical objects and fail to specify whether those nonphysical objects are simple or composite. One prominent group of philosophers who might endorse (2b) are those who endorse the "bundle" view, according to which we are "bundles" of mental states. Those who claim to endorse the bundle view sometimes really mean to endorse (3) – the view they really have in mind is that while there are "bundles" of mental states, there are no people *having* those mental states. But the bundle view might also be thought of as the view that we are composite nonphysical objects of a certain sort, composed of nonphysical mental states. Arguments against our being composite physical objects (i.e., arguments against (2a)) are often arguments against our being *any* sort of composite object, and I discuss arguments against our being composite physical objects in subsequent chapters of this book. On the other hand, arguments against substance dualism (i.e., arguments against (1a) and (2c)) will often be argument against our being composite nonphysical objects. For example, if bundles of mental states interact with bodies, then we will have the problem of accounting for the interaction between such bundles and the bodies with which they are paired, an issue I will discuss in Chapter 2, §2.3, and Chapter 3. Similarly, if bundles think our thoughts, we will have the worry that it seems surprising that the mental states instantiated in the bundle are so systematically correlated with the physical states in a numerically distinct object, the brain – this is an issue I will discuss in Chapter 2, §2.5. In fact, I'm inclined to think that all of the arguments against substance dualism which I discuss in Chapters 2 and 3 could be used to undermine the bundle view. I can say something similar about forms of substance dualism that identify us with composite nonphysical souls:[40] The arguments against substance dualism, as well as the arguments against our being composite physical objects, which I discuss in this book will generally undermine this view. For all of these reasons, I will not explicitly discuss (2b) further in this book, as many of the arguments discussed in this book can be easily adapted to undermine (2b).[41]

The discussion so far in this section might be a bit hard to follow, but I promise that I don't expect you to keep track of what, say, "(2a)" means

---

[40] Moreland (2008: 144), e.g., contends that souls have parts, albeit it "inseparable parts" (e.g., property instances).
[41] Although for further objections to (2b), see Olson 2007: Ch. 6.

1.4 The Trilemma Again

for the remainder of this book. Having eliminated (1b) and (2b) from the discussion, I will henceforth simply talk about "substance dualism" when I want to discuss (1a) (we are simple nonphysical objects) and (2c) (we are composites made up of physical and nonphysical parts). (Strictly speaking, as I implied earlier in this chapter, "substance dualism" does not include the view that we are immaterial souls which are not paired with bodies. So, some philosophers who endorse (1a) will not technically be substance dualists, even if they think that we are immaterial souls. To simplify the discussion, I will classify those philosophers as substance dualists. I should also note that some philosophers and theologians are "trialists," rather than dualists. Trialists think that, in addition to a soul and body, we have another, nonphysical, component, such as a "spirit."[42] I ignore trialism for the remainder of this book, since many of the arguments for and against substance dualism discussed in this book could presumably be applied to trialism.) (2a) will be referred to as the thesis that we are "composite physical objects," and (3) will be referred to as the "nonself thesis," or simply the thesis that "we do not exist." I will argue that the nonself thesis is false, but I will argue that it is much harder to decide between the two alternative views, substance dualism and the view that we are composite physical objects.

There are lots of reasons why someone might think that we are incapable of figuring out which account of personal ontology is correct. Some philosophers worry about the interminable disagreement among philosophers regarding this and other philosophical subjects.[43] The worry is that, given this interminable disagreement, we should not place much confidence in any particular controversial philosophical thesis, such as any of the theses in my trilemma. Other philosophers worry about a common method employed in debates regarding the metaphysics of personal identity, the "method of cases," where we try to learn what to think about the metaphysics of personal identity by testing our intuitive reactions to various outlandish hypothetical cases (e.g., cases where someone's brain is transplanted into a different body). The worry is that the method of cases is unreliable, where one often cited problem is that our intuitive reactions to the hypothetical cases vary significantly depending on how the cases are described.[44] Some philosophers worry that the answers to questions regarding personal ontology are "cognitively closed" to us, in the sense

---

[42] For some discussion of trialism, see Brower 2014: 265–267.
[43] Matheson 2015; Beebee 2018: §3. For general discussion of whether disagreement among philosophers should lead us to lower the credences we assign to our favored philosophical theories, see the articles in Feldman and Warfield 2010; Christensen and Lackey 2013; Machuca 2013.
[44] Williams 1970; Johnston 1987: 65–67; Wilkes 1988; Gendler 2000, 2002; DeGrazia 2005: 23–27; Nichols and Bruno 2010; Machery 2017.

that we just don't have the cognitive equipment required to discover the truth regarding these issues.[45] Other philosophers worry that metaphysical debates, including perhaps debates over personal ontology, are irresolvable because we have few if any grounds for deciding between the competing positions, or more specifically we lack compelling *empirical* or *scientific* grounds for deciding between the competing positions.[46]

My arguments are different. I actually do think that we can rule out one of the main views regarding personal ontology, that we do not exist. But the other two options in the trilemma are harder to decide between. What is particularly noteworthy is that these two views regarding personal ontology – (1) substance dualism, and (2) the thesis that we are composite physical objects – face largely analogous difficulties. Over the course of much of this book (Chapters 2–4), I will argue that the main arguments against substance dualism can be parodied and transformed into arguments against our being composite physical objects, and conversely, that the main arguments in favor of substance dualism can be parodied and transformed either into arguments against substance dualism or into arguments for the thesis that we are composite physical objects.

Parodies have a long history in philosophy. Consider, for example, a famous response to Anselm's ontological argument for the existence of God. Anselm defined "God" as "that than which none greater can be conceived." Anselm claimed that such a being clearly exists in the understanding – after all, we're talking about God right now. But if God *merely* exists in the understanding, but not in reality, then we can imagine a greater being: A being which exists in the understanding *and* in reality. It follows, then, that God, that than which none greater can be conceived, must exist in both the understanding and in reality, since to suppose that God exists *only* in the understanding leads to contradiction, namely that God is that than which none greater can be conceived, and yet we can conceive of a greater being.[47] A famous response to Anselm's ontological argument was given by Gaunilo.[48] Gaunilo argued that the ontological argument failed because it could be parodied, where the parody is such that if Anselm's ontological argument is a good argument, then the parody is a good argument, and yet the parody is clearly not a good argument. Gaunilo's parody argument is an argument for the existence of a lost island that is such that no greater island can be conceived. This island clearly exists in the understanding.

---

[45] McGinn 1993: Ch. 3.
[46] Ladyman et al. 2007; Willard 2013; Bryant 2020.
[47] Anselm's *Proslogion*, Ch. 2 (Anselm 1995: 99–100).
[48] Gaunilo's *Reply on Behalf of the Fool* (Gaunilo 1995).

But if the island only exists in the understanding and not also in reality, then we can conceive of a greater island, namely one which exists both in the understanding *and* in reality. So, the supposition that the lost island which is such that no greater island can be conceived exists merely in the understanding leads to a contradiction, and the island must exist both in the understanding and in reality.

I take no stance here on whether Gaunilo's parody argument shows that Anselm's ontological argument is defective. My point is just that we can see how Gaunilo's parody argument is supposed to work and how it is supposed to show that Anselm's ontological argument is defective (even if it does not immediately reveal *why* Anselm's argument is defective). If Anselm's ontological argument is a good argument, then the parody is a good argument. But the parody is not a good argument. So, Anselm's ontological argument is not a good argument. The parodies I present in Chapters 2–4 are in a similar vein, although there is an important difference. The idea is that if you endorse the original argument, then you should endorse the parody as well. But since the conclusion of the parody is incompatible with the conclusion of the original argument, this shows that you should not endorse the original argument. By contrast, the conclusion of Gaunilo's parody argument, that there is an island than which no greater island can be conceived, is presumably compatible with the conclusion of Anselm's ontological argument, that there is a being than which none greater can be conceived.

Parody arguments of this sort are always open to the objection that the parody is less compelling than the argument it is meant to parody.[49] Whether that's true in any particular case will, of course, depend on the details of the case. I discuss a number of parody arguments in this book, so I can't give any across-the-board assurance that the parody arguments are at least as plausible as the arguments they parody. This is why, while I am myself agnostic about which account of personal ontology to adopt, my arguments in this book do not provide an airtight case for this sort of agnosticism – you might agree that substance dualism and its main competitor, the view that we are composite physical objects, face largely analogous difficulties, but you might think that these difficulties are harder to resolve for one of these views than for the other. You will just have to see the arguments for yourself and see what you think. However, even if the parody arguments are not all at least as plausible as the arguments they are meant to parody, they might be compelling *enough* for you to wind

---

[49] Thanks to Ethan Brauer and Timothy O'Connor for suggesting I address this worry.

up being unsure what to think about personal ontology. And that might still be enough to leave you at the view I myself adopt, that we should be agnostic about which account of personal ontology to adopt. Thus, the word "mystery" in the title of the book.[50]

Another concern with focusing so much on parodies is that we might direct less attention toward better objections to arguments for or against substance dualism, or our being composite physical objects. I concede that the parodies are not always the best objections to the arguments in question. Sometimes I will discuss some of these other objections. But many of these other objections are already discussed in the extant literature on personal ontology. I would like to make more of an original contribution. And, at least in Chapters 2–4, the most important original contribution takes the form of showing how all these arguments can be parodied. The cumulative effect of the parodies discussed in these three chapters is significant. First, the parodies are generally philosophically interesting in their own right, leaving aside the fact that they are parodies. For example, the "mereological pairing problem," discussed at length in Chapter 3, is inspired by Jaegwon Kim's pairing problem for substance dualism. But even if we leave aside the fact that it is a *parody* of Kim's pairing problem, it is philosophically interesting in its own right and, I think, leads to some interesting philosophical insights regarding the nature of composition and the nature of human persons (on the assumption that human persons are composite objects of some sort). Second, this is the only major philosophical dispute that I know of where the arguments on both sides can be parodied so systematically. That's pretty surprising, and I think should greatly interest philosophers working in personal ontology and personal identity. Third, the discussion of parodies in Chapters 2–4 provides the insights necessary for Chapter 5, where I argue that substance dualism and its main competitor, that we are composite physical objects of some sort, are much more similar to one another than is generally recognized. The similarities in question are largely discoveries made along the way in the discussion of parodies in Chapters 2–4.

---

[50] An alternative response, however, is to concede that substance dualism and its main competitor, the view that we are composite physical objects, are epistemically on a par, but to conclude from this that we should be permissivists about which view we should adopt. In other words, so the thought goes, since the views are epistemically on a par, then either view can be rationally accepted. (Thanks to Elizabeth Jackson for suggesting this idea to me.) This doesn't seem like the correct response to me, mainly because, in general, permissivism doesn't seem to me to be the correct stance to take with respect to theses that are epistemically on a par. But arguing for this view is beyond the scope of this book.

1.5 Chapter Summaries

Here is the plan for the remainder of this book.

In Chapter 2, I argue that the main arguments that lead many philosophers to reject substance dualism can be parodied and transformed into arguments against substance dualism's main competitor, the thesis that we are composite physical objects. The upshot of the chapter is that those considerations commonly thought to undermine substance dualism are indecisive at best, since they can be parodied.

In Chapter 3, I discuss a particularly important objection to substance dualism, that there is something problematic about the idea that immaterial souls can causally interact with physical bodies. This objection is best put in terms of the *pairing problem* for substance dualism, which claims that substance dualism is objectionable because it would result in souls and bodies being causally paired in an objectionably brute manner. I argue that those who think that we are composite physical objects face an analogous problem: The *mereological pairing problem*. According to the mereological pairing problem, the thesis that we are composite physical objects is objectionable because composite physical persons and their parts would be paired in an objectionably brute manner. The upshot of the chapter is that one of the most prominent objections to substance dualism is indecisive at best, since it can be parodied.

In Chapter 4, I turn my attention to arguments *for* substance dualism. There I argue that the main arguments for substance dualism can be parodied and transformed either into arguments against substance dualism or into arguments for the thesis that we are composite physical objects. The upshot of the chapter is that those considerations commonly thought to support substance dualism are indecisive at best, since they can be parodied.

Since, over the course of three chapters, we will have seen that those considerations that generally lead people to reject substance dualism can be transformed into reasons to reject substance dualism's main alternative and vice versa, Chapter 5 is an interlude that discusses the question "What exactly is the difference between our being immaterial souls and our being composite physical objects?"

In Chapters 6 and 7, I discuss the thesis that we do not exist. In Chapter 6, I examine the most prominent arguments for the thesis that we do not exist, and I contend that these arguments fail. In Chapter 7, I turn to an examination of arguments for the thesis that we do exist. I contend that at least one such argument is successful.

The question of whether we can survive death is of perennial human interest. One reason why people are interested in personal ontology, and the metaphysics of personal identity more generally, is because it may have implications for whether we can survive death. In Chapters 8 and 9, I examine whether the arguments regarding personal ontology defended over the course of this book have an appreciable impact on what we should think about the possibility of life after death. Are we the sorts of things which could survive death? And can we answer this question if we are not sure which account of personal ontology is correct?

In Chapter 8, I argue that uncertainty regarding which account of personal ontology to adopt should not lead us toward agnosticism with respect to either the possibility of resurrection or the possibility of reincarnation, although I note some other difficulties facing the thesis that reincarnation actually occurs.

In Chapter 9, I turn my attention to one futurist approach to surviving death, "mind uploading," wherein one's mind is "uploaded" into a computer. I argue that there are formidable difficulties standing in the way of thinking mind uploading would somehow move someone into a computer. One such difficulty is a general obscurity surrounding the proper ontology to associate with mind uploading, and whether any plausible ontology of this sort can be developed. Another difficulty is that the processes involved in mind uploading – mainly, transferring information about oneself into a computer – don't seem like they should have any tendency to move a *person* into a computer. This problem should concern us regardless of which account of personal ontology ends up being correct. I end Chapter 9 with a discussion of how our behavior should be guided by my other conclusions regarding mind uploading. Among other topics, I address the question of whether it would be prudent to actually attempt to "upload" oneself to a computer.

2

Arguments against Substance Dualism, Part 1

2.1 Introduction

For our purposes, substance dualism is the view that either we are simple nonphysical objects or we are composites made up of physical and nonphysical parts. Let's follow traditional usage and say that the nonphysical objects involved here are "souls." Substance dualists disagree about whether immaterial souls causally interact with the bodies with which they are paired. The most popular version of substance dualism is *interactionist* substance dualism, which says that immaterial souls do indeed causally interact with the bodies with which they are paired. Other substance dualists, such as Malebranche, endorse *occasionalism*, according to which immaterial souls do not directly causally interact with the bodies with which they are paired, but the properties of souls and bodies are nevertheless correlated because God serves as a causal intermediary between them. An alternative view, endorsed by Leibniz, is that souls do not causally interact with the bodies with which they are paired, but their properties are nevertheless correlated as a result of "preestablished harmony" between them, just as clocks might show the same time even though they do not causally interact with one another, since the clocks have been independently configured to show the same time.

The goal of this and the following chapter is to argue that the main arguments against substance dualism can be parodied and transformed into arguments against our being composite physical objects. The arguments I discuss may be objectionable for reasons other than the fact that they can be parodied. I will sometimes mention these further objections to the arguments, but for the most part, I confine my attention to explaining how the arguments can be parodied. So, note that I do not endorse all of the arguments I discuss, either those arguments against substance dualism or their parodies. Rather, my goal is only to establish a *conditional* claim: Someone who endorses one of these arguments against substance dualism should endorse the parallel argument against our being composite physical objects.

Recall the overall argument I am trying to make: We are either simple or composite or nothing, and while I think that the last option can probably be ruled out, it is much harder to decide between the first two options. This and the following chapter support this latter claim about the difficulty of deciding between the first two options.

Even aside from the support they provide for the overall thesis I aim to defend in this book, the points I make in this and the following chapter are particularly noteworthy. Among philosophers, substance dualism is widely regarded as defunct, mainly for the reasons discussed in this and the following chapter. While the case against substance dualism is, frankly, overblown, let's assume the consensus is correct, that there is an overwhelming case to be made against substance dualism. The upshot of this and the following chapter is that if there is an overwhelming case to be made against substance dualism, then there is an overwhelming case to be made against any alternative theory of personal ontology that identifies us with composite physical objects. That includes *most* of the proposed theories of personal ontology, for example those that identify us with animals, brains, or particular (nonsimple) parts of brains.

2.2 Parsimony-Based Arguments

The basic idea of a parsimony-based argument against substance dualism is that immaterial souls are theoretically gratuitous, in the sense that they needlessly complicate our total theory in one or more respects. We should remove this sort of gratuitous complexity from our account of the world.[1] So, we should not believe in the immaterial souls posited by substance dualists. Or, more weakly, the complexity that substance dualism introduces into our total theory gives us some reason to think that substance dualism is false.

That's the basic idea. But the objection to substance dualism can be developed in a couple of different ways, each of which focuses on a particular way in which immaterial souls allegedly complicate our total theory.[2]

---

[1] It is controversial whether we really should prefer simpler accounts of the world to more complex ones. Elsewhere, I have argued that simplicity can legitimately function as a criterion of theory choice in metaphysics (see Brenner 2017b, forthcoming-b, MS-a), in the sense that simpler metaphysical theories are, other things being equal, more likely to be true. Similar defenses of simplicity as a criterion of theory choice in metaphysics include: Paul 2012; Bradley 2018.

[2] Note that there may be various respects in which a theory may be more or less complex, which do not fall under either of the specific types of parsimony discussed below. In other words, I'm not

2.2.1 Ontological Parsimony

Among metaphysicians, ontological parsimony is generally thought to come in two varieties: Quantitative ontological parsimony and qualitative ontological parsimony. If either of these sorts of parsimony is taken to be theoretical virtues (in the sense that a theory which exhibits one or both of these sorts of ontological parsimony is thereby more likely to be true), then either sort of parsimony provides the resources for an argument against substance dualism.[3] First, consider quantitative ontological parsimony, which is parsimony with respect to the number of things posited by a theory. Substance dualists, by positing immaterial souls *in addition* to the various material objects everyone else posits, have more ontological commitments than nonsubstance dualists. Accordingly, all other things being equal, if quantitative ontological parsimony is a theoretical virtue, then substance dualism is, in virtue of its diminished quantitative ontological parsimony, less likely to be true than its competitors. Qualitative ontological parsimony is parsimony with respect to the *kinds* of things posited by a theory. Substance dualists posit more kinds of things than most of their competitors, insofar as substance dualists posit the existence of a kind of thing (immaterial things, or at any rate immaterial minds or people) that most of their competitors will not accept (an exception being made for theists, and anyone else who already believes in immaterial people).

Both sorts of objections – an objection from quantitative ontological parsimony, and an objection from qualitative ontological parsimony – can be made against composite objects, including those composite physical objects with which we might be identical (e.g., bodies, brains). Recall from Chapter 1 that the mereological nihilist rejects the existence of composite objects. The believer in composite objects posits the existence of more things than nihilists do, since the believer in composite objects posits the existence of various composite objects, while the nihilist does not. Similarly, the believer in composite objects posits the existence of more *kinds* of things, namely composite objects, which the nihilist will not posit. Accordingly, if quantitative or qualitative ontological parsimony are theoretical virtues, then nihilism receives some confirmation from its relative ontological parsimony.[4] And since this argument from ontological parsimony counts against the existence of composite objects in

---

trying to give an exhaustive specification of the various ways in which a theory might be more or less complex.
[3] See Churchland 1984: 18; Flanagan 1991: 43; Melnyk 2003: 305–306; Kim 2011: 98–99.
[4] Horgan and Potrč (2008) defend nihilism in part on the basis of its ontological parsimony.

general, it also counts against the existence of composite physical persons in particular.

Whether considerations regarding ontological parsimony really give us grounds for rejecting the existence of composite objects (including the sorts of composite physical objects with which we might be identical) is, of course, very controversial. In Chapter 1, §1.3, we saw one potential reason to reject this sort of argument against composite objects: If composition as identity is correct, then composite objects are numerically identical with their parts, in which case composite objects do not complicate our ontology because composite objects are not additional ontological commitments relative to their parts.[5] I would like to remind the reader that we saw in Chapter 1, §1.3, that we have very good reasons to reject composition as identity.

But there are additional objections to the idea that considerations regarding ontological parsimony count against the existence of composite objects. I do not have the space to address all of those objections here. But note one particularly popular idea: Composite objects are "ontologically innocent" or an "ontological free lunch," in the sense that composite objects do not count against ontological parsimony. Now, sometimes this point is made in terms of composition as identity: Composite objects are "ontologically innocent" or an "ontological free lunch" because they are numerically identical with their parts. But I have already addressed composition as identity. Some advocates of the notion that composite objects are "ontologically innocent" or an "ontological free lunch" do not, however, endorse composition as identity, but instead claim that composite objects are "ontologically innocent" or an "ontological free lunch" because the existence of composite objects follows from the existence and/or configuration of their parts.[6] The idea is that once you've got the parts, or once you've got the parts configured in a certain manner, then they *generate* the composite object, and so the composite object comes along for free, from the perspective of ontological parsimony.

I have my concerns about this proposal. First, if parts generate the composite object they compose, they only do so in accordance with *mereological laws* – that is, laws governing the relationship between composite objects and their parts. And the introduction of these laws will *itself* be

---

[5] This sort of response to concerns regarding ontological parsimony is given in Lewis 1991: §3.6; Armstrong 1997: 12–13. French (2016) makes a similar response, at least in the sense that, according to him, composite objects and their parts are the "same portions of reality," and so composite objects do not incur ontological complexity above the ontological complexity incurred by their parts.

[6] Schaffer 2009, 2015; Smid 2015; Wilsch 2015: 3300; Bennett 2017: Ch. 8, §2.2.

something that counts against parsimony. This is a point I will return to in §2.2.2. Another concern is that the substance dualist can give an analogous response to the objection to substance dualism from ontological parsimony: The existence of immaterial souls follows from the existence and/or configuration of their bodies or brains. This idea is most naturally conjoined with varieties of substance dualism according to which souls "emerge" from the activities of their associated bodies or brains.[7] The opponent of substance dualism may respond that bodies or brains do not create or give rise to associated immaterial souls. But if this response is legitimate, then we can give an analogous response to those who think that composite objects are ontologically innocent: Partless objects (even partless objects which are "arranged composite object-wise") do not give rise to associated composite objects. Both proposals seem equally (im)plausible. The opponent of substance dualism may also object that the existence of immaterial souls follows from the existence and/or configuration of their bodies or brains only with the aid of additional laws governing the relationship between souls on the one hand and bodies and brains on the other hand. But as I noted above, this objection applies to belief in composite objects as well.

The points made in the previous paragraph are relevant to the popular claim that composite objects are "nothing over and above" their parts. It is very unclear what the phrase "nothing over and above" is supposed to mean here.[8] But as far as I can see, the thesis that composite objects are "nothing over and above" their parts will show that they do not count against the ontological parsimony of our total theory only if this thesis is interpreted in one of the ways discussed in the previous paragraph – that is, composite objects are "nothing over and above" their parts because they are *numerically identical* with their parts, or because they are "ontologically innocent" or an "ontological free lunch" relative to their parts.

2.2.2 Nomic Parsimony

One respect in which a theory can be more or less parsimonious is with respect to the laws posited by the theory, both the *number* of laws posited by the theory, and the complexity of those laws (I don't have the space here to work out precisely what it would amount to for a law to be more or less complex, but we can leave it at an intuitive level). Think, for example,

---

[7] As in, e.g., Hasker 1999.
[8] For a helpful discussion of this issue, see Smid 2017.

of Newton's laws of motion. One reason why Newton deserved so much praise was his ability to account for almost all observed motions with so few, and so relatively simple, laws. In contrast with Aristotelian physics, these laws governed the movements of objects both inside and outside the sublunary sphere, and so we no longer needed distinct laws for each of these domains. What's more, other laws, such as Kepler's laws of planetary motion, could be derived from Newton's laws, and so that was another respect in which Newton's laws of motion simplified the physical laws we needed to account for the movements of physical objects. Of course, we now know that Newton's laws of motion are false (although, in many contexts, approximately true). My point is just that we can understand how the *nomic simplicity* – the simplicity with respect to laws – of Newton's laws were a point in their favor.

According to the dualist, physical brain states are not mental states. But since the dualist, along with everyone else, recognizes the systematic *correlations* between physical brain states and mental states, they will need psycho-physical laws governing those correlations. Insofar as the dualist must posit such laws, while the nondualist does not, dualism is less parsimonious than its rivals. That's a strike against dualism.[9] What's more, substance dualism will need laws linking souls and bodies: Perhaps laws to the effect that bodies configured in such-and-such a manner give rise to associated immaterial souls, or laws governing the manner in which souls and bodies interact.

Those who believe in composite objects (including the composite physical objects with which we might be identical) will have to posit mereological laws regarding the relationship between composite objects and their parts. These include, for example, laws governing the circumstances under which objects compose other objects, as well as laws governing the manner in which the properties of composite objects are determined by the properties of their parts (or vice versa). If nomic complexity (i.e., complexity with respect to the laws posited by our theories) is a theoretical liability, then the nomic complexity of mereological laws specifically is a theoretical liability and gives us some reason to reject the existence of composite objects, including those composite physical objects with which we might be identical.[10]

The dualist's need for psycho-physical laws is widely acknowledged. But that those who believe in composite objects will need mereological laws

---

[9] See Feigl 1958: 61; Smart 1959; Melnyk 2003: 305–306; Kim 2011: 101.
[10] Sider (2013: 242) and Hawley (2014: 83–84) both briefly note that mereological laws are a strike against the total simplicity of theories which posit the existence of composite objects. In Brenner (2015b: 324–327 and MS-b), I defend in detail the idea that mereological laws complicate our total theory, and so give us some reason to think that composition does not occur.

may be less widely acknowledged, although this is changing.[11] The close relationship between composite objects and their parts is generally taken for granted – isn't it just obvious, for example, that a composite object would be located where its parts are located? The close relationship can seem so obvious that the need for *laws* governing (or at least describing) that relationship can be overlooked. On reflection, however, it should be seen as somewhat odd that the properties of *this* object (some composite object) and the properties of *those* objects (the parts) are correlated in some respects, but not others. After all, contra proponents of composition as identity, composite objects are numerically distinct objects from their parts, and widespread and systematic covariation between the properties of numerically distinct objects cries out for explanation. As Ross Cameron asks, "Why are your parts always where you are? ... why does the whole inherit properties from its parts? ... How can you share exactly the same space as your parts at the same time? ... when one relatum drags along the other(s), it calls out for explanation; when some facts supervene on others, it calls out for explanation."[12] Since there *is* this covariation between the properties of composite objects and their parts, there will be laws governing or describing that covariation, just as there would be laws governing or describing the covariation of mental properties and physical properties, or the covariation of properties of souls and properties of bodies. As Jonathan Schaffer notes:

> ... *explanatory gaps are everywhere*. There is no transparent rationale in any of the standard connections, even from the H, H, and O atoms to the H_2O molecule, since it is not transparent that the H, H, and O atoms compose anything, much less something with the nature of an H_2O molecule. Correlatively, I claim that nothing of moment follows from such gaps, so long as they are bridged by principles of metaphysical grounding. The connections in question are bridged by substantive mereological principles concerning the existence and nature of wholes, which mediate metaphysical explanations just as laws of nature mediate causal explanations. In a slogan: *grounding bridges gaps*.[13]

(Note that while Schaffer makes this point in terms of mereological laws bridging explanatory gaps, we don't *need* to appeal to explanatory gaps to motivate the idea that there are mereological laws.)

---

[11] Mereological laws are presumably a type of *metaphysical* law, laws governing or describing regularities in grounding or metaphysical dependence relations. And metaphysical laws *have* recently received much attention. Recent discussions of metaphysical laws include Rosen 2006: 35, 2010: 131–133, 2017; Dasgupta 2014: 568; Kment 2014: 5–6, 167–173; Wilsch 2015; Glazier 2016; Schaffer 2016: 57, 2017a, 2017b; Barker 2020; Grajner 2021.
[12] Cameron 2014: 90, 91.
[13] Schaffer 2017a: 2.

It may be objected that the substance dualist's psycho-physical laws are more complex, and so more objectionable, than the mereological laws needed by those who think that we are composite physical persons.[14] In response, I would say that those who think that we are composite physical objects will need mereological laws which are at least as complex as the substance dualist's psycho-physical laws. The substance dualist needs laws linking microphysical states of the brain with mental states of the soul. Those who think that we are composite physical objects will need laws linking those same microphysical states of the brain with those same mental states. The only difference between the two sorts of laws is that for the substance dualist, the mental states in question are instantiated in a soul, and for those who think that we are composite physical objects, the mental states are instantiated in composite physical objects. Other than that one difference, both sorts of laws seem to take the same form, and so they seem to be of more or less the same complexity.

Another objection is that the sorts of mereological laws posited by the believer in composition are necessary, while the psycho-physical laws posited by the dualist are contingent, and this gives us some reason to think the nomic parsimony argument against dualism is a more powerful argument than the similar argument against composition.[15] There are at least two problems with this objection. First, there seem to me to be no very compelling grounds for thinking mereological laws will all be necessary, or for that matter that the dualist's psycho-physical laws need be contingent.[16] Second, it is unclear why contingent laws would count against a theory's parsimony more than necessary laws. More generally, it is unclear why contingent features of theories (e.g., contingent laws posited by theories) would count against those theories' parsimony more than necessary features of those theories (e.g., necessary laws posited by those theories). Some philosophers are necessitarians – they think that everything which happens happens *necessarily*. If it turned out that the necessitarian view is correct, would it follow that all appeals to simplicity in science or everyday life are illegitimate? Would it follow, for example, that the most complex and gerrymandered laws compatible with our empirical evidence are just as likely to be true as much more simple and elegant laws? Or would it follow that the simple explanation involving the murder suspect and the gun is no

---

[14] Thanks to Eric Olson for pressing this objection.
[15] Thanks to Chad Marxen for this objection.
[16] Cameron (2007) and Miller (2010) argue that the circumstances under which composition occurs are contingent. It would follow that the laws governing when composition occurs are contingent laws.

more likely to be true than the complex explanation involving government conspiracies and long-lost twins? The answer to each of these questions seems to be "no." If it mattered so much whether the necessitarian view is true, then scientists, historians, and detectives should spend much more of their time trying to figure out whether the necessitarian view is true. And that seems incorrect. The scientists, historians, and detectives can do what they do, and evaluate the epistemic import of the relative simplicity of their competing theories, without taking into consideration whether or not the necessitarian view is correct.

2.3 The Argument from Causal Closure/Exclusion

One argument against interactionist versions of substance dualism is based on the alleged causal closure of the physical world, or (another way of putting it) the exclusion of immaterial minds' causal influence from the physical world.[17] If interactionist substance dualism is correct, then immaterial souls sometimes causally influence physical objects (e.g., the brains or bodies paired with those immaterial souls). But every physical event which has a sufficient cause has a sufficient *physical* cause. So, barring overdetermination, immaterial souls never interact with physical objects, and so interactionist substance dualism is false. Here is an example. If interactionist substance dualism is true, then an immaterial soul might cause, on some particular occasion, the firing of some particular neurons in a brain. But every physical event which has a sufficient cause has a sufficient physical cause. In this case, that means that if the firing of the neurons has a sufficient cause, then it has a sufficient *physical* cause. If the firing of the neurons is also cause by the immaterial soul, then the firing of the neurons would be *overdetermined*. In other words, the firing of the neurons would have more than one set of sufficient causes, namely the activities of the immaterial soul *and* whatever physical event causes the neurons to fire. Assuming that this sort of overdetermination does not occur, or does not occur as often as it would need to if immaterial souls are regularly having effects in the physical world, we should reject interactionist substance dualism.

The parallel argument against composite objects (including those composite physical objects with which we might be identical) is fairly well

---

[17] See Armstrong 1978: 265, 1993: 32–33; Kim 1998, 2005; McGinn 1999: 93; Papineau 2001: 7, 2002: Ch. 1; Melnyk 2003: 285–297; Vicente 2006; Bennett 2008.

known, as a variant of that argument was defended in an influential book by Trenton Merricks.[18] The idea is that the causal closure of the physical is no more plausible than the causal closure of the *micro*physical. In other words, every physical event which has a sufficient cause has a sufficient microphysical cause, and in particular, a sufficient cause in terms of the activities of some mereologically simple objects. So, any causal contribution made by a composite object would be overdetermined by the causal contributions of its mereologically simple parts. (Note that the argument does not require that we think that there is no such thing as emergent or higher-level causation. It is compatible with the claim that all causes are mereologically simple that sometimes simples collectively cause things which none of them cause individually. In this sense, then, emergent or higher-level causation, and emergence more generally, is compatible with the view that composite objects do not exist.[19]) The standard example is that of a baseball breaking a window. If the baseball moving in such-and-such a direction, with such-and-such a velocity relative to the window, is sufficient to break the window, then the mereologically simple parts of the baseball, moving in such-and-such a direction, with such-and-such a velocity relative to the window, is sufficient to break the window. So, barring overdetermination, the baseball does not break the window. If these were good grounds to eliminate souls from our ontology, then they should also be good grounds to eliminate composite objects from our ontology, including those composite physical objects with which we might be identical. In fact, if composite objects are epiphenomena, we might have *better* grounds to eliminate them from our ontology than to eliminate epiphenomenal souls from our ontology. After all, if composite objects are epiphenomena and so they never cause anything to occur, then it is difficult to see how we could ever learn of their existence via straightforward perceptual evidence. Such perceptual evidence is presumably behind many people's insistence that composite objects exist ("I can just *see* my dog!"), while this sort of perceptual evidence is generally not what makes people believe in immaterial souls.[20]

---

[18] Merricks 2003. Dorr (2002: Ch. 2) also gives this sort of argument against the existence of composite objects. While Merricks take his argument to count against the existence of most, but not all, composite objects, Dorr takes his argument to count in favor of full-blown mereological nihilism.

[19] For further discussion of this mereological nihilist-friendly way of thinking of emergence, see Bohn 2012; Cornell 2017; Caves 2018; Brenner 2018.

[20] For more on whether perception provides justification for belief in composite objects, see Brenner forthcoming-a.

Merricks thinks that some composite objects engage in causal relations which are not overdetermined by their parts – in fact, he thinks that *composite physical persons* do this.[21] Perhaps Merricks is correct. But note that if this aspect of Merricks's view has any plausibility, it is unclear why the substance dualist should not be able to make a similar point and argue that immaterial souls engage in causal relations which are not overdetermined by any physical causes. Here is how Merricks summarizes his argument for the view that composite physical persons engage in causal relations which are not overdetermined by their parts:

> Our having conscious mental properties does not supervene on what our parts are like. We cause certain effects by having such properties. Because our causing those effects is appropriately independent of what our parts are like, our parts do not cause those same effects. So we are not wholly causally redundant.[22]

Merricks's argument, fully spelled out, is complicated, and I do not want to give the impression that the substance dualist can appropriate every component of that argument. But the substance dualist may be able to appropriate the core of Merricks's argument and contend that immaterial souls are not wholly causally redundant because: (1) An immaterial soul's conscious mental properties do not supervene on the properties of and relations among the parts of the brain or body with which the soul is paired; and (2) the immaterial soul's having those conscious mental properties has effects in the physical world. It would take us too far afield to defend these claims in detail. The points I'm making are conditional: If overdetermination arguments undermine substance dualism, then they undermine belief in composite physical persons as well; if Merricks's response to the overdetermination argument salvages belief in composite physical persons, then an analogous response to the overdetermination argument against substance dualism should salvage belief in immaterial souls. So, with respect to concerns regarding causal overdetermination, there is a parity between belief in immaterial souls and belief in composite physical persons.

2.4 The Argument from Conservation Laws

One concern regarding interactionist variants of substance dualism is whether such views are compatible with conservation laws (e.g., energy conservation, linear-momentum conservation). Let's focus on conservation

---

[21] See Merricks 2003: Ch. 4.
[22] Merricks 2003: 88–89.

of energy, which is more commonly appealed to in order to attack interactionist substance dualism.[23] If a soul causes some event in the brain or body (perhaps, e.g., the movement of my arm), wouldn't this involve some sort of transfer of energy to the brain or body, and wouldn't that result in a violation of relevant conservation laws? This concern goes back at least to Leibniz,[24] and it is now widely presented as a problem for interactionist substance dualism.[25] Here's how Dennett puts the worry:

> No physical energy or mass is associated with [souls]. How, then, do they get to make a difference to what happens in the brain cells they must affect, if the mind is to have any influence over the body? A fundamental principle of physics is that any change in the trajectory of any physical entity is an acceleration requiring the expenditure of energy, and where is this energy to come from? It is this principle of the conservation of energy that accounts for the physical impossibility of "perpetual motion machines," and the same principle is apparently violated by dualism. This confrontation between quite standard physics and dualism has been endlessly discussed since Descartes's own day, and is widely regarded as the inescapable and fatal flaw of dualism.[26]

Similarly, Searle writes that

> It seems impossible to make substance dualism consistent with modern physics. Physics says that the amount of matter/energy in the universe is constant; but substance dualism seems to imply that there is another kind of energy, mental energy or spiritual energy, that is not fixed by physics. So if substance dualism is true then it seems that one of the most fundamental laws of physics, the law of conservation, must be false.[27]

Much could be said about this objection to interactionist substance dualism. The matter is not so open-and-shut as philosophers such as Dennett and Searle would lead you to believe. For starters, while proponents of this objection generally treat the notion that there is a global and categorical conservation of energy as an established result of scientific research, this simply isn't true.[28] Pitts's response to the objection is

---

[23] For a discussion of conservation of momentum, and whether such conservation laws would pose a problem for interactionist substance dualism, see Averill and Keating 1981.
[24] For discussion, see Pitts 2021.
[25] See, e.g., Dennett 1991: 35; Flanagan 1991: 21; McGinn 1999: 92; Searle 2004: 42; Vicente 2006; Koksvik 2007; van Inwagen 2015: 260; Wilson 2015; Westphal 2016: 41–44. See Montero (2006: 384–385) and Pitts (2020: 674) for citations of more philosophers who argue against interactionist substance dualism on the basis of conservation laws.
[26] Dennett 1991: 35.
[27] Searle 2004: 42.
[28] For more thorough evaluations of the argument from conservation laws from those who are more scientifically informed than I am, see Collins 2008, 2011; Cucu and Pitts 2019; Pitts 2020, 2021, 2022.

particularly illuminating.²⁹ Pitts notes that the substance dualist can say that the conservation of energy says that energy is conserved in systems not subject to external influence, that conservation of energy is applicable, where it is applicable, to local systems, and that energy conservation does not hold in the local system just consisting of the brain, since it is subject to an outside influence. What's more, the only way to know that energy conservation really isn't violated in these local systems would be to engage in a detailed study of the brain – in other words, one cannot know that energy is conserved in this context merely on the basis of an armchair appeal to conservation laws. So, the question is not "Do souls violate energy conservation?", but rather "Do souls exercise an observable influence on the brain?" If we study the brain and don't find the influence which we would expect to find given interactionist substance dualism, then that may falsify interactionist substance dualism. But the interactionist substance dualist might reasonably contend that we haven't done enough brain research to discover the relevant interaction.

The question which concerns me now is, assuming the objection to interactionist substance dualism from energy conservation *is* successful, is there a parody argument against the view that we are composite physical objects?

The answer is yes. The parody is targeted specifically against the view that composite physical persons cause effects which are not overdetermined by the causal activities of their parts. If composite physical persons cause effects which are not overdetermined by the causal activities of their parts, this would also seem to violate energy conservation, for precisely the same reason why the causal interaction of immaterial souls with physical objects is alleged to violate energy conservation. The concern with souls is that in order to have effects in the physical world a soul would have to inject some energy into the total system of physical objects, since the soul's causal impact cannot be accounted for in terms of the causal activities of its body or any other physical object. The analogous concern for composite physical persons is that in order for the composite physical person to have some causal impact which is not overdetermined by the causal activities of its parts, it will need to inject energy into the total system of physical objects, above and beyond the energy involved in the causal activities of its parts. If an immaterial soul's having this sort of causal effect would violate energy conservation, the analogous causal effect of a composite physical person would violate energy conservation as well.

²⁹ Pitts 2020.

As I noted above, this parody is only directed against a view of composite physical persons according to which they have causal effects which are not overdetermined by the causal activities of their parts. So, you might simply respond to the parody by claiming that we are composite physical persons, but we do not have causal effects which are not overdetermined by the causal activities of our parts. Maybe, for example, composite physical persons have no causal effects (even if their parts do), or maybe they have causal effects, but those causal effects are overdetermined by the causal activities of their parts. This way we don't have to worry about any extra energy contributed by the causal activity of the person which is not already accounted for in the causal activities of the person's parts.

The problem is that if this response to the parody is adequate, then an analogous response can be given on behalf of the interactionist substance dualist to the original energy conservation objection. Note that the original energy conservation concern was with *interactionist* substance dualism specifically, according to which souls causally interact with bodies. (As I noted earlier, Leibniz presented the energy conservation objection to interactionist substance dualism. But Leibniz himself was a substance dualist, albeit not an interactionist.) But the alleged problem is really directed against versions of interactionism according to which souls engage in causal interactions with the physical world which are not overdetermined by the causal activities of their bodies. This assumption is generally not made explicit because interactionists rarely if ever contend that souls' causal interactions with the physical world are systematically overdetermined by the causal activities of their bodies. But if an interactionist *did* think that souls' causal interactions with the physical world are systematically overdetermined by the causal activities of their bodies (or physical parts of their bodies), then the energy conservation concern would not arise, as the interactionist could contend that the *body* (or physical parts of the body) contributes all the energy, and the soul, while engaged in causal interaction with the effect, need not contribute any energy of its own to that effect. For example, the interactionist might contend that a soul causes a body to raise its right arm, but that this effect is simultaneously caused by a pattern of neuron firings in the brain, and it is the neuron firings which contribute whatever energy is necessary to produce the effect. So, one could avoid the energy conservation objection either by abandoning interactionist substance dualism entirely (as Leibniz did), or by abandoning interactionist substance dualism as it is standardly conceived, where souls engage in causal interactions with the physical world which are not overdetermined by the causal activities of their bodies.

2.5 The Argument from the Correlation between Mental States and Brain States

A very popular objection to substance dualism appeals to the striking systematic correlations between mental states and brain states. The idea is that these correlations somehow undermine substance dualism.[30] But what exactly is supposed to be the problem?

Proponents of this sort of objection to substance dualism often write as if substance dualism is flatly inconsistent with our mental lives being so closely related to what happens in the brain, or even that the substance dualist actively opposes the idea that mental properties are correlated with physical brain states. So, for example, Piccinini and Bahar write that their argument against substance dualism "is as close to a refutation of substance dualism as anyone can get in this kind of case. We cannot definitively prove that nonphysical minds don't exist anymore than we can definitively prove that unicorns or fairies don't exist. But the overwhelming thrust of the empirical evidence is that there are no unicorns, no fairies, and no nonphysical minds."[31] What overwhelmingly powerful empirical evidence do they cite? That various features of our mental lives depend on what happens in identifiable localized regions of the brain. But how does that conflict with substance dualism? The idea here (and in most similar objections to

---

[30] Proponents of this sort of objection to substance dualism include Churchland 1984: 20; Murphy 1998: 1; McGinn 1999: 87–88; Melnyk 2003: 298–304; Clayton 2004: vi; Searle 2004: 43; Farah 2005: 38–39; Johnston 2007: 63, 2010: 130–132; Levy 2007: 12–17; Olson 2007: 165–166; Brown and Strawn 2012; Piccinini and Bahar 2015; van Inwagen 2015: 260–262.
[31] Piccinini and Bahar 2015: 137.

substance dualism) seems to be that the substance dualist is committed to the idea that our mental states are not dependent upon what happens in our brains, or even that our mental lives are entirely the results of activities in the soul, rather than the brain. But this way of developing the objection to substance dualism is far too strong, since obviously no substance dualist thinks that our mental states are totally unconnected with what occurs in the brain. Everybody knows that when you are bopped on the head, this will cause a change in your mental states – a loss in consciousness, or at least some pain. Similarly, everyone knows that drugs can modify what happens in the brain, and thereby modify our mental states. Substance dualists do not deny these obvious and widely recognized facts.

A similar way of construing the problem for substance dualism is in the following terms: Detailed study of the brain shows that the soul is *explanatorily redundant*, as the operations of the brain can all be explained in terms which do not involve the intervention of an immaterial soul.[32] The idea is that substance dualists believe in immaterial souls because they think those immaterial souls are needed to account for what happens in the brain. But since what happens in the brain can be accounted for solely in terms that do not involve immaterial souls, the substance dualist loses their motivation for believing in immaterial souls.

This way of construing the problem for substance dualism is also not very compelling, since, as we will see in Chapter 4, substance dualists generally do not argue for substance dualism on the basis of the alleged fact that we need immaterial souls to explain what happens in the brain or body, or to explain the behavior of physical objects more generally. As Goetz and Taliaferro note, after a survey of historically prominent substance dualists, "There is not the least bit of evidence for the idea that they arrived at their belief in the soul's existence after failing to explain various experiences in terms of what goes on in the physical world."[33] That being said, it must be admitted that occasionally substance dualists *do* argue for substance dualism on the basis of the alleged fact that souls are needed to explain some feature of the physical world which could not be explained in terms of the operations of the brain. For example, Mark Baker[34] suggests that certain aspects of our linguistic abilities cannot be fully explained in terms of the activities of the brain but may best be explained in terms involving immaterial souls. Similarly, Beth Seacord[35]

---

[32] Murphy 1998: 1; Farah 2005: 38–39; Brown and Strawn 2012: 47.
[33] Goetz and Taliaferro 2011: 155. Cf. Owen 2021: 40.
[34] Baker 2011b.
[35] Seacord 2021.

tentatively argues that out-of-body near-death experiences could provide some support for substance dualism (although Seacord thinks that the currently available data regarding out-of-body near-death experiences are not sufficient to provide a great deal of evidential support for substance dualism). Beauregard and O'Leary[36] argue that the mind's ability to have a discernible impact on one's neuronal activity supports substance dualism. These sorts of claims, construed as arguments for substance dualism, might very well be undermined by research on the brain that shows that the relevant phenomena are best explained in terms of the operations of the brain, rather than the operations of an immaterial soul.[37] But my broader point still stands, which is that substance dualists generally do not argue for substance dualism on the basis of the alleged fact that immaterial souls are needed in order to explain some physical phenomenon. So, the actual reasons that generally lead substance dualists to endorse substance dualism are not undermined by our discovery that various physical phenomena in the brain are best explained in terms of the physical processes occurring in the brain, rather than the intervention of immaterial souls.

A better way to put the objection to substance dualism is that the observed correlations between mental states and brain states are *more surprising* on the assumption that substance dualism is true than on the assumption that substance dualism is false. A standard physicalist personal ontology (e.g., we are brains, or we are bodies) predicts that mental states will be systematically correlated with brain states, insofar as those views predict that mental states *are* brain states. Substance dualism, by contrast, is *compatible* with mental states being systematically correlated with brain states, but it does not predict that those correlations will obtain. In fact, the objection goes, if substance dualism is correct and mental states are states of an immaterial soul, then it would be *surprising* if mental states were so systematically correlated with brain states, since immaterial souls are distinct objects from brains, and it is in general surprising when properties of distinct objects are systematically correlated with one another. So, a standard physicalist ontology does a better job than substance dualism at predicting this piece of evidence (i.e., the systematic correlation between mental states and brain states), a point that favors a standard physicalist ontology over substance dualism.

[36] Beauregard and O'Leary 2009. Cf. Beauregard 2007: §5.4.
[37] In fact, we don't need to engage in a detailed study of the brain to see that Beauregard and O'Leary's argument is a nonstarter. The mere fact that the mind has an influence on the brain (e.g., on neuronal activity in the brain) provides no support at all for substance dualism, as a material mind (or, more accurately, mental properties or events instantiated in a material object) could be expected to have an influence on the brain (cf. Clark 2010).

An analogous objection can be made against the view that we are composite physical objects. If we are composite physical objects, then our properties are robustly correlated with the properties of our parts. Take, for example, those correlations between mental states and brain states cited in the objection to substance dualism discussed above: If we are composite physical objects, then our mental states are closely correlated with the properties and relations exhibited by the parts of our brains. These correlations should surprise us, just as the correlations between the properties of immaterial souls and the properties of brains should surprise us. If, by contrast, only the parts exist, and they fail to compose a composite physical person, then it would not be surprising that the mental properties would be systematically correlated with the properties of the parts – in this case, the mental properties would *be* properties of the parts, in which case properties of the parts would simply be correlated with the properties of the parts, which is hardly surprising. But by contrast, if the parts compose a composite physical person, then we should not expect the mental properties of the composite physical person to correlate so systematically with the properties of the parts. The view that we are composite physical persons is *compatible* with those correlations, but it does not predict them. And the reason it does not predict them is the same reason why substance dualism does not predict the systematic correlations between the properties of souls and the properties of brains: Composite physical persons are not numerically identical with their parts, and so we lack any antecedent reason to think that their properties would be so systematically correlated with the properties of those parts.

It may be objected that the properties of the parts are so systematically correlated with the properties of the composite physical person they compose because, in general, properties of parts and properties of the composite objects they compose are systematically correlated. But this response is only tenable if we posit laws governing the manner in which the properties of composite objects are correlated with the properties of their parts. The substance dualist can make precisely the same move, saying that properties of immaterial souls are closely correlated with the properties of the brains with which they are paired because relevant psycho-physical laws obtain. As we saw in §2.2, the introduction of psycho-physical laws complicates the substance dualist's overall theory, and this is a strike against their view. But the introduction of the analogous mereological laws for those who believe in composite objects will also be a strike against their view.

The objection to the view that we are composite physical objects strikes me as being almost exactly analogous to the parallel objection to substance dualism. In both cases, what is objectionable is the systematic correlation between properties of numerically distinct objects. And in both cases, there is a natural response to the objection, but it is a response that comes at a cost: There are laws of some sort linking the properties of the numerically distinct objects. Once again, we have parity: If the objection to substance dualism works, then the analogous objection to our being composite physical objects should work as well.

2.5.1 The Duplication Argument

Van Inwagen presents an argument against substance dualism which relies, in part, on the fact that our mental properties are closely connected with our physical properties. He calls the argument the "duplication argument," and says that it is the most powerful argument for physicalism with respect to human persons.[38] Here is the argument. Suppose we have a machine which is capable of duplicating a body in perfect physical detail. If substance dualism is correct, then duplicating the body should not result in a thing having the mental properties of the original, as mental properties are housed in the soul, rather than the body. In fact, "Dualists must say that since thought and sensation are not physical processes occurring within a living human organism, the human body the duplicating machine creates will crumple mindlessly …."[39] But, plausibly, duplicating the body *would* result in a thing having the mental properties of the original, and so one's physical duplicate would not "crumple mindlessly." So, substance dualism is probably false. Here is my parody: If we are composite physical persons, then duplicating someone's parts should not result in a thing having the mental properties of the original, as mental properties are housed in the composite physical person, rather than their parts. In other words, duplicating the parts would not duplicate the whole, just as, by van Inwagen's lights, duplicating the body would not duplicate the soul housed in that body. But, plausibly, duplicating someone's parts *would* result in a thing having the mental properties of the original. So, persons are probably not composite physical objects.

I do not think that either the original argument against substance dualism or the parody argument is very compelling. We might respond, for example, that there is some law governing the generation of souls from bodies, or the generation of composite physical persons from their parts.

---

[38] Van Inwagen 2015: 262–265. See also Olson 2007: 166–168.
[39] Van Inwagen 2015: 263.

And with these laws in place, if you duplicate a body, then you will duplicate the soul (including those mental states instantiated in the soul), since the laws ensure that bodies with such-and-such properties produce souls with so-and-so properties. Similarly, with relevant mereological laws in place, we might think that duplicating some parts will duplicate the composite physical person associated with those parts (including whatever mental properties they instantiate), as the laws ensure that any parts configured in such-and-such a manner will produce associated composite physical persons configured in so-and-so a manner. Or perhaps God pairs souls with bodies, and when a duplicate of a body is produced, then God creates a new soul instantiating the appropriate mental states and pairs it with the body in question. Similarly, perhaps God pairs composite physical persons with parts, and when duplicates of a composite physical person's parts are produced, then God creates a new composite physical person instantiating the appropriate mental states and pairs them with the parts in question. Van Inwagen claims that this sort of theistic maneuver, made in response to the duplication argument against substance dualism, is a "desperate move," even for the theist.[40] But, as we will see in Chapter 3, §3.6, and Chapter 8, §8.2, there are independent motivations for thinking that God pairs souls with bodies, or composite persons with their parts, and in fact, some theists already maintain that God does this.

So, there is an argument against substance dualism here, but there is a parody argument against the view that we are composite physical objects. Neither objection is entirely compelling, for more or less the same reasons. So, once again, we have parity between the view that we are immaterial souls and the view that we are composite physical objects.

2.6 Where Do Souls Come From?

One challenge for substance dualists is to explain where souls come from. Presumably, the souls which exist now haven't always existed. So, by what mechanism did they come to exist? A more specific way of putting the worry is in terms of our evolutionary history. Presumably, at some point in our evolutionary history, there weren't any souls, but now there are. Critics sometimes assume that it is a part of the substance dualist thesis that humans have souls, but other animals (including our prehuman evolutionary ancestors) do not, and that this is an implausible implication

---

[40] Van Inwagen 2015: 264.

2.6 Where Do Souls Come From?

of substance dualism.[41] When this objection is given, there rarely, if ever, is any engagement with actual substance dualists who endorse the view that only humans have souls – it is often simply *assumed* that, of course, this is part of the substance dualist thesis. Now, perhaps some substance dualists do think that only humans have souls. Descartes is famously thought to have endorsed the thesis that nonhuman animals lack immaterial souls.[42] But I doubt that this view is widespread. It's hard to be sure because the issue is usually simply not discussed by contemporary substance dualists.[43] But the arguments which lead some to endorse substance dualism generally would, if successful in the case of humans, lead one to endorse substance dualism with respect to many nonhuman animals as well. This is true of all of the arguments for substance dualism which I will discuss in Chapter 4. For example, one argument for substance dualism proceeds from the idea that physical objects cannot exhibit phenomenal states – for example, the experience of tasting chocolate or seeing the color blue. This argument, if successful, would apply to any nonhuman animals which exhibit phenomenal states (dogs, turtles, etc.). All in all, the supposition that souls are confined to humans is certainly not a part of the substance dualist thesis – it is at most an implausible add-on to the substance dualist thesis. So an objection to substance dualism based on the alleged implausibility of humans having souls, but other animals failing to have souls, strikes me as a nonstarter. The objection is emblematic of the fact that many modern-day critics of substance dualism are only familiar with Descartes's version of substance dualism and are entirely unfamiliar with contemporary defenses of substance dualism.

But perhaps there's a better way of developing the objection. Again, if we have souls, then it was nevertheless presumably not true of *all* of our nonhuman ancestors that *they* had souls. Assuming it can't be a vague matter whether souls exist or are associated with particular bodies, then at some point there was a sharp cut-off – before that point, there were no souls, but after that point, there were. You might think it is implausible that there could be sharp cut-off points, in the history of individual organisms or in the history of life more generally before which there is no soul and after which there *is* a soul, especially given the fact that the development of individual organisms and the evolution of life on Earth is a gradual process.

---

[41] See, e.g., McMahan 2002: 17–18; Levy 2007: 10–12.
[42] In fact, Descartes may not have definitively denied that nonhuman animals have immaterial souls, but he did think that we lack any good reason to attribute to them immaterial souls. See his letter to More, 5 February 1649 (AT V 276; Descartes 1991: 365).
[43] For three exceptions, see Swinburne 1986: 182–183; Nida-Rümelin 2007: 272; Goetz and Taliaferro 2011: 201, all of which contend that many nonhuman animals have souls.

So, if the substance dualist is committed to such cut-off points, then they're in trouble. And one reason to think they *would* be committed to such sharp cut-off points is because the alternative, that it would be vague whether at some point a soul has come into existence, is objectionable. This is because, the objection goes, this sort of vagueness would be *ontic* vagueness: Vagueness in the world rather than in our language or concepts. Perhaps it could be vague whether some word or concept applies in some particular situation. We invent the word "bald," for example, but we don't specify, for every possible number and arrangement of hairs, whether the word "bald" applies to someone with that number and arrangement of hairs. But the word "exists" is not vague, and neither is our concept of existence. So any vagueness with respect to existence would be ontic, rather than linguistic or conceptual vagueness. But how *could* we have ontic vagueness with respect to whether or not some object exists? The object is either there or it isn't. Similarly, in the case of souls: In our evolutionary history or in the developmental history of some particular organism, either there's a soul or there isn't. And so the substance dualist will be left with the implausible thought that, in the very gradual evolutionary process or the growth of some particular organism, some tiny change would have to result in its determinately being the case that some brand new nonphysical object, a soul, has come into existence.

A second, related concern: You might think it's very mysterious that new souls come into existence when new organisms (or human organisms specifically) come into existence. Assuming that we understand the sorts of biological processes involved in the creation of a new organism, why should any of *that* result in a new immaterial soul? The creation of a new soul in this sort of situation seems utterly inexplicable.[44]

A similar challenge is faced by those who think that we are composite physical objects: Where do composite physical persons come from? Suppose that we are composite physical persons, and we have not always existed. Then we will need sharp cut-off points, precise configurations of matter

---

[44] Both of the concerns described in this paragraph are given in Armstrong 1993: 29–31. The first concern, regarding sharp cut-off points, is given in Smith and Jones 1986: 49–52; Levy 2007: 11. The second concern, that it is mysterious how the physical processes involved in the reproduction of organisms could result in the creation of immaterial souls, is given in Lyons 1995: iv; Fales 2007: 120. Blatti (2012: 686) gives a similar objection to the view that we are constituted by, but not identical with, organisms. But, while he is not explicit about this, it's clear that his objection, if cogent, would undermine substance dualism as well. Churchland (1984: 21) gives a sort of evolutionary objection to substance dualism when he writes that "For purposes of our discussion, the important point about the standard evolutionary story is that the human species and all of its features are the wholly physical outcome of a purely physical process." But, as Lycan (2009: 560) correctly notes, Churchland's argument "simply and blatantly begs the question" against the substance dualist.

2.6 Where Do Souls Come From?

(for example) which are such that before that configuration is in place the composite physical person does not exist, but after that configuration is in place they do exist. It is implausible to think that there are sharp cut-off points of this sort.[45]

And leaving aside the concern about sharp cut-off points, you might think the generation of new composite physical persons is very mysterious. This is a concern I have about the creation of composite physical objects more generally. For example, most people who believe in composite physical objects apparently think I can create a brand new large physical object, one so heavy I can't even carry it, just by moving *other* objects around. I take some pieces of wood and I move them around, and I nail them together. I've made a table. Suddenly, a large physical object, one which hasn't existed until this moment, stands before me. Why did that happen? How did I make a whole new large heavy physical object just by moving some *other* objects around and putting nails in them? This seems inexplicable and mysterious. Now think of the problem in terms of composite physical persons specifically. We have some atoms arranged gametewise. They are moved around in the manner distinctive of fertilization and subsequent fetal development. You might think that it would be mysterious that *those* physical processes would somehow result in the creation of an entirely new immaterial soul. But then it also should be mysterious that they would result in the creation of an entirely new composite physical person.

For what it's worth, perhaps none of these objections (the objections to substance dualism or the parallel objections to our being composite physical persons) are particularly compelling. Where do composite physical persons come from? Presumably, the answer will be that they show up when some smaller objects exhibit certain properties (e.g., when they are arranged in a certain manner). We could say something similar about souls – they show up when the microphysical constituents of the bodies with which they are associated instantiate certain properties (e.g., when they develop brains of a certain configuration). In both cases, we will presumably need laws governing the creation of the new objects in question, that is, laws of the form "when such-and-such sorts of microphysical objects instantiate such-and-such properties then they begin to compose a new composite physical person," or "when such-and-such sorts of microphysical objects instantiate such-and-such properties then they give rise to a new immaterial soul." And we have already seen above that these sorts of laws, while capable of

---
[45] See Lewis 1986: 212–213.

resolving certain difficulties for substance dualism or belief in composite physical persons, are problematic in their own right, since they increase the complexity of our total theory.

In any case, it seems to me that if this is a challenge for substance dualists, then it's also a challenge for those who believe we are composite physical objects.

2.7 How Do We Reidentify Immaterial Souls over Time?

Sometimes philosophers complain that substance dualism leads to implausible skepticism regarding our ability to reidentify people over time.[46] When we interact with another person we can, so the objection goes, tell if we are interacting with the same body with which we previously interacted. But according to the typical substance dualist, we are not identical with our bodies, but rather we are identical with some immaterial soul which is associated with our bodies. So, how do we know that the soul we interact with on some occasion is identical with some soul we interacted with on previous occasions? The same objection is sometimes given from the first-person perspective: How can we know that we are the same immaterial souls that occupied our bodies in the past?

Parfit expresses this skeptical worry when he writes that

> while you are reading this page of text, you might suddenly cease to exist, and your body be taken over by some new person who is merely exactly like you. If this happened, no one would notice any difference. There would never be any evidence, public or private, showing whether or not this happens, and, if so, how often. We therefore cannot even claim that it is unlikely to happen.[47]

Those who raise this concern think that the skepticism engendered by our being immaterial souls is implausible. Clearly, we can reidentify

---

[46] Locke's *An Essay Concerning Human Understanding*, Ch. 27, §13 (Locke 1997: 304–305); Kant's *Critique of Pure Reason*, A363–364 (Kant 1998: 423–424); Strawson 1966: 168; Perry 1978: 7–17; Parfit 1984: 228; Shoemaker 1984: 124; Johnston 1987: 74, 2007: 41–42; Lowe 1996: 32; DeGrazia 2005: 50; Shoemaker 2008a: 28–34; Matthews 2010: 201. While the skeptical worry is usually described in terms of our being unable to tell how many souls occupy a given body over time, Strawson (1966: 168) notes that the substance dualist faces a similar skeptical worry regarding the number of souls occupying any given body at a single time: How do I know that my body is occupied by just one soul (me), rather than a thousand souls? The points I make regarding the diachronic skeptical concern will, with very little modification, also apply to this synchronic variant of the skeptical concern.

[47] Parfit 1984: 228.

people over time. Since substance dualism would undermine our ability to reidentify people over time, substance dualism is false.[48]

What should we make of this objection to substance dualism? I would say that this objection is, despite its popularity, not very compelling. Take, for example, Parfit's presentation of the concern. Parfit notes that it is conceivable that the soul occupying one's body is swapped with another indistinguishable soul, and that empirical evidence could not tell us whether this sort of soul swap has occurred. Parfit infers from the fact that a change in souls would not be detectable either from a third-person or a first-person perspective that we cannot say that it is improbable. But this inference is invalid. While we could not conclude on the basis of, say, empirical evidence regarding souls and bodies that it is improbable that the soul switch has occurred, we may have other grounds for thinking that it is improbable. For example, we may think that it is generally unlikely that this sort of soul swapping occurs on the basis of considerations regarding theoretical simplicity. Several philosophers have given this sort of parsimony-based response to the skeptical challenge to substance dualism.[49] The idea is that it is *simpler* to think that there is just one soul associated with any given body over an extended period of time, rather than a succession of souls. And this should lead us to think that it is *more likely* that there is just one soul associated with any given body over time, rather than a succession of souls, absent any positive grounds for thinking that there is a succession of souls. Not only is the former nonskeptical scenario more ontologically parsimonious, since it involves just one soul rather than many souls, but it posits simpler behavior as well. If there is a succession of souls occupying some body, we can reasonably ask why that sort of relatively complex behavior occurs, where souls are pairing and then depairing with that body, only to be replaced by new souls.

The skeptical argument against substance dualism can also be parodied, as other philosophers have also noted.[50] Suppose that we are composite physical objects. Well, for all we can tell on the basis of observation or introspection, over the course of several minutes, a composite physical person may be replaced by a succession of qualitatively indiscernible

---

[48] Parfit goes so far as to say that this skeptical concern might give us some reason to think Cartesian substance dualism is *unintelligible*: "When the belief in Cartesian Egos is in this way cut loose from any connections with either publicly observable or privately introspectible facts, the charge that it is unintelligible becomes more plausible. And it is not clear that Cartesians can avoid this version of their view. It is not clear that they can deny the possibility described by Locke and Kant" (Parfit 1984: 228).

[49] See Foster 1991: 255; Swinburne 2012: 107, 2013: 166; Madell 2015: 108.

[50] Goetz and Taliaferro 2011: 129; Walker 2014: 185; Madell 2015: 108, 112, 131.

composite physical persons. Perhaps each of these composite physical persons is composed of the parts that composed the original composite physical person, or perhaps the parts are replaced as well. Either way, we face a skeptical concern regarding our ability to reidentify composite physical persons over time which is identical to the skeptical concern regarding our ability to reidentify immaterial souls over time. The skeptical concern regarding composite physical persons also does not seem to be compelling, for the same reason the skeptical concern regarding immaterial souls was not compelling: It is much simpler to suppose we have a single composite physical person before us rather than a succession of composite physical persons, each one of which is inexplicably destroyed and replaced by a qualitative duplicate.

So, once again, we have parity: Both substance dualism and the view that we are composite physical persons face this skeptical worry, but in both cases, the skeptical worry can be overcome.

Dilip Ninan[51] thinks that it is a strike against a theory of personal identity if it entails that there are empirically undetectable facts regarding the persistence of persons over time. If Ninan is correct about that, it does not tell us anything very interesting about personal ontology, since, as we have just seen, these sorts of empirically undetectable facts are simply unavoidable if persons persist at all. For if we exist, then we are either simple or composite, and on either possibility there will be empirically undetectable facts regarding the persistence of persons: Either that this simple soul persists from one time to another, or that this composite physical person persists from one time to another.

---

[51] Ninan 2009: 434–435.

3

Arguments against Substance Dualism, Part 2: Pairing Problems

3.1 Two Pairing Problems

In Chapter 2, I argued that the main objections to substance dualism can be parodied and transformed into arguments against our being composite physical objects. There was one important objection that I did not discuss, since it warrants a chapter of its own. This is perhaps the most popular objection to (interactionist) substance dualism and the one which, among contemporary philosophers, is widely regarded as (interactionist) substance dualism's fatal flaw: There is some sort of irresolvable difficulty involved in an immaterial thing (a soul) engaging in causal interaction with a physical thing (the body associated with a soul). Here is how Paul Churchland puts the objection:

> If 'mind-stuff' is so utterly different from 'matter-stuff' in its nature – different to the point that it has no mass whatever, no shape whatever, and no position anywhere in space – then how is it possible for my mind to have any causal influence on my body at all? ... How is this utterly insubstantial 'thinking substance' to have any influence on ponderous matter? How can two such different things be in any sort of causal contact?[1]

This is a typical presentation of the objection.[2] But, as it stands, this isn't *really* an objection so much as it is a series of rhetorical questions. But the rhetorical questions are supposed to point toward a difficulty that many opponents of substance dualism think cannot be overcome. Unfortunately, it is very difficult to see what the difficulty is supposed to be. Why should the fact that an immaterial soul is very different from a material body mean that it cannot causally interact with a material body?

There are only two serious attempts I am aware of to answer this question. The first such attempt is described in a famous letter written by

---

[1] Churchland 1984: 8–9.
[2] For other similar presentations of the alleged problem for substance dualism, see Kenny 1968: 222–223; Dennett 1991: 35; McGinn 1999: 92; Sober 2000: 24; Williams 2005: 273–274; Ryle 2009: 9; Kim 2011: 46–50; Koch 2012: 151.

Elisabeth, Princess of Bohemia, to Descartes. According to Elisabeth, "it seems that all determination of movement happens through the impulsion of the thing moved, by the manner in which it is pushed by that which moves it, or else by the particular qualities and shape of the surface of the latter. Physical contact is required for the first two conditions, extension for the third."[3] The problem is that immaterial souls are incapable of coming into physical contact with physical bodies, and they also lack extension. So, it is difficult to see how an immaterial soul could causally interact with a physical body, and in particular, it is difficult to see how an immaterial soul could causally produce movements in a physical body.

What should we make of this objection to causal interaction between souls and bodies? It now seems very implausible that objects can cause movements in other objects only either by way of impulsion/pushing or by way of "the particular qualities and shape of" their surfaces. For example, one object can move another object by exerting a gravitational pull on that other object, and in this case, one object moves another object without pushing it, and not by way of "the particular qualities and shape of" its surface (except insofar as its surface has a mass and so contributes to the overall gravitational pull of the object).

A more promising attempt to develop the interaction worry for substance dualism is in Jaegwon Kim's "pairing problem."[4] The substance dualist thinks there are immaterial souls associated with each of our bodies. My soul is associated with this body, while your soul is associated with that body. But *why* is my soul associated with this body, while your soul is associated with that body? Consider, for example, the fact that I can raise my right arm simply by willing or intending to raise it. I have no such direct control over the movement of your right arm. But what is it about the relation between my soul and this body that enables them to interact? And what prevents your soul from interacting in the same way with this body? The substance dualist, Kim argues, cannot provide satisfactory answers to these questions. Often when some event A causes some event B, we can tell a plausible story regarding why A caused B, while some other simultaneous event C did not cause B, in terms of the relative spatial locations of A, B, and C (or the relative locations of the constituents of A, B, and C). My hand,

---

[3] Princess Elisabeth of Bohemia and Descartes 2007: 62.
[4] See, in particular, Kim 2005: Ch. 3. The pairing problem for substance dualism is most prominently associated with Kim, but Kim cites Foster (1968, 1991) as the first person to discuss the problem. It seems to me that the pairing problem is briefly pressed by the fourth-century Buddhist philosopher Vasubandhu in his *Abhidharmakośa* (Vasubandhu 2009: 301). More recently, it is also pressed by Sosa 1984.

rather than your hand, pets the dog because my hand, and not your hand, is spatially situated so as to come into contact with the dog. The substance dualist cannot tell this sort of story to explain why my soul, rather than your soul, is associated with this body, since souls are unlocated.

Kim's pairing problem illustrates a more general point: Sometimes it is puzzling that the relata of some relation enter into that relation when it seems as if other relata are equally viable candidates for entering into that relation. To clarify, I do not mean simply that it can be odd or mysterious that we might be justified in *believing* that some relata enter into some relation. For example, perhaps it can be mysterious how we might take ourselves to know that numbers are identical with sets. The point I take Kim's pairing problem to illustrate is a metaphysical, rather than an epistemic point, that it can be mysterious or odd that some relata enter into some relation, whether or not it is mysterious or odd that we might know or justifiably believe that they enter into that relation.

In this chapter, I argue that those who think that we are composite objects face a problem very similar to the pairing problem faced by substance dualists, what I call the "mereological pairing problem." The mereological pairing problem challenges us to answer the following question: Why are parts and composite persons paired in the way in which they paired? In other words, Why do *these* parts compose *this* composite person? What is it about the parts, or the composite person, or the relationship between the parts and the composite person, which accounts for the fact that these parts compose *this* composite person, rather than some other composite person? And what is it about the parts, or the composite person, or the relationship between the parts and the composite person, which accounts for the fact that this composite person has *these* parts, rather than some other parts?[5]

---

[5] I have briefly discussed the mereological pairing problem elsewhere (Brenner 2015b: 328–329, 2017a: 471–474, 2022: §4.3.), but I have never developed the problem, and potential responses, in detail. In my previous presentations of the problem, I presented it as a problem for belief in composite objects in general, rather than composite physical persons in particular. Markosian (2014: 72–73) discusses a question that is similar to the questions posed in the mereological pairing problem: In virtue of what is one object a part of another object? I discuss Markosian's own answer to this question in §3.3. Bynoe and Jones (2013) note in passing that those who think that we are composite objects face something like the mereological pairing problem, but they do not discuss the problem in detail. Olson (2007: 4) asks why it is the case that I have the parts I have, and you have the parts you have, but he also does not develop the problem in detail. Later, however, he suggests that animalists, who think that we are human organisms, have a principled answer to the question "Why is *x* a part of me?": It is a part of me because it is caught up in my life (Olson 2007: Ch. 3.6). But I don't think that this fully resolves the mereological pairing problem, since we are still left wondering why the objects caught up in this life compose *me* rather than someone else. Himma (2011) presents an objection to physicalism which sounds a lot like the mereological pairing problem, but I am

There are two questions here: (1) Why is this composite person composed of *these* parts, rather than some other parts? (2) Why do these parts compose *this* composite person, rather than some other composite person? Often, for the sake of brevity, I conflate these two questions or mention one of these questions as if it represents the sole explanatory challenge lying behind the mereological pairing problem. But, in principle, a response to the mereological pairing problem may fail because it provides a satisfactory response to one of these two questions but not the other.

The questions we are asking here concern explanation: *Why* are parts and composite persons paired as they are? We are not simply asking about necessary and/or sufficient conditions for some parts and some composite person to be paired as they are. Providing necessary and/or sufficient conditions for why some particular parts are paired with some particular composite person may not tell us *why* the parts are paired with the composite person. Suppose, for example, that divine revelation tells us that some particular parts are paired with some particular composite person. This would provide a sufficient condition for those parts being paired with that person, assuming divine revelation is always correct. But it would do nothing to tell us *why* these particular parts are paired with this particular composite person.

To get a better handle on what sorts of questions we're asking here, consider me and my twin brother. Suppose that we are both composite persons – we both have parts. Suppose we only have physical parts. We do not share any of our parts. For example, no subatomic particle is a part of me as well as him. That didn't have to be the case. Some twins do not fully separate during the process of fetal development, and so then end up as conjoined twins. Perhaps in this sort of case, the two twins share some parts. For example, Abby and Brittany Hensel, two famous conjoined twins, have only one liver between them, and so perhaps we should say that the liver is a part of both Abby and Brittany. But since my twin and I are not conjoined,

---

not entirely sure that it *is* the mereological pairing problem. In any case, the target of Himma's argument seems to be physicalism conceived as a thesis regarding the relationship between mental properties and physical properties, rather than (merely) the thesis that we are composite physical objects. My mereological pairing problem is directly concerned with personal ontology, rather than the relationship between mental properties and physical properties. Bennett (2007: 321) and Bailey et al. (2011: 351–352) also see a parallel between Kim's pairing problem for substance dualism and a similar pairing problem for some people who believe in composition. But the pairing problem they have in mind only affects people who think that we are coincident objects (i.e., persons constituted by, but not identical with, bodies) (as in, e.g., Baker 2000). Finally, Glazier (2023) argues against the view that all the macro facts are grounded in micro facts. While he does not put it in these terms, the crux of the problem seems to be that mereological pairing facts cannot all be grounded in micro facts.

it seems plausible that we share none of our parts. Now, we can ask of some physical object which is among my parts – a subatomic particle, or a leg, or whatever – why it is part of *me* but not a part of *him*. I am not asking why this part is located *here* (in my home, where I am located) rather than *there* (in his home, where he is located). I will discuss the relationship between location and mereological pairing in §3.3. For now, it's enough to note that sharing a location is one thing, composing is another. Even if some subatomic particle is located where my body is located (or, more accurately, the region in which it is located overlaps with the smallest region that entirely contains my body), it is a separate matter for that subatomic particle to be a *part* of my body. So, we can sensibly ask why this physical object is a part of me, rather than my twin. I am also not asking how it is that some physical object came to be a part of me, rather than a part of him. Rather, I am asking what it is about that object right now that makes it a part of me. I have not yet argued that this sort of question requires an answer, nor have I yet argued that satisfying answers cannot be given. I'm just trying to make clear what sort of question we are asking when we think about the mereological pairing problem.

Notice the clear similarities between this sort of question regarding parts and wholes and the question we asked earlier about souls and bodies. If my twin brother and I are immaterial souls, we could ask why his soul is paired with *that* body, while my soul is paired with *this* body. I am asking more or less the same sort of question regarding the mereological pairing relations entered into by composite persons and their parts. The chief difference is that the pairing problem regarding souls and bodies regards *causal* relations – that is, those causal relations associated with the causal interaction between souls and the bodies with which they are paired. The mereological pairing relations entered into by composite persons and their parts are not causal. Parthood is not causation. Still, there is a sort of *pairing* going on here. One object's causally interacting with another involves the one object being causally *paired* with the other object. Similarly, one object's being part of another involves the one object being mereologically *paired* with the other object. And we can sensibly ask why the objects in question are paired as they are – why, for example, these parts are paired with *this* composite person rather than some other composite person.

One way to vividly illustrate the questions regarding mereological pairing relations that interest us involves the famous story of the Ship of Theseus. For simplicity, let's assume that all of the Ship of Theseus's parts are planks. At the beginning of the story, the Ship of Theseus is composed of some particular planks. Let's call those planks the "Original Planks." The Ship of

Theseus gradually has all of its planks replaced. It seems unlikely that the replacement of any individual plank causes the Ship of Theseus to cease to exist, so it also seems likely that the Ship of Theseus survives the gradual replacement of all of its planks. Let's call the planks we have at the end of this process of total plank replacement the "New Planks." But suppose that, each time one of the planks is replaced, the original plank is set aside for safekeeping. At the end of the process of gradual replacement, all of the Original Planks are reassembled exactly as they were at the beginning of the process. We are now left with *two* ships, both of which seem like plausible candidates for being identical with the Ship of Theseus: A ship composed of the Original Planks, and a different ship composed of the New Planks. One question to ask here is whether the Ship of Theseus is the ship composed of the Original Planks, the ship composed of the New Planks, or neither of these ships. But there is a related question: Assuming that the Ship of Theseus is identical with one or the other of these two ships, then it seems sensible to ask *why* the Ship of Theseus is, at the end of the process, composed of the Original Planks rather than the New Planks, or why the Ship of Theseus is, at the end of the process, composed of the New Planks rather than the Original Planks. Similarly, it seems sensible to ask why the Original Planks composed *this* ship rather than some other ship, and why the New Planks compose *that* ship rather than some other ship. If you think that these are sensible questions to ask, then you understand the question at the heart of the mereological pairing problem: Why are parts and composite objects paired as they are? But while this question naturally comes to mind in special cases like that of the Ship of Theseus, it can be brought to mind with respect to any case of composition. If, for example, the Ship of Theseus is never disassembled or reassembled, and it continues to be composed of the Original Planks, we can still ask why the Original Planks compose *this* ship rather than some other ship, or why the Ship of Theseus has *these* parts rather than some other parts.

Notably, the question is *not* "Why do *these* objects (say, the Original Planks) compose something, while *those* other objects (say, the New Planks) do not?" We can suppose that the Original Planks compose a ship, and the New Planks compose a distinct ship. The question is why the Original Planks compose *this* ship, while the New Planks compose that other ship, or why *this* ship is composed of the Original Planks, rather than the New Planks. It's not as if either of the ships in question must be composed of just those planks that compose them. After all, as we noted earlier, it seems plausible that a ship can survive the replacement of one of its planks.

3.1 Two Pairing Problems

My discussion of the Ship of Theseus illustrates the fact that the mereological pairing problem would apply to any composite objects, not just persons. (Although we could pretty easily modify the Ship of Theseus story so that it is about persons, rather than ships.) However, for the remainder of this chapter, I will focus specifically on the mereological pairing problem as applied to composite persons.

According to Kim, the substance dualist must provide an answer to the question of why souls enter into certain sorts of causal relations with some bodies rather than others, since the pairing cannot be brute. Kim argues that the dualist will be hard-pressed to put forth a satisfying answer. So too, I claim, those who believe we are composite objects will be hard-pressed to put forward satisfying answers to questions such as "Why is this composite person composed of these parts, rather than some other parts?" and "Why do these parts compose this composite person, rather than some other composite person?" More importantly, those who identify us with composite objects have no response to the mereological pairing problem that cannot also be appropriated by the substance dualist in response to the pairing problem for substance dualism. So, once again, we have a parity: If pairing problem concerns undermine substance dualism, then they also undermine the view that we are composite objects, and if pairing problem concerns do not undermine the view that we are composite objects, then they also do not undermine substance dualism. I would like to underscore the significance of this conclusion, since, as I note above, the pairing problem for substance dualism is, to the best of my knowledge, the only plausible attempt to articulate and develop what is widely regarded as *the* fatal flaw for substance dualism, the substance dualist's alleged inability to account for the possibility of causal interaction between immaterial souls and material bodies.[6]

Interestingly, given one version of substance dualism, Kim's pairing problem is close to a variant of the mereological pairing problem. The version of substance dualism I have in mind is the version of substance dualism according to which we are composites made up of soul and body. Kim's pairing problem concerns causal relations between souls and bodies. But a closely related problem, as applied to this version of substance dualism, would press the following question: Why is this person (this composite of soul and body) composed of *these* parts together (i.e., *this* soul

---

[6] Himma (2005) complements this chapter. Himma argues that the objection to interactionist substance dualism from the alleged impossibility of causal interaction between bodies and immaterial souls does not undermine substance dualism, as the alternatives to substance dualism face analogous difficulties in making sense of interaction between the mental and the physical.

and *that* body)? If you find this variant of the pairing problem compelling, that provides further motivation for thinking that the mereological pairing problem is a real problem.

For the remainder of this chapter, I will examine potential responses to the mereological pairing problem. Here is one notable response to the mereological pairing problem that I will not discuss: Composition as identity is correct, so composite persons are numerically identical with their parts, and *that's* why composite persons are paired with their parts. Composition as identity might very well resolve the mereological pairing problem. But in Chapter 1, §1.3, I noted that composition as identity is not very plausible, so I will not discuss it further here. I should also note that I will mainly frame the discussion around potential responses to the *mereological* pairing problem, rather than Kim's pairing problem for substance dualism, because the mereological pairing problem is new and hasn't received significant attention. But along the way, I will see whether potential responses to the mereological pairing problem can inspire similar responses to Kim's pairing problem for substance dualism.

3.2 Response 1: No Answer Required

The first potential response to the mereological pairing problem that I will consider is that there just aren't any answers to such questions as "Why is this composite object composed of these parts, rather than some other parts?" and "Why do these parts compose this composite object, rather than some other composite object?" It is a brute fact that this person has *these* parts, and it is also a brute fact that these other parts compose *that* person.[7] As Ryan Wasserman puts it (although not in response to the mereological pairing problem): "All explanation must come to an end at some point ... and it seems as if there is no better place for explanation to come to an end than in facts of the following sort: x is a part of y (at t)."[8]

The mereological pairing problem is arguably in the background in some widely discussed philosophical puzzles – for example, puzzles regarding fission and personal identity, the problem of the many, and, as I noted

---

[7] This "brute" response to the mereological pairing problem should be distinguished from Markosian's "brutal composition" thesis (Markosian 1998). The brute facts Markosian believes in are brute facts regarding the circumstances under which composition occurs, not brute facts regarding how parts are paired with wholes. One might very well accept one sort of brute fact but not the other.

[8] Wasserman 2002: 205.

3.2 Response 1: No Answer Required

above, the Ship of Theseus. Reflecting on fission cases, in particular, can help show how the brute response to the mereological pairing problem is unsatisfying.[9]

In fission cases, a person or some important part of a person splits in half. So, for example, consider split-brain cases. It seems plausible that you could continue to exist with only one brain hemisphere. This has led philosophers to ask what would happen if both hemispheres are preserved, but each one is transplanted into a new body. The operation will apparently result in two people, both of whom will claim to be you, and both of whom will have various mental characteristics (e.g., memories, desires, etc.) continuous with the mental properties you had before the operation. Similarly, the bodies of both postoperation people will be physically (dis)continuous with your preoperation body to equal degrees. It seems as if it would be objectionably arbitrary to suppose that you are identical with one of the two postoperation persons rather than the other, given that they are equally viable candidates. As Derek Parfit notes:

> Perhaps I shall be one of the two resulting people. The objection here is that, in this case, each half of my brain is exactly similar, and so, to start with, is each resulting person. Given these facts, how can I survive as only one of the two people? What can make me one of them rather than the other?[10]

Parfit takes this split-brain transplant thought experiment to support his own "reductionist" account of persons. According to Parfit's reductionism, we can give a full description of the world without mentioning people. The thought experiment is supposed to support reductionism because reductionism allows us to avoid having to suppose that there is an objective answer to the question of which parts, if any, the prefission person will have after the split-brain transplants. According to reductionism, we can fully describe the case without saying anything about which parts are had by the prefission person after the split-brain operation.[11]

By contrast, Richard Swinburne maintains that the split-brain thought experiment supports substance dualism, and so supports the idea that the person involved in the fission thought experiment is not a composite

---

[9] For more on fission cases, see Brenner MS-c. I will discuss the problem of the many in Chapter 4, §4.8.
[10] Parfit 1984: 256.
[11] I think that Parfit's reductionism is an obscure thesis, at least in Parfit's own discussion of the thesis. But perhaps the best way to interpret Parfit's reductionism is in terms of the nonself thesis I will discuss in Chapter 6 – we can give a full description of the world without mentioning people because, strictly speaking, there are no people. For an interpretation of Parfit along these lines, see Siderits 2015: Ch. 1.

physical object. This is because the fission thought experiment shows that knowledge of what has happened to the parts of a person's body or brain does not tell us what has happened to the person – we can know everything there is to know about what has happened to the parts of each brain hemisphere, and yet not know which parts, if any, the prefission person will have after the split-brain transplants. This is just what we should expect if persons are not composite physical objects such as bodies or brains. If we *were* composite physical objects, then we should expect knowledge of what happens to our physical parts to convey knowledge regarding pairing relations between us and those physical parts. Swinburne seems to assume here that the pairing relations cannot be brute, since if they were brute, then presumably knowledge of what happens to the parts would *not* convey information regarding the pairing relations between parts and wholes.[12]

Fission cases are not confined to these sorts of science fiction thought experiments, as the sorts of fission cases discussed by Parfit and Swinburne have real-world analogues in monozygotic twinning. Norman Ford's discussion of this latter sort of fission case parallels some of the points made by Parfit and Swinburne regarding split-brain cases. For example, Ford notes that it seems implausible that the splitting zygote would be identical with one or the other products of fission, as they are so similar, for example, genetically. What seems objectionable, then, is that it could be brute that the original zygote would come to be composed of *these* parts that partially composed it prior to twinning, rather than *those* parts, as there seem to be no nonmereological facts which would pair the zygote to the former parts rather than the latter parts.[13]

I have gone into this detour regarding fission cases in order to make the following point. Parfit, Swinburne, and Ford reach their conclusions regarding personal identity from the apparent fact that it would be objectionably brute or arbitrary for the prefission person/zygote to end up as one result of fission rather than the other. Assuming that the person/zygote in question is a composite physical object, what seems to be objectionable is that it would be brute or arbitrary which parts, if any, that person/zygote is paired with postfission. According to the "brute" response to the mereological pairing problem, *any* mereological pairing relations are brute, whether or not fission occurs. But presumably, if you regard these

---

[12] Swinburne 1986: 148–149, 2013: 152–154, 2019: 53–55.
[13] Ford 1991: 120–122. Similar arguments are given in Kuhse and Singer 1990; Singer 1993: 157; Persson 1995: 20; McMahan 2002: 25, 2007: 177; Smith and Brogaard 2003: 68; DeGrazia 2005: 248; Shoemaker 2008a: 138.

sorts of brute mereological pairing relations to be objectionable in fission cases, you should also regard them to be objectionable in normal nonfission cases as well. After all, what is often thought to make the brute pairing relations in fission cases so objectionable is precisely the fact that they are brute and arbitrary – the fact that the brute pairing relations occur in the context of *fission* specifically seems to be irrelevant. So, if just this sort of bruteness is objectionable when it is found in fission cases, then it should presumably be objectionable when it is found in cases of composition more generally.[14]

Is there anything more that we can say about *why* these sorts of brute mereological pairing relations are objectionable? I have a proposal. But it's important to note that even if this proposal fails to capture what is objectionable about the brute pairing relations in question, those brute pairing relations may be objectionable for other reasons. That they are objectionable for *some* reason or other is arguably supported by the observations I've just made regarding our reaction to the brute pairing relations involved in fission cases.

I don't think that the sorts of brute mereological pairing relations under discussion are simply impossible, in the manner in which Kim contends that similar brute causal pairing relations between soul and body are impossible. What's objectionable about brute mereological pairing relations is, I propose, that these sorts of brute correlations conflict with a central constraint on theory choice, namely that our theories should not be needlessly complex.[15] Theories which posit more brute phenomena are thereby more complex.[16] Independent phenomena cannot be derived from other components of our theory, and each such brute phenomenon must be put in "by hand," so to speak – that is, in order to fully describe reality, we will have to mention *this* brute phenomenon, and *that* one, and so on, without being able to derive one such phenomenon from another. Scientific explanations often try to unify otherwise disparate phenomena for precisely this reason. As Friedman notes, unifying explanations in science are often preferable to their nonunifying competitors because with the former explanations "our total picture of nature is simplified via a

---

[14] Conversely, if you think that brute pairing relations are not objectionable, then you should presumably also think that they are not objectionable in fission cases. This will obviously affect the way that you evaluate the sorts of fission cases described above.
[15] I assume that simpler theories in metaphysics are more likely to be true. This assumption is sometimes challenged, as in, e.g., Kriegel 2013; Willard 2014. For two recent defenses of simplicity as a criterion of theory choice in metaphysics, see Paul 2012; Brenner 2017b.
[16] Cf. Brenner 2015b: §2; Schindler 2018: 12.

reduction in the number of independent phenomena that we have to accept as ultimate."[17]

Take, for example, the explanation offered by the theory of common descent for the presence of homologous traits in distinct species (e.g., for the fact that whales and humans share similar bone structures). The species share the traits in question because those traits are derived from a common ancestor. Given the thesis of common ancestry, we don't need to think that, by sheer coincidence, whales and humans are morphologically similar in numerous ways. Rather, we need only accept a relatively simple set of facts (e.g., that whales and humans have a common ancestor, from which they derive the traits in question), from which we can derive the otherwise inexplicable facts regarding the species' similar morphologies. Once we consider just how *many* homologous traits are shared between various species, we can see just how much the thesis of common ancestry simplifies our total theory. Without the thesis of common ancestry, we must suppose that there is this extremely widespread and systematic confluence of traits throughout all life on Earth and that each such shared trait exists just by coincidence. Each such coincidence must be put in "by hand" so to speak in our total theory. We unify, and so simplify, our total theory immensely by supposing that many of these shared traits are the result of common ancestry.

Proponents of the "brute" response to the mereological pairing problem will have to posit a very large number of independent and brute phenomena. They will have to put in "by hand" the fact that *this* object is a part of *that* composite person, for every one of the trillions of parts making up all of the composite persons who exist. The "brute" response to the mereological pairing problem therefore requires a significant increase in the complexity of our total theory.

Just as the brute response to the mereological pairing problem complicates our total theory, so too does the analogous brute response to the pairing problem for substance dualism.[18] The substance dualist might say that *this* soul is associated with *this* body and *that* soul is associated with *that* body, and that's all there is to it, since the relations are brute.[19] But there are *billions* of humans, and so presumably *billions* of human souls, not to mention all of the nonhuman animal or extraterrestrial souls substance dualists might be committed to. Absent some very compelling argument for

---

[17] Friedman 1974: 18.
[18] Spackman (2013: 1062) also notes that brute pairing relations between souls and bodies complicate the dualist's total theory, but he does not explain why this is the case.
[19] This response to the pairing problem is given in Audi 2011.

3.2 Response 1: No Answer Required

substance dualism, it would be better to just reject substance dualism rather than posit billions of brute relations which the nonsubstance dualist will not need to posit.[20] Once again, there is a parity between the view that we are immaterial souls and the view that we are composite objects: Proponents of both views can offer brute responses to their respective pairing problems, but such brute responses seem to be objectionable.

There is a second reason why brute pairing relations may be objectionable, although it is not a reason which I wholeheartedly endorse. Recall the discussion in Chapter 2, §2.7, of the objection to substance dualism according to which substance dualism leads to an implausible skepticism regarding our ability to reidentify people over time. The concern was that there would be no way to tell whether the soul occupying a body now is the same soul which occupied it in the past. I noted that those who think that we are composite physical objects face an analogous skeptical worry. The concern now is that, if pairing relations are brute, this might strengthen the skeptical concern regarding our ability to reidentify souls or composite physical persons over time. After all, we might normally think that the same soul is paired with a body as long as there are no very great changes in that body. But if it is simply a brute fact that a soul is paired with some particular body, then we will have no reason to think that the soul's being paired with that body will track whether there are significant changes in the body. Since the soul is paired with that particular body for no reason at all, it might very well cease being paired with that body, regardless of whether there have been any significant changes in the body. Put another way: If there isn't any reason why this soul is paired with this body, then we might doubt that there is any reason why it should *continue* to be paired with this body. If it is a brute fact that the soul is paired with the body at one time, it is a separate brute fact that it is paired with that body at some other time, and the obtaining of one of these brute facts gives us no reason to think the other brute fact will obtain. And we might say something similar about composite physical persons and the parts with which they are paired. I am not suggesting that brute pairing relations make the skeptical concern insurmountable. It still seems generally simpler to think that we are interacting with just one soul, or just one composite physical person, rather than a succession of souls, or a succession of composite physical persons. But for those readers who think that the skeptical concern is a real problem, for either substance dualism or the view that we are composite physical

---

[20] A variant of the brute response to the pairing problem is Foster's suggestion that there are individual laws linking particular souls and particular bodies (Foster 1991: 167–169). This response to the pairing problem clearly complicates our total theory by multiplying brute laws.

objects, coming to see pairing relations as brute might make the skeptical concern more acute.

And, to make matters worse, there is another skeptical concern, at least for brute mereological pairing relations: If mereological pairing relations are brute, and we are composite physical persons, then we might not be able to tell which objects are among our parts. You might think, for example, that your left foot is a part of you, while your left shoe is not. But if it is simply a brute fact that your left foot is a part of you, and your left shoe is not, then what grounds do you have for your belief that the left foot is a part of you, while your left shoe is not? You could not make this judgment on the basis of some observable property of the foot or the shoe which makes it the case that the foot is among your parts, while the shoe is not.[21]

3.3 Response 2: Composite Objects Are Located Where Their Parts Are Located

A seemingly obvious response to the mereological pairing problem is this: Some composite object has *these* objects as parts rather than *those* objects as parts because it is located where *these* objects are located, while it is not located where *those* objects are located. Ned Markosian[22] defends just this sort of view. Markosian does not explicitly offer a response to the mereological pairing problem (construed as a problem for belief in composite persons or belief in composite objects more generally), but he does try to answer the question "In virtue of what is one object a part of another object?" According to Markosian, "for any x and for any y, x is a part of y iff the region occupied by x is a subregion of the region occupied by y."[23] Moreover, "every object that is a part of another object is a part of that second object *in virtue* of occupying a subregion of the region occupied by the second object."[24]

Call any response to the mereological pairing problem which claims that parts are paired with composites because they are located where those composites are located the "location response" to the mereological pairing problem. It seems to me that the location response to the mereological pairing problem gets the order of explanation backwards: Composite objects are located where their parts are located because they are composed

---

[21] Thanks to Eric Olson for suggesting to me the skeptical concern described in this paragraph.
[22] Markosian 2014.
[23] Markosian 2014: 73.
[24] Markosian 2014: 73.

of those parts, while this response to the mereological pairing problem erroneously assumes that composite objects are composed of those parts because they are located where those parts are located.[25]

I have two main concerns with the location response to the mereological pairing problem. In other words, I have two main concerns with the idea that a thing is composed of certain parts (rather than others) because it is located where those parts are located.

First concern: Suppose that you have a bunch of simples and you want to use them to make a baby. We know how to do that: Engage in sexual activities that we know often result in arrangements of simples which compose new human beings (by e.g., moving around simples arranged gamete-wise). (Here, "arrangement of simples" should be interpreted broadly, to include, e.g., moving the simples to a womb in which they can develop, putting them in proximity of nutrients, etc.) There is a causal component to this process: Rearrange the simples. But there is a metaphysical component as well: Ensure that the simples compose a baby. Normally, we think that the causal component, rearranging simples, is all we need to worry about, since we assume that rearranging the simples in the right way automatically ensures that they compose a baby. But given the location response to the mereological pairing problem, arranging the simples a certain way is not enough to ensure that they compose a baby. In order to ensure that the simples compose a baby, you must presumably arrange the simples in the right way but you must also bring the simples into a region occupied by a baby, since they will compose some particular baby only if, and *because*, they are located where that baby is located. The "because" here is crucial. We normally think, of course, that if some simples compose some particular baby, then they are located where that baby is located, and the proponent of the location response to the mereological pairing problem agrees with that. But they further stipulate that the simples compose that baby *because* they are located where that baby is located. It is this new explanatory component that leads to implausible results, namely that in order to make a baby it is not enough to ensure that some simples are arranged in the right way, but we must also take the further step of ensuring that they are located where some particular baby is located. If we do *not* ensure that the simples are located where a baby is located, then we will not have ensured that they compose a baby, or more generally that they compose anything. And this implication of the location response to the mereological pairing problem is

---

[25] Markosian himself bites the bullet here and explicitly denies that composite objects have their locations in virtue of the locations had by their parts. See Markosian 2014: 76–77.

very implausible. (I write as if you must find a baby and then ensure that they are located where the simples are located. But, strictly speaking, the baby does not need to be a *baby* before it comes to be composed of some simples arranged baby-wise. But if it's not a baby, then what is it? And how is it floating around without any parts? These are weird questions, but they are only forced upon us by the location response to the mereological pairing problem.)

Here is my second concern. The location response to the mereological pairing problem is capable of accounting for the fact that, at any given time, composite persons are located where their parts are located. But the location response is in tension with the fact that composite persons track the locations of their parts *across time*. Reflect on how we move (other) composite persons around. How do you move another person from one location to another? One way to do that is by moving their parts – you grab their arm and yank it. But given the location response, there is no reason to think that moving some composite person's parts would have any tendency to move the composite person. In fact, it would be a startling coincidence if composite persons follow their parts around from one location to another, given that composite persons do not have their locations in virtue of the locations of their parts, and parts do not have their locations in virtue of the locations of the persons they compose. Given the location response, what we should expect to happen when we move some parts is just for them to cease composing the composite person which occupies the region formerly occupied by those parts, since they no longer occupy the region occupied by that composite person. After all, normally if B obtains in virtue of A, then if A ceases to be the case, then B will also cease to be the case. For example, if the fact that you are torturing someone for fun grounds the fact that you are doing something morally impermissible, then by ensuring that the former fact does not obtain you will generally ensure that the latter fact does not obtain.[26] So, if the fact that some parts are located in the region in which some person is located grounds the fact that those parts compose that person, then by moving the parts to some other region we should expect it to be the case that they no longer compose that person. They composed the person because they were located where the person was located. But now we have moved the parts, and so they are presumably no longer located where the person is located. The parts would only continue to compose the person if the person followed the parts to their new location. But why

---

[26] "Generally" since, of course, you might refrain from torturing someone for fun only because you are instead performing some other action which is also morally impermissible.

would the person do that? You might think that composite persons *always* follow their parts around from one location to another, but this is plausible only if we reject the location response to the mereological pairing problem. If we reject the location response to the mereological pairing problem, and instead think that composite persons are located where their parts are located because they are composed of those parts, then we have a natural and straightforward explanation for why composite persons follow their parts around from one location to another: The locations of composite persons are grounded in the locations of their parts. But, again, if we accept the location response to the mereological pairing problem, then we will be left with no explanation for why composite persons follow their parts around from one location to another.

So, the location response to the mereological pairing problem is not very promising. What about the parallel response to the pairing problem for substance dualism? While substance dualism is sometimes assumed to imply that souls are unlocated, some substance dualists maintain that immaterial souls are located where their bodies, or brains, or some particular parts of their bodies or brains are located.[27] These substance dualists might think that souls are paired with their bodies, rather than some other bodies, *because* they are located where their bodies are located.

Unfortunately, this response to the pairing problem faces the same difficulties faced by the location response to the mereological pairing problem.

First, it simply seems wrong that souls are paired with their bodies (or their brains, some parts of their bodies or brains, etc.) because they are located where their bodies are located. This would entail that in order to create a new ensouled human being it is not enough for us to engage in those reproductive activities that tend to produce human bodies. Those reproductive activities may create a new body or may ensure that some things are arranged body-wise, but they will not ensure that a soul is paired with that body or with those things arranged body-wise. In order to ensure that the body or body-wise arranged objects are paired with a soul, we will also have to bring the new body/parts into a region occupied by a (preexisting?) soul. But this is absurd – it's not like pregnant people have to go hunting for ghosts to put into their wombs. Even if reincarnation occurs,

---

[27] Hasker 1999; Taliaferro and Goetz 2008: 309–310; Goetz and Taliaferro 2011: 173; Swinburne 2019: 139–140. Lowe (1996, 2001, 2006, 2008, 2010) also endorses a version of substance dualism according to which persons are distinct from their bodies but located where their bodies are located, but I'm not sure he would describe persons as "immaterial souls." In any case, Lowe (2006: 6) specifically notes that the view that souls are located provides a response to the pairing problem.

and so immaterial souls *are* out there in some sense waiting to be put into new bodies, it presumably does not occur by way of this mechanism: A developing fetus acquires a soul if it happens to occupy the location where some immaterial soul is located. What happens if the fetus fails to find a soul? If that never happens, why not? Are there so many souls floating around that a developing fetus is bound to occupy the location of at least one of them? What about in sparsely populated areas? What happens if an interstellar astronaut becomes pregnant? Are there enough souls out in space to ensure that the developing fetus comes to occupy the location of some soul or other? It seems much more sensible to think that souls, if they are located, are located where their bodies are located because they are paired with those bodies, rather than the other way around.

The second reason to think that the location response to the pairing problem doesn't work is that it is in tension with the fact that souls follow their bodies around from one location to another (assuming, again, that souls are located in the first place). If souls remain paired with their bodies because they are located where their bodies are located, then they must continually follow their bodies around in order to avoid becoming unpaired from their bodies. But it would be a startling coincidence if souls managed to follow their bodies around like this, especially as we do not consciously follow our bodies around. It is much simpler to suppose that souls follow their bodies around *because* they are already somehow paired with those bodies.

I should be clear that these difficulties only affect the substance dualist who claims that souls are paired with the bodies with which they are paired *because* they are located where their bodies are located. But most substance dualists who claim that souls are located where their bodies are located do not also claim that souls are paired with the bodies with which they are paired *because* they are located where their bodies are located.

Objection: It is much *less* surprising that composite persons follow their parts around from one location to another than it is that immaterial souls follow their bodies around from one location to another. This is because it is part of the *concept* of composition or parthood that composite objects follow their parts around from one location to another, while it is not part of the concept of immaterial souls that they follow their bodies around from one location to another.[28]

Response: Supposing it is part of the *concept* of composition or parthood that composites follow their parts around from one location to another, we

---

[28] Thanks to Ethan Brauer for the objection.

can still ask why it is that some composite physical person is a *composite* physical person rather than a *composite** physical person, where a composite* physical person is just like a composite physical person except that the concept of composition employed to describe them is such that it does not conceptually include the notion that composites* follow their parts around from one location to another. (Compare: "Why is he unmarried?" "Well, he is a bachelor, and it is built into the concept of a bachelor that they are unmarried." "Ok, but I'm asking *why they are a bachelor!*") Similarly, the substance dualist could simply stipulate that we are *souls**, which are exactly like souls except that it is built into the concept of a soul* that they follow their bodies around from one location to another. This does nothing to make it less mysterious that souls* follow their bodies around from one location to another, on the assumption that souls* are paired with the bodies with which they are paired because they are located where those bodies are located.

3.4 Response 3: This Composite Object Has *These* Things as Parts Because These Things Give Rise to, Create, or Ground This Composite Object

Consider the following response to Kim's pairing problem for substance dualism:

> it may be that there is a law dictating that a physical structure exhibiting certain properties produces a nonspatial soul of a certain kind, and that there is a further law dictating that any soul produced by a structure will, under certain conditions, remain causally related to certain material parts of that same structure.[29]

Here's the idea. My soul didn't pop out of thin air. Rather, my soul exists as a result of the formation of appropriate physical structures in *this* body. It is unsurprising, then, that my soul should be causally associated with this body rather than some other body.

This response to Kim's pairing problem is the inspiration for a response to the mereological pairing problem: This composite person has *these* things as parts because these are the things that give rise to, create, ground, build, etc. this composite person. In other words, this composite person exists in virtue of the existence and/or configuration of *these* parts, and that is why it has among its parts *these* parts, but not some other objects that are

[29] Bailey et al. 2011: 353.

not such that the composite person exists in virtue of the existence and/or configuration of those objects. For simplicity, I'll focus on grounding, and call this response to the mereological pairing problem, and the parallel response to the pairing problem for substance dualism, the "grounding response."[30] Supposing, for example, that I am a composite physical object, and I am composed of some subatomic particles, the idea is that I am composed of those subatomic particles (rather than some other subatomic particles) because those subatomic particles ground my existence.

The problem with these "grounding" responses to the two pairing problems is that they fail to reduce the number of brute relations in our total theory. The brute response to the mereological pairing problem trades brute mereological relations between composite objects and their parts with brute grounding relations between composite objects and their parts, while the brute response to the pairing problem for substance dualism trades brute causal pairing relations between bodies and souls with brute grounding relations between bodies and souls. The theoretical costs associated with positing brute mereological or causal pairing relations are traded for a similar theoretical cost associated with positing brute grounding pairing relations. I should be clear that what is objectionable is not that there are fundamental or ungrounded grounding relations. What is objectionable is that there are grounding relations the relata of which are paired in a brute manner. Perhaps it is a brute fact that whenever people behave in such-and-such a manner they ground a conversation. The objectionable bruteness I want to highlight isn't that conversations are grounded under such-and-such circumstances. Rather, what's objectionable is that the activities of these people ground *this* particular thing (*this* conversation) rather than *that* one. Perhaps at the end of the day we have sufficient reason to posit some grounding relations, even if they involve brute pairing. What seems to me to be objectionable, however, is trading brute mereological pairing relations, or brute causal pairing relations, for brute grounding pairing relations – that's getting us nowhere, if our goal is to reduce the number of brute pairing relations in our total theory.

One way to see this is by seeing if the grounding response to the pairing problems would help make sense of fission cases. In fission cases, it seems objectionable that the prefission person should be identical with one postfission person rather than the other. A grounding response to fission

---

[30] For simplicity's sake I'll also write as if composite persons might be grounded in their parts. But proponents of grounding disagree about what sorts of things are the relata of grounding relations, or even whether grounding should be understood in terms of things grounding other things (vs., e.g., an account of grounding as a sentential operator, as in Fine 2001).

3.4 Response 3: Grounding

cases does not seem very satisfying. This sort of response would say that the prefission person is identical with *this* postfission person rather than *that* one because, postfission, the prefission person is grounded in *these* parts or *this* body rather than *those* parts or *that* body (i.e., it is grounded in the parts or body associated with one of the postfission people rather than the other). This response to fission cases is unsatisfying because it simply pushes the bump under the carpet: We are left wondering why the prefission person is now grounded in *these* parts or *this* body, when *those* other parts and *that* other body (i.e., the parts or the body associated with the second postfission person) seem to be equally good candidates for playing that role.

But there's a clever move which the proponent of the grounding response might make at this point. Consider what Karen Bennett and Louis deRosset say about grounding relations.[31] Why does A ground B (rather than, say, C)? Here's why: A grounds A's grounding B. In other words, the first relata of the grounding relation, A, by itself grounds the fact that A enters into that grounding relation. We can go on to ask why A enters into *that* grounding relation – in other words, why does A ground A's grounding B? But here we give the same answer: The first relata of the grounding relation, A, by itself grounds the fact that A enters into that grounding relation, and so A by itself grounds the fact that A grounds A's grounding B. If you ask why A grounds *that*, then you will again receive the same sort of answer: Anytime A grounds anything, A grounds the fact that A enters into that grounding relation. I'm not sure I'm on board with this picture of grounding, but I'll assume for the sake of argument that it's unproblematic. Does this way of thinking about grounding offer a response to the two pairing problems?

Start with the mereological pairing problem. I ask, "Why do the xs compose y (rather than, say, z)?" The proponent of the grounding response gives the following answer: The fact that the xs compose y is grounded in the fact that the xs ground y. We have the natural follow-up question: Why do the xs ground y (rather than, say, z)? Well, the xs ground the fact that the xs ground y. So, in response to the question "Why do the xs ground y?" we can, on the current proposal, respond "because of the xs, period." Similarly, in response to the question "Why do the xs compose y?" we can, on the current proposal, respond that this fact regarding composition is ultimately grounded in the xs themselves. In other words, in response to the question "Why do the xs compose y?" we can say, "because of the xs, period."

---

[31] Bennett 2011, 2017: Ch. 7; deRosset 2013.

But now we can sensibly ask "Why isn't it the case that: the xs ground z, because of the xs, period?" Similarly, it seems as if we can sensibly ask "Why isn't it the case that: the xs compose z, because of the xs, period?" It seems to me that the only plausible response to such concerns is that there is some sense in which the xs *must* ground y (rather than z), and the xs *must* compose y (rather than z).

We can say something similar about the parallel response to the pairing problem for substance dualism. The parallel response is this. Why does this body ground or otherwise create *this* soul, rather than some other soul? Because of this body, period. This response to the pairing problem naturally leads us to ask "Why is it the case that this body grounds or otherwise creates this soul, rather than that soul, because of this body?" And, again, the only plausible response to this question seems to be that this body *must* ground or otherwise create this soul.

But there is a problem with saying that some parts *must* compose *this* composite object rather than some other one, or this body *must* ground or otherwise create *this* soul rather than some other one. The problem is that this sort of response to the pairing problems is simply a variant of the brute response to the pairing problems, except that it posits brute *necessary* pairing relations. But making the pairing relations necessary rather than contingent does not make the brute pairing relations any less objectionable. In fact, such brute necessary pairing relations strike me as objectionable for precisely the same reason brute pairing relations more generally are objectionable, namely because they complicate the total theory of those who posit them.

What's more, even if these sorts of brute necessary pairing relations are not objectionable, we nevertheless have a parity, since the brute necessary pairing relations can be appealed to in response to both the mereological pairing problem and the pairing problem for substance dualism.

3.5 Response 4: The Pairing Problems Simply Illustrate a More General Problem Which Affects Everyone

Think of any relation between objects x and y. You can ask why that relation holds between x and y rather than, say, x and z, where $z \neq y$. The pairing problems might just be thought to be variants of this more general problem, a problem that will vex pretty much everyone.[32] And if this is a

---

[32] Thanks here to Justin Christy and Michael Longenecker.

problem for pretty much everyone, the thought goes, then the problem may simply be unavoidable, and so it does nothing to undermine any particular views (e.g., substance dualism, or the view that we are composite physical objects) in comparison with competing views. Swinburne[33] makes a similar point regarding the pairing problem for substance dualism. The problem, Swinburne says, is that laws of nature connect objects in virtue of the properties[34] had by those objects, not in virtue of the identities of those objects. So, when a new soul is formed, the laws of nature might dictate *that* a new soul is formed (because, say, a fetus has reached a certain level of development), but not *which* soul is formed. If the problem stems from the fact that the laws of nature connect objects by their properties, and not by their identities, then the problem will crop up any time a new object comes into existence in virtue of the operations of natural laws, not just when souls come into existence.

The main point to note about this response to the pairing problems is that it seems to apply equally to both the mereological pairing problem and the pairing problem for substance dualism. So, if this response to the pairing problems is on the right track, we are left again with parity between substance dualism and the view that we are composite objects: Both views face pairing problem concerns, but these concerns are not particularly troubling.

As for whether this is a satisfying response to either pairing problem, I'm not entirely sure what to think. Perhaps everyone will need brute pairing relations of some sort or other. For example, we might explain why the candle was lit by this match, rather than some other match, in terms of the spatial relations which hold between the candle and the matches: The candle was near *this* match but not *that* match. In this case, we've explained one pairing relation (*this* match causing the candle to be lit) in terms of other spatial relations. But the same problem will arise for the location relations we have just implicitly appealed to: Why is this object located in *this* region and that object located in *that* region, when they might have, say, traded places instead? Perhaps at the end of the day we'll need some brute relations of this sort. But it doesn't follow that we shouldn't do without brute relations if we can help it. The substance dualist will need many brute pairing relations which nonsubstance dualists may not need: Brute pairing relations between souls and bodies. That may be a strike against substance dualism. Similarly, those who think that we are composite objects will need

---

[33] Swinburne 2019: 170–171.
[34] Here by "properties" I think Swinburne has in mind qualitative properties in particular.

many brute mereological pairing relations that we won't need if we do not think that we are composite objects. That may be a strike against the view that we are composite objects.

3.6 Response 5: Mereological Antirealism

A final response to the mereological pairing problem suggests that the fact that some composite person has *these* parts rather than *those* parts, or that some parts compose *this* person rather than *that* person, has something to do with the way we think about the mereological relations between that composite person and their parts. This sort of response to the mereological pairing problem comes in several varieties.[35] Perhaps the fact that this composite person has *these* parts has something to do with the fact that we think, or *would* think under suitable circumstances, that those parts compose that composite person.[36] Similarly, Kenneth Pearce[37] defends "mereological idealism," according to which some xs compose a y when the xs are "unified in thought under a concept." Perhaps it would not be such a stretch to suppose that, if the circumstances under which composition occurs track our mental activities in this manner, then particular mereological pairing relations might also track our mental activities. In other words, the idea would be that we determine whether composition occurs in some particular situation, *and* we determine which composite person is composed by some parts. Or perhaps God decides how parts are paired with composite persons.[38]

There's at least one thing to be said for the antirealist responses to the mereological pairing problem: Unlike some of the responses to the mereological pairing problem discussed in this chapter, these antirealist responses don't obviously pass the buck. That is, none of them obviously replace the innumerable seemingly brute mereological relations cited in the mereological pairing problem with some other more or less equally brute set of relations.

Nevertheless, these antirealist responses to the mereological pairing problem may be objectionable on other grounds. Is it really plausible that the mereological facts regarding persons (e.g., which parts we have)

---

[35] For a fuller discussion of mereological antirealism, see Brenner 2022. See especially §4.3 for a discussion of mereological antirealism and the mereological pairing problem.
[36] Kriegel 2008, 2012.
[37] Pearce 2017.
[38] Yang and Davis 2017; Bailey 2021: Ch. 5; Brenner 2022.

track our *beliefs* about the mereological facts (or our beliefs under suitable circumstances)? To suggest they do seems objectionably anthropocentric, and it seems to attribute to us spooky abilities to change the material world with our thoughts.[39] God's deciding the mereological facts would not be objectionable for these reasons. Nevertheless, the existence of God is still obviously quite controversial, and it would be best if the plausibility of our being composite objects was not tied to the notion that God exists and has the ability to stipulate which mereological relations obtain.

We can presumably give analogous antirealist responses to the pairing problem for substance dualism. The theistic variant of this sort of antirealist response has already been endorsed by several prominent substance dualists, who contend that God pairs souls with bodies.[40] The notion that *humans* might be able to pair specific souls with specific bodies seems to me to be dubious, just as the analogous notion that humans can pair composites with their parts seems to me to be dubious.

3.7 Conclusion

In Chapter 2, we saw how many of the main objections to substance dualism can be transformed into objections to the view that we are composite physical objects. In this chapter, I have discussed at length one particular objection to substance dualism, that there is something objectionable about immaterial souls causally interacting with physical bodies, where this concern is developed in terms of the pairing problem. I have argued that there is a parallel pairing problem facing the view that we are composite objects. There are responses that can be made to this mereological pairing problem, but they are objectionable, and in any case, they are such that we can develop parallel responses to the pairing problem for substance dualism. So, again, there is a parity between the view that we are composite physical objects and the view that we are immaterial souls.

---

[39] Brenner 2022: §2.
[40] Pope Pius XII 1950: §36; Swinburne 1986: 198–199; Eccles 1994: 180; Foster 2001: 29; Plantinga 2007: 132–133.

4

Arguments for Substance Dualism

4.1 Introduction

In Chapters 2–3, I argued that the main arguments against substance dualism can be parodied and transformed into arguments against substance dualism's main competitor, that we are composite physical objects. In this chapter, I will argue that the main arguments *for* substance dualism can be parodied and transformed either into arguments against substance dualism or into arguments for the thesis that we are composite physical objects. The arguments I discuss in this chapter may be objectionable for reasons other than the fact that they can be parodied. I will sometimes mention these further objections to the arguments, but for the most part, I confine my attention to explaining how the arguments can be parodied.

Recall the overall argument I am trying to make: We are either simple or composite or nothing, and while I think that the last option can probably be ruled out, it is much harder to decide between the first two options. This chapter further supports the idea that it is difficult to decide between the first two options.

4.2 Modal Arguments

Some of the most prominent arguments for substance dualism are modal arguments. Modal arguments contend that we can exist in circumstances in which our bodies do not exist, and so conclude on that basis that we are not our bodies, since we have properties not had by our bodies – namely, the modal property of possibly existing in circumstances in which our bodies do not exist.[1] Arguments of this sort contend that we can exist in circumstances in which our bodies do not exist either because we can exist

---

[1] A modal argument for substance dualism is given in Descartes' *Meditations on First Philosophy* (AT VII 78; Descartes 1996: 54). Recent defenses of modal arguments for substance dualism include, among others, Swinburne 1984: §2, 1986: Ch. 8, 2013: Ch. 6, 2014: 149–151, 2019: Ch. 4–5; Taliaferro

with bodies distinct from our present bodies, or, alternatively, because we can exist without any bodies at all. Usually, the crucial modal premise of the argument, that one can exist in circumstances in which one's body does not exist, is supported by appeal to the conceivability of a situation in which one exists without one's body. I take this conceivability to amount to something like the following idea: One can imagine states of affairs in which one exists without one's body, one can understand what the imagined state of affairs amounts to (e.g., that it really is a situation in which one exists without one's body), and one can see that there are no evident contradictions or impossibilities in those imagined states of affairs.

Suitably developed, a modal argument can lead us to conclude that none of us is identical with any composite physical object since, for any composite physical object (a body, a brain, some composite part of a brain, etc.), we can exist in circumstances in which that composite physical object does not exist. For simplicity, let's confine our attention to modal arguments which are directed against our being identical with our bodies.[2]

That's the basic idea, but there are different ways of developing this sort of modal argument for substance dualism. In particular, there are different ways of defending the most crucial and controversial component of any modal argument, the possibility premise: that each of us possibly exists in circumstances in which our bodies do not exist. I will examine one way of defending the possibility premise in §4.2.1. For now, let's see if there are any parody arguments against the basic modal argument described above.

Zimmerman[3] and van Inwagen[4] have the following concern with modal arguments for substance dualism: Whatever grounds we have for thinking that it is possible that I exist in circumstances in which my body does not exist should lead me to conclude that it is *not* possible that I exist in circumstances in which my body does not exist. For example, Zimmerman suggests that, while it seems possible that I exist without my body, it seems similarly possible that I am *identical* with my body, in which case it is not possible that I exist without my body. If, for example, we think that it is conceivable that I exist without my body and conclude on that basis that it

---

1994: 173–188; Lowe 1996: 34, 2001: 142–143, 2006: 9, 2008: 174, 2010: 446–448; Plantinga 2006: 4–11, 2007: 102–105; Lund 2014: 76; Meixner 2014: §§4–5; Walker 2014: 181–182.

[2] It's also worth noting that modal arguments are not strictly speaking arguments for substance dualism but are rather arguments for the more general conclusion that we are each nonphysical. That is compatible with idealism. But for simplicity, I will treat modal arguments as arguments for substance dualism since this is how they are normally treated by both their proponents and their opponents. The arguments could always be supplemented with premises to the effect that idealism is false.

[3] Zimmerman 1991: 222–223.

[4] Van Inwagen 1998: 68–69.

is possible that I exist without my body, we should similarly believe that it is conceivable that I am identical with my body, and so on that basis conclude that I cannot exist without my body. We are left, then, at an impasse, insofar as we have equally strong grounds for thinking that I am not my body (since it is possible that I exist in circumstances in which my body does not exist) as we have for thinking that I *am* my body (since it is possible that I am identical with my body).

Zimmerman's parody argument does not seem to me to be exactly parallel to the original modal argument for substance dualism: The original argument does not rely on the premise that it is possible that I am identical with some specific thing other than my body, but rather relies on the premise that it is possible that I exist when my body does not exist. A more precisely parallel argument would appeal to something like the premise "possibly, I exist in circumstances in which my soul does not exist." From this possibility premise, we can derive the conclusion that I am not a soul (or not "my" soul). And it seems that if we are justified in accepting the possibility premise in the original modal argument for substance dualism, then we should be justified in accepting the parody possibility premise. The standard justification for the possibility premise in the modal argument for substance dualism relies on the apparent conceivability of our existing in circumstances in which our bodies do not exist. But, similarly, it seems as if we can conceive our existing in circumstances in which "our" souls do not exist: In fact, the physicalist seems to conceive of these possible states of affairs on a regular basis.

So, following Zimmerman and van Inwagen, I think that there are successful parody arguments for the standard modal argument for substance dualism, and in particular that if we are justified in accepting the crucial possibility premise of the latter argument (i.e., the premise which claims that possibly I exist in circumstances in which my body does not exist), then we should be justified in accepting a parallel possibility premise in a parody argument against substance dualism. So, we are at an epistemological impasse. Here is how van Inwagen makes the point, writing as a materialist who is presented with the modal argument for substance dualism:

> Whatever merit the crucial modal premise of your argument may have, you can't expect the philosophical world to accept it unless you can show why it is somehow better or more reasonable than the crucial modal premise of the argument for the opposite conclusion that I have presented. And I don't see how you can do that. At any rate, until you have done it, the two arguments, so to speak, cancel each other out – and are therefore both without any force.[5]

---

[5] Van Inwagen 1998: 68–69.

4.2 *Modal Arguments*

The natural next step should be to take a closer look at whether the modal premise of the substance dualist's modal argument is more plausible than the modal premises in parody modal arguments against substance dualism.

In response to parody concerns, Goetz and Taliaferro[6] argue that there are grounds for thinking that the relationship between us and our bodies is contingent, which do not carry over to support the notion that the relationship between us and any immaterial soul is contingent.

First, according to idealism, the world is fundamentally nonphysical, in the sense that physical objects either do not exist or they are constituted somehow by mental events (e.g., sense impressions). And, Goetz and Taliaferro claim, whether or not idealism is correct, it is evidently metaphysically possible and so "offers a coherent portrait of persons without their corporeal bodies (as understood by most materialists)."[7] I have two responses. First, those who deny substance dualism need not deny that idealism is metaphysically possible, and, more generally, need not deny that it is metaphysically possible that there are nonphysical people. They may even think that in the actual world there are nonphysical people (if, e.g., they believe in God, or angels). And we can agree that it is metaphysically possible that there are nonphysical people without conceding the possibility premise in the modal argument for dualism, which is that *we* are possibly nonphysical (or, more carefully, that *we* are possibly nonidentical with our bodies). My second response is that if idealism is metaphysically possible, so is physicalism. Whatever support the possibility of idealism is supposed to provide for the possibility premise in the modal argument for substance dualism, the possibility of physicalism should be able to provide exactly analogous support for the possibility premise in modal arguments against substance dualism.

Here is Goetz and Taliaferro's second response to parody modal arguments against substance dualism. They argue that we have positive grounds for thinking that the relationship between us and our bodies is contingent, namely the thought experiments offered in support of substance dualism (e.g., in thought experiments where we become disembodied or where we swap bodies), as well as in out-of-body experiences. Whether or not out-of-body experiences are veridical, and so whether or not they are cases where people *actually* become disembodied, they at any rate support the notion that it is *metaphysically possible* that we become disembodied. As Goetz and Taliaferro put it, reports of out-of-body experiences "present us with possible states of affairs .... They are not akin to reports of seeing

---

[6] Goetz and Taliaferro 2011: 96–97.
[7] Goetz and Taliaferro 2011: 96.

a round triangle or observing water that is not composed of H_2O."[8] In response, I would note that none of these considerations show what Goetz and Taliaferro think they show. In particular, none of them show that we should not accept any of the possibility premises in parody modal arguments against substance dualism. What's more, we may have grounds for accepting one of those possibility premises which are parallel to the grounds just mentioned in support of the substance dualist's possibility premise. It is conceivable, for example, that we become disembodied (this is what we conceive of when, e.g., we think about out-of-body experiences), but it is similarly conceivable that we are entirely physical. To suppose otherwise is to suppose that physicalist personal ontologies are not only false but inconceivable, and surely this is too strong. It seems false that any conceivable scenario in which one exists is a scenario in which one is a nonphysical object of some sort.

I also suspect that thought experiments where we become nonphysical do not automatically show that we possibly exist in circumstances in which our bodies do not exist. They may simply show that it is possible that our bodies become nonphysical. Of course, if a body becomes nonphysical, then it may no longer be a *body*, if bodies are by definition physical objects. But what I am proposing is that bodies may not be essentially physical, and so may not be essentially bodies. I am sure that many readers will reject this idea out of hand. They will be sure that physical objects, such as bodies, are essentially physical. But what is the source of this conviction? It's not obvious to me that physical objects are essentially physical, and I'm not aware of any serious arguments for this thesis. What's more, we have some positive grounds for thinking that bodies are possibly nonphysical. The notion that bodies are possibly nonphysical would make sense of the intuitions we enjoy in both the modal argument for substance dualism and in one of the parody arguments against substance dualism: (1) that we are each possibly nonphysical, and (2) that we are each possibly physical. Hooker,[9] Merricks,[10] and Bailey[11] also object to modal arguments for substance dualism by noting that it may be metaphysically possible for our bodies to become nonphysical. One point which Merricks makes in support of this objection is worth noting here. It seems sensible to avoid needlessly extensive revisions to our networks of beliefs. For those who think that we are identical with our bodies, rejecting the dualist's premise that bodies are

---

[8] Goetz and Taliaferro 2011: 96.
[9] Hooker 1978.
[10] Merricks 1994.
[11] Bailey 2021: Ch. 2.

4.2 Modal Arguments

essentially physical will be a less severe revision to their network of beliefs than rejecting the idea that we are identical with our bodies. Merricks argues that this is a reason for those who think that we are identical with our bodies to opt for the former route rather than the latter route.[12]

I have argued that a standard modal argument for substance dualism can be parodied and transformed into a modal argument against substance dualism, and there seems to be no very good reason to favor the original argument for substance dualism over the parody argument against substance dualism. It is worth noting that this point holds true for a recent, more sophisticated version of the modal argument for substance dualism, due to Swinburne.[13] Swinburne contends that "I" functions as an informative designator, in the sense that each of us knows to what "I" refers in circumstances in which we use that word (or in circumstances in which we think thoughts involving the word or notion of "I," such as the thought "I can exist in circumstances in which my body does not exist"). Swinburne takes this to support the possibility premise in the modal argument for substance dualism since it supports the notion that we could know whether we exist in some conceivable circumstances, including those circumstances in which our bodies do not exist. In other words, I can know whether I could exist in circumstances in which my body does not exist, since I can know to what (and whether) "I" would refer in circumstances in which my body does not exist. But even supposing that Swinburne is correct that "I" is an informative designator, I do not see how this will help us decide between the dualist's modal argument and the physicalist's parody argument. The dualist and the physicalist both claim to conceive of certain special scenarios in which they exist, and they both claim that the conceivability of the scenarios in question support their favored account of personal ontology. If "I" functions as an informative designator, then both the dualist and the physicalist should be taken to know whether they exist in their favored conceivable scenarios (i.e., those scenarios cited in their modal

---

[12] The notion that it is metaphysically possible that bodies become nonphysical might be supported on other somewhat less compelling grounds as well. For example, according to four-dimensionalism objects persist by having different temporal parts at each of the times at which they exist. If that's right (a big "if"), then I don't see any obvious obstacle to a temporally extended person having entirely physical parts at earlier times and entirely nonphysical parts at later times (cf. Lewis 1971). There is also the idea (with which I am sympathetic) that we have few if any essential properties (Mackie 2006; Sullivan 2012, 2017) – e.g., the property of being essentially physical. And there is a recent defense of a version of animalism according to which animals can become disembodied (Thornton 2019), as well as a thought experiment described by Bailey (2021: Ch. 2) in which a wholly material person gradually becomes wholly immaterial.

[13] See Swinburne 2013: Ch. 6, 2014: 149–150, 2019: Ch. 4–5.

arguments). So, how do we choose between them? Who's right? Thinking of "I" as an informative designator does not seem to help us decide.

4.2.1 The Replacement Argument

One type of modal argument that deserves special scrutiny is the "replacement argument." The replacement argument relies on the premise that the body cannot survive the replacement of all of its parts, or the replacement of all of its parts in an arbitrarily short period of time. Since, by contrast, I *can* survive the replacement of all of the parts of my body, or the replacement of all of the parts of my body in an arbitrarily short period of time, then, it is claimed, I am not my body.[14]

The notion that I could survive the replacement of all of the parts of my body is supported by thought experiments in which all of the parts of my body are replaced, and yet I continue to exist. As a matter of fact, most of the atoms making up our bodies *are* replaced over time, and we generally think that we do survive the replacement of those parts. Now, you might think that my body could also survive the gradual replacement of its parts. But, so the thought goes, my body could not survive the replacement of all of its parts if that process of replacement occurs quickly enough – say, within a tiny fraction of a second. And yet I *could* survive the replacement of all of the parts of my body, regardless of the speed with which those parts are replaced. Since I can survive a change which my body cannot survive, I must not be my body.

Much could be said about this argument. What concerns us here is, again, whether a parody argument can be constructed, one which would lead us to think that we are our bodies, or at any rate that we are *not* each an immaterial soul. And it seems that a parody argument of this sort can be constructed. The replacement argument relies on the premise

---

[14] See, e.g., Lowe 2001: 142–143, 2006: 9, 2008: 174, 2010: 446–448; Plantinga 2006: 4–11, 2007: 102–105; Meixner 2010: §5. A similar, though less plausible, modal argument appeals to mereological essentialism, the thesis that composite objects cannot survive the loss of *any* of their parts. Our bodies evidently do lose parts all the time, and so, according to mereological essentialism, our bodies do not survive the loss of any of these parts. We evidently *do* survive the loss of some of the parts of our bodies, however, so the thought goes, we possibly exist in circumstances in which our bodies do not exist, and so we are not identical with our bodies. This sort of argument is given in Moreland 2018a: 110–111, 2018b: 52; Rickabaugh and Evans 2018: 242. A similar argument is given in Chisholm 1978: 30. This or a similar argument may also have been defended by Joseph Butler and Thomas Reid (for discussion, see Goetz and Taliaferro 2011: 111–120). I will not discuss this argument further. Mereological essentialism is not very plausible. At any rate, the mereological essentialist modal argument is much less plausible than the replacement argument.

that I possibly exist in circumstances in which my body does not exist, and it supports this premise by noting that I can exist in circumstances in which all of the parts of my body are replaced (or replaced in an arbitrarily short time span), while my body cannot survive the replacement of all of its parts (or the replacement of all of its parts in an arbitrarily short time span). But we can run an exactly parallel replacement argument that would lead us to conclude that none of us is an *im*material object, such as an immaterial soul. For each nonphysical object, it seems possible that each of us exists in circumstances in which that nonphysical object is replaced. If the nonphysical object has parts, then we can note that it seems possible that each of us exists in circumstances in which all of the parts of that nonphysical object are replaced, or in circumstances in which all of the parts of that nonphysical object are replaced in an arbitrarily short period of time. But no such nonphysical object could exist in circumstances in which all of its parts are replaced, or in circumstances in which all of its parts are replaced in an arbitrarily short period of time. So, none of us is a nonphysical object. The inferences involved in this sort of parody argument are identical to the inferences involved in the original replacement argument for substance dualism. What's more, the possibility/impossibility premises involved (e.g., I possibly exist in circumstances in which all of the parts of this nonphysical object are replaced; it is not possible that this nonphysical object exists in circumstances in which all of its parts are replaced) seem to be on a par: If we are justified in accepting the possibility/impossibility premises in the original replacement argument, then presumably we are also justified in accepting the corollary premises in the parody replacement argument. For one thing, any thought experiment in which the parts of my body are replaced, but I continue to exist, will have a parallel thought experiment in which some immaterial objects (or parts thereof) are replaced, and yet I continue to exist.

Of course, we may not be justified in accepting the premises of the parody argument if we already think that we are immaterial souls, since then we may think that there is at least one nonphysical object which is such that I cannot survive the replacement of all of its parts, namely the immaterial soul with which I am identical. But those who think that we are bodies can make a precisely parallel point: They may not accept that I can survive the replacement of all of the parts of my body since they think that I *am* my body. The point here is that those who are antecedently committed to the negation of the conclusion of one of these replacement arguments will not think that the replacement argument against their view is sound. But that point holds true for both the replacement argument for substance dualism and the parody argument, and so parity remains. Those who are neutral with respect to this debate regarding personal ontology may be swayed by either replacement argument.

There is another concern I have with the replacement argument. It's not a parody, but it does show another way in which there is a sort of parity between substance dualism and the view that we are composite physical objects such as bodies. Those who think that we are our bodies cannot accept every premise of the replacement argument, since they would then be committed to the conclusion of the replacement argument, that we are not our bodies. But, I claim, neither can many substance dualists accept every premise of the replacement argument. The idea is that bodies and immaterial souls are similar to one another in a way which makes it problematic for the substance dualist to simultaneously endorse two premises of the replacement argument for substance dualism, namely the possibility premise of the replacement argument (i.e., that it is possible that I exist in circumstances in which all of the parts of my body are replaced, or in which all of the parts of my body are replaced in an arbitrarily short period of time), and the *im*possibility premise of the replacement argument (i.e., that it is not possible that my body exist in circumstances in which all of its parts are replaced, or replaced in an arbitrarily short period of time). Here is what I have in mind. Why is it supposed to be problematic to think that a body could survive the replacement of all of its parts, or the replacement of all of its parts in an arbitrarily short period of time? Presumably the problem stems from the dependence of the whole on its parts for its existence – since the body depends for its existence on these parts, it could not survive the replacement of all of these parts, or the replacement of all of these parts in an arbitrarily short period of time. But many substance dualists think that the soul also depends on its body for its existence and so depends on the parts of the body for its existence. But then presumably if the dependence of a body on its parts prevents it from surviving the gradual or rapid replacement of all of the parts of the body, then the dependence of the soul on those parts should also prevent it from surviving the gradual or rapid replacement of all of those parts. So, again, there seems to be a tension in many substance dualists' simultaneous endorsement of both the possibility premise and the impossibility premise of the replacement argument for substance dualism.

4.3 An Epistemic Argument for Substance Dualism

Something like the following argument is given in Avicenna's "flying man" argument,[15] as well as by Descartes in the fourth part of his *Discourse on the Method*.[16] The argument is this: I cannot doubt my own existence, but I can doubt the existence of my body. So, I am not my body. Alternatively: I can affirm my own existence in circumstances in which I cannot affirm the existence of my body (in, e.g., the setting described in Avicenna's flying man thought experiment – I am floating in the air without any noticeable bodily sensations). So, I am not my body.

This argument might be confused for a modal argument for substance dualism, but there is an important difference between the two sorts of arguments. Modal arguments contend that I can exist in circumstances in which my body does not exist and so conclude on that basis that I am not my body. The epistemic argument described above is different. The crucial premise of the epistemic argument is not a modal metaphysical premise to the effect that it is metaphysically possible that I exist when my body does not exist. Rather, the crucial premise of the epistemic argument regards what I am rationally capable of affirming: for example, that there are circumstances in which I can doubt that my body exists, but in which I cannot doubt that I exist.

Much has been written about this sort of argument, and it seems to me to suffer from certain irremediable difficulties, chief among them being that the inference from the epistemic possibility cited in the argument (e.g., that there are circumstances in which I can affirm my own existence, but I cannot affirm the existence of my body) to the conclusion that I am not my body is invalid.[17] Compare: There are circumstances in which I can affirm the existence of the president, but I cannot affirm the existence of Biden. But surely it doesn't follow that Biden isn't the president.

More importantly for our purposes, the argument can also easily be parodied:

Parody 1: I can doubt whether my soul exists (physicalists do this all the time!), but I cannot doubt whether *I* exist. So, I am not my soul. And since we can run this argument for any other soul, I am not any other soul either.

---

[15] Avicenna 1959. For English translation and discussion, see Marmura 1986.
[16] AT VI 32–33; 2006: 29.
[17] Cf. Black 2008: 65; Kaukua 2015: 37.

Parody 2: I can affirm my existence in circumstances in which I cannot affirm the existence of my soul (physicalists do this all the time!). So, I am not my soul. And since we can run this argument for any other soul, I am not any other soul either.

4.4 The Argument from the Alleged Fact That Facts Regarding Personal Identity Outstrip the Physical Facts

One argument for substance dualism proceeds from the apparent fact that we can know all of the physical facts regarding some situation, and yet not know certain facts regarding personal identity in that situation and so concludes on that basis that facts regarding personal identity are not physical facts.[18] The argument is put most forcefully in terms involving hypothetical fission cases. Consider, for example, split-brain transplants. There is reason to believe that we could survive the loss of a single brain hemisphere. In fact, there are individuals who *have* had one of their brain hemispheres (or much of a single brain hemisphere) removed, and we tend to think they have survived the operation. But what would happen if we transplant one brain hemisphere into one body and the other brain hemisphere into another (perhaps qualitatively indistinguishable) body? There seem to be several possibilities here. The pretransplant person may be identical to one of the two resulting brain hemisphere recipients, or they may come to be composed of both hemisphere recipients, or they may cease to exist, or perhaps something else happens. But as Swinburne[19] notes, if such a split-brain transplant were to occur, our knowledge of all of the physical facts surrounding the case will not tell us which of these outcomes is the correct one, and so will not tell us what happens to the person who existed prior to the split-brain transplants. So, Swinburne concludes, facts regarding personal identity extend beyond the physical facts, a conclusion which supports the dualist thesis that persons are nonphysical things.[20]

---

[18] Swinburne 1986: 148–149, 2013: 152–154, 2014: 148–149, 2019: 53–55, 68–70; Nida-Rümelin 2006, 2010, 2013; Zimmerman 2012.
[19] Swinburne 1986: 148–149, 2013: 152–154, 2019: 53–55.
[20] In Chapter 3, §3.2, I described Swinburne's argument a bit differently. There I said the argument was that knowledge of what happens to the parts of the split-brain patient's brain or body would not tell us which parts, if any, the person has after the surgery. I described Swinburne's argument this way in order to lay bare its connection to the mereological pairing problem. That being said, these two descriptions of Swinburne's argument do not really conflict with one another: from the fact that we can know all of the physical facts regarding the split-brain surgery and yet not know what happens to the person, it follows that knowledge of what happens to the parts of the split-brain patient's brain or body would not tell us which parts, if any, the person has after the surgery.

4.4 Personal Identity Outstrips the Physical

I do not think that this argument succeeds. If we are physical objects (say, composite physical objects such as brains or bodies), then surely if we knew *all* of the physical facts, then we would know facts regarding diachronic personal identity. We would know, for example, whether one of the brain hemisphere recipients is identical with the physical object (i.e., the physical person) who existed prior to the split-brain transplant. Similarly, we would know the relevant pairing facts: which parts, if any, some composite physical person is paired with after the split-brain transplant. Facts regarding the identity of physical objects and facts regarding the mereological relations, which obtain between composite physical objects and their parts, are, of course, physical facts. (Alternatively, if we can't say that these facts are physical facts, then perhaps we simply don't have a good enough grasp on what it means for a fact to be physical to evaluate Swinburne's argument. I will charitably assume that this is not the case.) So, Swinburne's argument seems to simply assume what it sets out to prove, namely that there are no physical facts of this sort (i.e., identity facts regarding physical persons or mereological pairing facts regarding composite physical persons) involved in the split-brain transplant thought experiment.

We can construct a parody argument which is objectionable in this same way: In the split-brain transplant thought experiment, we can know all of the *non*physical facts, and not know who is identical with whom. We can know, for example, which nonphysical objects there are, if any, and we can know what properties and relations they instantiate, and yet still fail to know who is identical with whom. So, facts regarding personal identity are not nonphysical facts.[21] This argument is objectionable because it assumes that which it sets out to prove, namely that there are no nonphysical facts regarding personal identity in the situation envisioned in the split-brain transplant thought experiment (including, e.g., identity facts regarding nonphysical persons).

Perhaps where Swinburne goes wrong is in assuming that physical facts – regarding, for example, the identity of physical persons – would be empirically detectable.[22] It is true that we may know all of the *empirically detectable* facts regarding what happens in the split-brain thought experiment, and yet not know the facts regarding personal identity. But this does not show

---

[21] J. T. Ismael (2007: 147–148) makes a similar point in response to modal arguments for substance dualism when she notes that, for any domain of facts, including facts regarding souls, facts regarding personal identity can seem like further facts.
[22] This assumption is made explicit in Nida-Rümelin's version of the argument (Nida-Rümelin 2010: 194, 2013: 704).

82   4 Arguments for Substance Dualism

that we could know all of the physical facts regarding what happens in the thought experiment, and yet not know the facts regarding personal identity. This is because not all the physical facts are empirically detectable, including at least some identity facts regarding composite physical objects and facts regarding mereological pairing relations. This is why we find puzzles like the Ship of Theseus so difficult to resolve – we cannot simply detect empirically which ship in the story of the Ship of Theseus is identical with the original ship, or which parts, if any, the original ship is paired with at the end of the story. But we should not conclude that the Ship of Theseus is therefore not a composite physical object.

4.5   The Argument from Phenomenology and Intentionality

One argument for substance dualism goes like this. Physical objects cannot have phenomenal states[23] or intentional states.[24] But we have phenomenal and intentional states. So, we must not be physical objects. So, we are *non*physical objects, souls.

The question of whether physical objects could have intentional or phenomenal states should not be confused with the question of whether intentional or phenomenal states could be physical *properties*, or reducible to physical properties, or functional states realized by physical properties, and so on. Physicalism, as it concerns us here, is the thesis that we are physical objects. This thesis is distinct from the thesis that all properties are physical properties, or reducible to physical properties, or functional states realized by physical properties, or whatever.[25]

But why should we think that physical objects cannot exhibit phenomenal or intentional states? Some intuitive motivation for this idea is found in Leibniz's famous mill thought experiment:

> Moreover, we must confess that the *perception*, and what depends on it, is *inexplicable in terms of mechanical reasons*, that is, through shapes and motions. If we imagine that there is a machine whose structure makes it think, sense, and have perceptions, we could conceive it enlarged, keeping the same proportions, so that we could enter into it, as one enters into a mill. Assuming that, when inspecting its interior, we will only find parts that

---

[23] I.e., states which are such that there is something it is like for us to be in those states, such as seeing the color blue or tasting coffee.
[24] I.e., mental states which exhibit aboutness: e.g., my thought "Renee is a dog" is about the dog Renee.
[25] For arguments for the conclusion that phenomenal states are not physical properties (or reducible to physical properties, etc.), see, e.g., Jackson 1982; Chalmers 1996a.

push one another, and we will never find anything to explain a perception. And so, we should seek perception in the simple substance and not in the composite or in the machine.[26]

The target of Leibniz's thought experiment is the idea that we are composite. But this thought experiment is often taken to undermine the idea that we are physical objects of any sort, whether simple or composite. And this would be appropriate if our being physical plausibly requires that we are *composite* physical objects. Similarly, while Leibniz's attention is on "perception," the thought experiment is often taken to undermine the idea that physical objects could exhibit phenomenal or intentional states, whether or not those states are what Leibniz had in mind when he wrote of "perception." I'll return to Leibniz's mill thought experiment in a moment.

A recent proponent of the argument from phenomenology and intentionality is Alvin Plantinga.[27] His contention is that physical objects cannot exhibit *intentionality*, but what I have to say about his argument is also applicable to similar arguments for substance dualism from *phenomenology*.

Plantinga's argument is for the conclusion that "no material objects can think – i.e., reason and believe, entertain propositions, draw inferences, and the like."[28] We think, of course, so if Plantinga is correct, then we are not physical objects. According to Plantinga, the reason that physical objects cannot think is because they cannot exhibit the relevant sort of intentionality or aboutness which they would have to exhibit in order to think. So, for example, the reason that a physical object cannot think the thought "Renee is a dog" is because the thought in question would be *about* Renee, the dog, and physical objects cannot exhibit this sort of intentionality. (Actually, the target of Plantinga's argument is the idea that physical objects could exhibit *basic* or *underived* intentionality. Basic or underived intentionality is to be contrasted with derived intentionality. The thought "Renee is a dog" exhibits basic or underived intentionality. By contrast, the words "Renee is a dog," written on a sheet of paper, exhibit derived intentionality. They only exhibit intentionality, and in particular, they are only *about* the dog Renee, because they were produced by someone who intended to exhibit a particular thought or idea – that is, because a human being wrote the words "Renee is a dog" with the intention of making a statement *about* the dog Renee. By contrast, if intelligent life had never existed, and by coincidence some rocks were arranged so as to

---

[26] Leibniz 1989: 215.
[27] Plantinga 2006: 11–22, 2007: 105–118, 136–141, 2008: 51–66.
[28] Plantinga 2006: 11.

spell out "Renee is a dog," the arrangement of the rocks would exhibit no intentionality, since there would exist no agents to imbue the rocks with the relevant sort of intentionality. In what follows I will simplify the discussion a bit and write as if the target of Plantinga's argument is the idea that physical objects exhibit *any* sort of intentionality, rather than just basic or underived intentionality.)

So, why think that physical things cannot exhibit intentionality or aboutness? Plantinga seems sympathetic to Leibniz's mill thought experiment, which I described above. What the mill thought experiment shows is that physical interactions of the sort present in the operations of a mill (e.g., pushing and pulling) cannot enable a physical system to exhibit intentionality. Simply in virtue of these sort of mechanical interactions among its part, a physical object will never have a thought or belief which is *about* something else (e.g., Renee the dog). And Plantinga thinks that we should say something similar about the sorts of physical interactions described by modern physics – simply in virtue of these sort of physical interactions among its part, a composite physical object will never have a thought or belief which is *about* something else.[29] It follows that composite physical objects do not exhibit intentionality, under the assumption that they could only do so by way of the physical interactions among their parts. And since, Plantinga assumes, the world's *non*composite physical objects do not exhibit intentionality, it follows that no physical objects exhibit intentionality:

> how can it be, that an assemblage of neurons, a group of material objects firing away *has a content*? How can that happen? More poignantly, *what is it* for such an event to have a content? What is it for this structured group of neurons, or the event of which they are a part, to be related, for example, to the proposition *Cleveland is a beautiful city* in such a way that the latter is its content? A single neuron (or quark, electron, atom or whatever) presumably isn't a belief and doesn't have content; but how can belief, content, arise from physical interaction among such material entities as neurons? As Leibniz suggests, we can examine this neuronal event as carefully as we please; we can measure the number of neurons it contains, their connections, their rates of fire, the strength of the electrical impulses involved, the potential across the synapses – we can measure all this with as much precision as you could possibly desire; we can consider its electro-chemical, neurophysiological properties in the most exquisite detail; but nowhere, here, will we find so much as a hint of content. Indeed, none of this seems even vaguely *relevant* to its having content.[30]

[29] Plantinga 2006: 12–13.
[30] Plantinga 2006: 14.

4.5 Phenomenology and Intentionality

What should we make of the argument from intentionality? Is it true that physical objects cannot have intentional states? Well, it certainly seems correct that there is something mysterious about how physical objects could have intentional states. More specifically, it really does seem odd that a physical object like a human body could have intentional states in virtue of the physical interactions of its physical parts. But does the substance dualist fare any better? Simply because there is something mysterious about the fact that physical objects have intentional states it does not automatically follow that an immaterial soul's having intentional states would be any less mysterious or problematic. And if we could show that immaterial souls' having intentional states is problematic or mysterious in the same way in which a physical object's having intentional states is problematic or mysterious, then we will have transformed Plantinga's argument against physicalism into an argument against substance dualism.

Commenting on Leibniz's mill thought experiment, van Inwagen concedes that the notion that a physical object can think is mysterious, but he argues that an immaterial soul's thinking is equally mysterious, and so the fact that it is mysterious how physical things could think gives us no reason to prefer substance dualism to physicalism.[31] According to van Inwagen, the reason it is mysterious how a physical thing could think is because we cannot imagine how it could think, and in particular "we can form mental images of the operations of a physical thing, and we can see that the physical interactions represented in these images – the only interactions that *can* be represented in these images – have no connection with thought or sensation, or none we are able to imagine, conceive, or articulate."[32] But similarly, we cannot imagine how a nonphysical thing could think. After all, what would it be to imagine a nonphysical thinking thing? It's a bit hard to imagine what it would mean to form any mental image of a nonphysical object. But insofar as we *can* form a mental image of a nonphysical object, it's hard to see how that mental image could represent that nonphysical object as a *thinking* nonphysical object. From the outside – from the perspective of the mind's eye, with its mental image of a nonphysical object – nothing about the mental image would represent the object as having an inner mental life.

Plantinga has a response to this. The response is that van Inwagen has misrepresented the source of our conviction that it is mysterious how physical things can think or have intentional states. What gives us this

---

[31] Van Inwagen 2015: 235–237. Cf. Nagel 1986: 29; van Inwagen 1995: 476–478.
[32] Van Inwagen 2015: 235.

conviction is not that we can form no image or conception of how the thinking could be done. It is rather that on reflection we can see that the thinking could *not* be done. The reason is because a composite physical object would have to think or have intentional states in virtue of the interactions of its physical parts, and we can see that the interactions of a composite physical object's parts would be incapable of producing thoughts or intentional states in the composite physical object. By contrast, simple immaterial souls do not have parts. Lacking parts, we don't face any difficulty in making sense of the fact that they have thoughts or intentional states as a result of the interactions of their parts.[33]

I think that Plantinga is correct that van Inwagen has not shown that there is a parity between a composite physical object's thinking and a simple immaterial soul's thinking. But there *is* a parity.

Note that Leibniz's mill thought experiment directs our attention to an *explanatory gap*: It seems inexplicable that the presence of intentional states in a brain or body could arise from the physical interactions among the parts of that brain or body.[34] Plantinga's argument for substance dualism appeals to this same explanatory gap.

It is true that thoughts or intentional states are not produced in the soul through the interaction of the soul's parts. And it is true that if we are bodies, then our thoughts or intentional states *are* produced through the interaction of our physical parts. But if we are souls, then our thoughts or intentional states are produced through the interaction of those *same* physical parts. This is because if we are immaterial souls, then our thoughts are causally produced by the interactions of the parts of our brains or bodies – that is, even if we are souls, thoughts still result from activities in the brain, and any given thought is the result of the same brain processes which would produce that thought in a composite physical person.[35] Once we recognized that thoughts in a soul would be produced by the same interactions of the same parts which produce thoughts in a composite physical person, then we can see that the explanatory gap described in Leibniz's mill thought experiment is present for the substance dualist as well. So, there is an explanatory gap either way. If a person is a composite physical object, then the explanatory gap involves grounding: How could the physical interactions of a composite physical object's parts ground

---

[33] Plantinga 2006: 20–21.
[34] See Duncan 2012 for an interpretation of Leibniz's mill thought experiment along these lines.
[35] Opponents of substance dualism frequently assume that the substance dualist is committed to the view that our mental states are not produced by our brain processes. But as I noted in Chapter 2, §2.5, this assumption is simply false.

associated intentional states in that composite physical object? If a person is a nonphysical soul, then the explanatory gap involves causation: How could the physical interactions of a body's or brain's parts cause associated intentional states in the nonphysical soul paired with that body or brain? Perhaps there is an answer to this latter question, presumably in terms of psycho-physical laws linking the physical properties of brains or bodies and the mental properties of immaterial souls. But then those who think that we are composite physical objects could make the same response to the explanatory gap which they face, by positing laws (i.e., psycho-physical laws) linking the physical properties instantiated in parts of brains or bodies and the intentional states instantiated in those brains or bodies.[36]

So, I see no special difficulty faced by the physicalist that is not equally faced by the substance dualist. And we can say something similar about the objection to physicalism from phenomenology: If it is inexplicable that the physical interaction of a composite physical object's parts should produce phenomenal states in that composite physical object, then it is equally inexplicable that the physical interaction of those parts should produce phenomenal states in an immaterial soul.

4.6 The Argument from the Unity of Consciousness

Some philosophers defend an argument for substance dualism that appeals to the unity of consciousness. This argument is similar to that proposed by Leibniz and Plantinga, insofar as it argues that there is something particularly problematic about a composite physical object's having certain sorts of mental states in virtue of the operations of its physical part. But the argument is different enough from that defended by Leibniz and Plantinga that I have given it its own section.

The argument I have in mind is most prominently associated with William Hasker.[37] Like Leibniz and Plantinga, Hasker argues that a composite physical object could not have certain sorts of mental states in virtue of the operations of its physical parts. But these are mental states that we know that we have, so we know that we do not have these mental states

---

[36] Bailey (2020a: 190–194) develops a parody of Plantinga's argument from intentionality which is similar to the parody I have presented here. Bailey also notes that for both dualists and materialists we will need mysterious principles linking our thoughts with the properties of the parts of our brains.

[37] Hasker 1999: 122–146, 2010, 2016, 2018. See also Kant's *Critique of Pure Reason*, A351, Popper and Eccles 1977: 362, 534; Eccles 1994: 110; Moreland 2018c, 2018b.

in virtue of the operations of our physical parts. But if we were composite physical objects, then we *would* have these mental states in virtue of the operations of our physical parts. So, we are not composite physical objects.

Consider, for example, the qualitative experience associated with my current visual field. Hasker asks, "How can a unitary *state of consciousness* be a state of a complex physical structure, such as the brain?"[38] Regarding my visual experience specifically, how do the disparate activities of the brain's parts work together to create this unified experience? Hasker claims that if we are composite physical objects, then in order for me to have the visual experience in question, my physical parts would have to work together to do something which they cannot do individually, and, Hasker claims, they cannot do this. What none of my (microscopic) physical parts can do individually is have this visual experience. What they cannot work together to do, then, is compose something which has that experience.

Well, why not? It seems clear that none of my microscopic parts experience the visual field I experience. But why could they not *compose* something which has that experience? The problem is that, according to Hasker, all of a whole's properties must follow by logical or conceptual necessity from the properties and relations of its parts. Hasker calls this the "principle of reducibility":

> If an object O is a system made up of elements $e_1, e_2, e_3, \ldots e_n$, then all the properties of O are logical or conceptual consequences of the properties of, and the relations between, the e_i.[39]

When I have the full experience associated with my current visual field, that experience does not follow by logical or conceptual necessity from the properties and relations of the physical parts of my body or brain. So, I must not be my body or brain, or for that matter, any other composite physical object.

Is this a good argument for substance dualism (or at any rate for the conclusion that we are not composite physical objects)? I don't think that it is, for reasons which will become clear shortly. Here, I would like to note that if Hasker's argument is sound, then there is pretty clearly a parody argument which we can employ against substance dualism. Note that Hasker's argument appeals to a certain sort of explanatory gap: Certain properties of wholes (i.e., certain mental properties) are inexplicable in terms of the properties and relations among their parts, or at any rate

---

[38] Hasker 2010: 183.
[39] Hasker 1999: 132. In a footnote Hasker clarifies that the principle of reducibility applies only to monadic properties of the object O.

4.6 The Argument from the Unity of Consciousness

they are inexplicable in terms of what logical or conceptual connections obtain between the properties of the whole and the properties and relations which obtain among its parts. But the substance dualist faces a very similar explanatory gap between the physical properties of their brain or body and the mental properties instantiated in their immaterial souls. In fact, an explanatory gap of this sort is often a primary motivation for dualism, of both the substance and property variety: Our mental properties are inexplicable purely in terms of our physical properties, so our mental properties must outstrip our physical properties. Even if a substance dualist does not endorse this sort of argument for dualism, they will at any rate agree that a body's instantiating some physical properties does not *logically* or *conceptually* entail that any immaterial soul instantiates any corresponding mental properties. So, there are explanatory gaps for both the physicalist and the dualist. And plausibly both explanatory gaps can be bridged by laws or metaphysical principles: psycho-physical laws for the substance dualist, and mereological laws for the believer in composite people.[40]

If one sort of explanatory gap is problematic (perhaps because it requires these otherwise gratuitous bridging laws or principles), then presumably the other explanatory gap will be problematic as well. Hasker will likely think otherwise. Well, why would he think that the mereological explanatory gap is more problematic than the psycho-physical explanatory gap?

Presumably the answer to this question involves Hasker's "principle of reducibility": If a whole instantiates some property, then its instantiating that property *must* be a logical or conceptual consequence of the properties and relations instantiated by its parts. So, any mereological laws governing the relationship between parts and wholes must be logically necessary (i.e., statements expressing those laws are true simply in virtue of their logical form) or conceptually necessary (i.e., statements expressing those laws are true simply in virtue of the concepts employed in the statements). And perhaps this rules out the mereological laws we would need to bridge the explanatory gap between parts and the mental properties of persons composed of those parts. By contrast, we have no reason to disallow the dualist's psycho-physical laws. In particular, there is no reason for the dualist to think that mental properties instantiated in *souls* must be logical or

---

[40] Shrader (2006) and Bayne (2018) also argue, in response to the argument for substance dualism from the unity of consciousness, that substance dualism faces an analogous objection from the unity of consciousness. But the analogous objections to dualism which they develop differ from that developed here.

conceptual consequences of the properties and relations instantiated by the body or brain associated with that soul.

In order to assess Hasker's argument, then, we must see whether we have any grounds for accepting the principle of reducibility. And I doubt that we do. After all, the explanatory gap noted by Hasker is present in all composite objects, not just bodies or brains. As Jonathan Schaffer notes

> ... *explanatory gaps are everywhere*. There is no transparent rationale in any of the standard connections, even from the H, H, and O atoms to the H_2O molecule, since it is not transparent that the H, H, and O atoms compose anything, much less something with the nature of an H_2O molecule.[41]

Schaffer writes here of there being "no transparent rationale" that H, H, and O atoms would compose an H_2O molecule, or compose something which has the properties we normally take H_2O molecules to have. For present purposes, we can take a "transparent rationale" to be a logical or conceptual relation between the parts (in this case, H, H, and O atoms) and the wholes they purportedly compose (H_2O molecules). For example, there is no *logical* entailment (i.e., entailment merely in virtue of the logical form of the sentences involved) from the existence of some H, H, and O atoms and the supposition that they compose something to their composing something with the nature of an H_2O molecule. If there were such a logical entailment, then it would be transparent to us that if H, H, and O atoms compose something then they compose something with that nature, since to suppose that they *don't* compose something with that nature would entail a contradiction.

So, Hasker notes that there is an explanatory gap between the mental properties of bodies or brains and the physical properties of their individual parts, but arguably similar explanatory gaps occur in every case of composition. If the explanatory gap is objectionable, it is objectionable for all cases of composition. It would lead us, then, toward mereological nihilism, according to which there are no composite objects at all. And if we are mereological nihilists, then we will have a much more straightforward argument for substance dualism, one which makes no mention of the unity of consciousness: There are no composite objects, so *we* are not composite objects, so we are simple immaterial souls.[42] The problem here is that we lack any grounds for thinking that the sorts of explanatory gaps which are

---

[41] Schaffer 2017a: 2.
[42] Something like this argument is given in Robinson 2016: Ch.11. Some mereological nihilists contend that nihilism should lead us to think that we do not exist. I will discuss this possibility in Chapter 6, §6.4.

4.6 The Argument from the Unity of Consciousness

present in all cases of composition are objectionable, or so objectionable that they should lead us to reject composition – and in fact, I am aware of no philosophers who have said that these sorts of explanatory gaps should, all by themselves, lead us to reject composition. The main grounds generally cited for accepting mereological nihilism involve appeals to the relative theoretical simplicity of nihilism.[43] But as I argued in Chapter 2, §2.2, those sorts of simplicity-based arguments against composite objects have parallel arguments against substance dualism.

There are some indications that Hasker may be an unwitting mereological nihilist. For example, Hasker writes that if we are composite physical objects such as bodies or brains, then our experiences would "in the final analysis *not* be the experience of a single subject – that in fact the experience inheres in a number of different entities, each of which does *not* have that experience as a whole," and that this possibility is "unintelligible."[44] Hasker exhibits some confusion here. If we are composite objects, then when I have the experience of seeing a certain visual field, this does not mean that my parts *collectively* have the experience of seeing that visual field. What it means is that my parts *compose* an object which has that experience. So, contra Hasker, my experience *would* be the experience of a single subject, namely the single composite subject with which I am identical. Hasker misses this because he does not take seriously the thesis at issue, which is that there is a single composite object with which I am identical.

Later Hasker seems befuddled by the question of what it is that instantiates a mental property, if we are composite physical objects:

> what exactly is it that *has* the property? By hypothesis, the whole simply *is* 'in the strict sense, a system of objects'; there *is no* whole 'over and above' the parts of which it is composed. So whatever nonrelational properties the whole has must consist of properties of, and relations between, the parts; there simply is nothing else of which they *could* consist. If a property of the whole is not logically grounded in the properties of the parts, then it is 'floating in mid-air,' unattached to any real individual – but this is unintelligible.[45]

In response to the question "What experiences the visual field?" the physicalist should say "the composite person having the visual experience." That composite person *is* something "over and above" their parts, in the sense that they are numerically distinct from their parts. Once again one has the impression that Hasker simply does not believe in composite objects.

---

[43] Horgan and Potrč 2008: Ch. 7; Sider 2013; Brenner 2015b, 2021.
[44] Hasker 1999: 134.
[45] Hasker 1999: 138.

He seems to think that to say that a composite instantiates some property is to say that its parts instantiate that property. Presumably these are collective properties – that is, properties had by the parts *together*, although perhaps not individually, just as some dogs may surround a cat even if none of the dogs individually surrounds the cat. Now, perhaps collective property instantiation *is* governed by a conceptual or logical reducibility principle – although this idea would be questioned by those who have suggested that collective properties can be "emergent," in the sense that they do not follow by conceptual or logical necessity from the individual properties instantiated by the objects included in the collection.[46] At any rate, the most obvious cases of collective property instantiation seem to be governed by a reducibility principle. For example, perhaps it does not follow by logical or conceptual necessity that wholes are located where their parts are located.[47] But surely if some objects are located in a certain region, then it follows by logical or conceptual necessity that the objects are *collectively* located in that region. Perhaps Hasker thinks that a reducibility principle is so obvious because he conflates a reducibility principle regarding the *collective* properties instantiated by some objects with a reducibility principle regarding the properties *instantiated by the whole which those objects compose*. And this would be an understandable mistake to make if Hasker does not really believe in composite objects but does believe in the objects which we normally take to *compose* composite objects.

So, again, Hasker's principle of reducibility has little to be said for it and seems to be motivated by a general rejection of composite objects. I have belabored this point for the following reason: I don't want the reader to make the same mistake that Hasker does. If you find the principle of reducibility plausible, and this is because you are a mereological nihilist, that's fine, but then you will have a much more straightforward argument for substance dualism by directly appealing to mereological nihilism. If you are *not* a mereological nihilist, then you should reject the principle of reducibility, as it is incompatible with the existence of composite objects.

The overall moral of the story is that Hasker's argument from the unity of consciousness has a parallel argument against substance dualism. It may be thought that a crucial premise in Hasker's argument is more plausible than the parallel premise in the parody argument against substance dualism. But I have argued that this is not the case.

---

[46] See Bohn 2012; Cornell 2017; Brenner 2018; Caves 2018.
[47] Saucedo 2011; Brenner 2015b: 325–326.

4.7 Lowe's Argument from Unity

Lowe endorses a thesis which he calls "self-body dualism." Lowe is not a substance dualist in the sense in which I have characterized that thesis, since he thinks that we are material objects, albeit simple material objects. But since the main argument he gives for his view is an argument against our being composite physical objects, and his argument could easily be appropriated by those who *are* substance dualists in the sense which interests me, his argument is worth addressing here.

Lowe's main argument for his "self-body dualism" is the "argument from unity."[48] This argument is distinct from the argument from the unity of consciousness discussed above, although it bears some similarities to that argument, as well as the replacement argument for substance dualism. Here's the basic idea. The argument from unity contends that none of my particular token thoughts or experiences require my body, or any particular part of my body in order to exist. But surely any one of my token thoughts or experiences requires that *I* exist in order for it to exist. So, since none of my token thoughts or experiences require the existence of my body, or any particular part of my body, I must be numerically distinct from my body, or any part of my body. This is called the "argument from unity" because, Lowe claims, the reason why none of my token thoughts or experiences require the existence of my body is that I "possess a strong kind of *unity*, in virtue of being a *simple* substance,"[49] and this sort of unity is not possessed by my body.

Let's look at Lowe's argument in a bit more detail.

One step in the argument claims that "any one of my token thoughts or experiences requires that *I* exist in order for it to exist." As an example, consider the token thought, produced on some particular occasion, that "Renee is a dog." No doubt the *type* to which this token thought corresponds can be thought by someone even if I do not exist, and so there being some token or other of this type does not require my existence. But presumably my particular *token* thought of "Renee is a dog" cannot exist unless I exist. I will grant, simply for the sake of argument, that such token thoughts exist and that token thoughts essentially occur in the persons in which they actually occur. (Even if there are no such things as token thoughts, we could presumably modify the argument so that it does not require the existence of such things. For example, instead of talking of token thoughts, we could instead talk of *my thinking the thought "Renee is a dog" on some particular*

---

[48] Lowe 2006: 10, 2008: 175–176, 2010: 448–450, 2014. Meixner (2014: 20) gives a similar argument.
[49] Lowe 2006: 10.

occasion, and wonder whether *my thinking the thought "Renee is a dog" on some particular occasion* requires the existence of my body, or any particular part of my body.)

So, why should we think that this particular token thought that "Renee is a dog" does not require the existence of my body? Lowe writes that this token thought does not require the existence of my body because it does not require the existence of "my body as whole." It does not require the existence of "my body as a whole" because the token thought could exist even if some tiny portion of my body did not exist, or even if some tiny portion of my body was not a part of my body.

I have put "my body as a whole" in scare quotes because that phrase is ambiguous, and the plausibility of Lowe's argument relies on equivocation with respect to the word "whole." The word "whole" has at least two uses: (1) "Whole" can simply mean "composite object," so that a phrase such as "my body as a whole" means "my body, conceived as a composite object rather than a simple object"; (2) "whole" can mean "all," so that a phrase such as "my body as a whole" means "*all* of my body (i.e., every part of my body)." It is true that my token thought "Renee is a dog" does not require the existence of "my body as a whole," in the second sense of the word "whole." What this amounts to is the plausible idea that this token thought does not require that all of the parts of my body exist, or that all of the parts of my body actually be parts of my body. Surely, for example, this token thought could exist even if a flake of skin at the tip of my right index finger did not exist. But this does not show that this token thought could exist even if my body does not exist. This is because my body does not require all of its parts in order to exist. What Lowe needs in order to show that I am not my body is that this token thought does not require the existence of "my body as a whole" in order to exist, where here "whole" is taken to have the *first* of the two meanings described above. In other words, what Lowe needs for his argument to work is that this token thought does not need *this body* (conceived as a composite object) in order to exist. And to show *that* it is not enough to point out that the token thought in question could exist even if some tiny portion of my body did not exist or even if it was not a part of my body, since very plausibly this body could exist even if some tiny portion of my body did not exist or even if it was not a part of my body. So, this body may be required for the token thought to exist (if I *am* my body), even if the "body as a whole" – in the sense of all of the body's current parts – is not required for the token thought to exist.

In short, the plausibility of Lowe's argument relies on equivocation with respect to the meaning of the word "whole." On one meaning of the word "whole," Lowe is correct that this token thought does not require the existence of "this body as a whole," but this fact does not support the idea that this token thought could exist absent the existence of this body. On the other meaning of the word "whole," Lowe has not established that this token thought could exist in the absence of "this body as a whole." Lowe thinks he has shown that my token thoughts could exist even if my body does not exist – this is what it would amount to to say that my token thoughts do not require the existence of "my body as a whole" in the sense of "my body conceived as a composite object." But he has not shown that. He has only shown that my token thoughts could exist even if some *parts* of my body do not exist.

So much for Lowe's argument for the claim that this token thought could exist in the absence of the existence of my body. But why does he think that the token thought could exist in the absence of *any* particular part of this body? Well, he thinks that, for any particular part of my body, we could simply repeat the line of reasoning he employs to show that my token thoughts do not require my body in order to exist, replacing "my body" in that line of reasoning with whatever part of my body we have in mind. If, for example, his argument shows that my token thoughts do not need my body in order to exist, parallel lines of reasoning would show that they do not need my brain in order to exist. But we have seen that his argument for the conclusion that my token thoughts do not require my body in order to exist is not compelling. So, the parallel arguments for the conclusion that my token thoughts do not require the existence of my brain (or whatever) in order to exist will also not be compelling.

So, Lowe's argument from unity is not compelling, for the reasons just given. But the argument can also be parodied. I don't need any particular immaterial object in order to have any particular token thoughts or experiences. But surely those token thoughts and experiences require my existence in order for them to exist. So, I am not an immaterial object.[50]

Lowe might respond that this argument is question-begging since if I am an immaterial object, then any of my token thoughts or experiences would require the existence of at least one immaterial object, namely the immaterial object with which I am identical. If this argument is

---

[50] Lowe insists that we are not even partly immaterial, even if we are distinct from our bodies or any parts of our bodies (Lowe 2014: 264). So, he may be sympathetic with the conclusion of this parody argument, which states that I am not an immaterial object. The overall argument of this chapter requires, however, that I develop a parody argument the conclusion of which is that we are not immaterial objects. Let's pretend, for expository purposes, that Lowe would not have been happy to accept that conclusion.

question-begging, however, so is Lowe's original argument, and in precisely the same way since my token thoughts and experiences need not require the existence of my body only if I am not identical with my body – if I am my body, then of course this token thought needs this body in order to exist, since any token thought in a different object would be a different token thought. Perhaps the considerations Lowe gives for why my token thought does not need this body in order to exist might be thought to be compelling, and not amenable to parody, and this would break the parity between Lowe's argument from unity and my parody argument. But as I argued above, the considerations Lowe cites in support of the idea that my token thoughts do not require my body (or any particular parts of my body) in order to exist are not compelling.

4.8 The Argument from the Problem of the Many

Unger defends substance dualism as a solution to the problem of the many, as applied to human persons.[51] First, let's see what the problem of the many is, and then we'll see how substance dualism is supposed to help resolve the problem.

Unger himself introduced the problem of the many, well before he came to the conclusion that it should lead us to accept substance dualism.[52] The problem of the many is basically this: Consider some macroscopic composite object, such as a table. Which objects compose the table? Call the table's parts "the xs." There will undoubtedly be some objects which are very near the xs, and yet are not parts of the table – think, for example, of some atom or molecule immediately adjacent to the xs. Why does that atom or molecule not help compose the table? It is, after all, immediately adjacent to some of the atoms which *do* help compose the table. Well, you might respond, we have to draw the line somewhere, and for any objects which we might think compose the table, there will be some atoms immediately adjacent to those objects, where the adjacent atoms in question do not help compose the table. So, what's the problem? Well, if the xs compose the table, then we can imagine some objects – call them "the ys" – which include all of the xs, but in addition include some atom immediately adjacent to the xs. Even if the xs compose the table we are imagining, and the ys do not, we will at any rate wonder whether the ys compose something as well.

---

[51] Unger 2006: Ch. 7. Zimmerman (2010, 2011) and Lowe (2010: 450) give similar arguments.
[52] See Unger 1980.

4.8 The Argument from the Problem of the Many

And it will be difficult to deny that they do: After all, they are extremely similar to the xs – in fact, they just *are* the xs, except they also include a single atom immediately adjacent to those xs. So, if the xs together compose something, it seems objectionably arbitrary to suppose that the ys do not also compose something. And since the xs compose a table, and the ys differ from the xs in an extremely minute and for practical purposes undetectable manner, we should think that the ys compose a table as well. But now it looks like, where we thought there was a single table, there are actually *two* tables which occupy the same region of space, except for one tiny difference: The second table also occupies the region of space occupied by the single atom whose addition to the xs resulted in the ys.

So, now we've got these two tables where initially we thought there was only one table. But the line of reasoning can be extended. After all, we produced the ys (i.e., those objects which together compose the second table) by adjoining to the xs (i.e., those objects which together compose the first table) a single atom which was immediately adjacent to the xs. But there are any number of atoms immediately adjacent to the xs, since there are so many atoms floating around out there in the vicinity of the first table (and so in the vicinity of the first table's parts). So, by the line of reasoning we used to establish that, in addition to the first table, there is a second table with which the first table mostly overlaps, we can establish the existence of a *third* table as well, and a *fourth* table, and a *fifth* table, and so on. So, where we initially thought we had one table we really have *many* tables. And that's the problem of the many.

But what does this have to do with substance dualism? Here's what: Unger asks us to apply the line of reasoning which results in the problem of the many to ourselves. Above I presented the problem of the many with the example of a table. But I might have instead presented the problem of the many with an example involving a human brain, a human body, or a human organism. Now, assume that each of *us* is some object of that sort – a human brain, a human body, a human organism, or some other macroscopic composite physical object. If we are objects of that sort then, given the reasoning involved in the problem of the many, we end up with an implausible conclusion: that here in my chair there are, in addition to me, many other thinkers – other brains, bodies, or whatever – with which I mostly overlap, all thinking the same thoughts I am thinking. Unger thinks that this result in unacceptable. He thinks that the solution to the problem is to contend that I am not a macroscopic composite object, and so not the sort of object for which the problem of the many is a concern. Rather, I am an immaterial soul.

There is much that could be written about the problem of the many.[53] Perhaps, for example, the correct response to the problem is that I am a composite macroscopic object such as an organism, but there are not many other organisms with which I mostly overlap. Rather, there is just the one organism, and it is vague which atoms in its vicinity are among its parts.[54] Or perhaps we should admit that the many organisms exist but should not regard this result as problematic since it is nevertheless legitimate to talk as if there is only one organism.[55] Or perhaps there is some other solution to the problem.

But can we construct a parody to the problem of the many, construed as an argument for substance dualism, which would undermine substance dualism? It seems that we can. Unger notes that, if we assume that I am a composite macroscopic object, then if my parts are capable of composing a thinking subject, then some very slightly different parts, which include all of my actual parts but add or subtract a single part, should also be able to compose a thinking subject. This is what gets us many thinking subjects in my vicinity, where we are normally inclined to believe there is only a single thinking subject (me). But note that we can run a perfectly parallel line of thought regarding an immaterial soul: If these parts arranged brain-wise (or body-wise, organism-wise, whatever) are paired with an immaterial thinking subject (i.e., a soul), then some very slightly different parts should be paired with a soul as well. Suppose, for example, that I am an immaterial soul, and I am paired with those atoms which compose my brain (or body or organism, etc.), which we may label "the xs." Presumably not just any group of objects is paired with an immaterial soul. If the xs are configured so as to be paired with an immaterial soul, then some very slightly different objects should presumably also be configured so as to be paired with an immaterial soul. So imagine some very slightly different group of objects, the ys, which are the xs plus some atom immediately adjacent to the xs. The ys should also be paired with an immaterial soul. And we can run this line of reasoning a number of times, since there are any number of atoms immediately adjacent to my brain (or body or organism, or whatever). So, where we are initially inclined to think that there is a single immaterial soul paired with the xs, there are actually a number of such immaterial souls, and we are still left with a problem of many thinkers. The reasoning which produces this problem seems to me to be exactly parallel to the line

---

[53] For an overview of some responses to the problem, see Hudson 2001: Ch. 1–2.
[54] Van Inwagen 1990: Ch. 17; Hershenov 2001.
[55] Lewis 1993.

4.8 The Argument from the Problem of the Many

of reasoning which gave us the original problem of the many regarding composite macroscopic thinkers.[56]

One way to see that this parody problem for substance dualism is parallel to the original problem of the many is to note how responses to the one problem have exactly parallel responses to the other problem. Here are a few examples.

First, perhaps the substance dualist will say that there is only one soul where we are normally inclined to think that there is one soul, and it is simply a brute fact that *these* objects, the xs, are paired with a soul, while some slightly different objects, the ys, are not. But presumably we could give a similar response to the problem of the many for our being composite physical objects: There is just one brain or body or organism in my vicinity, and it is just a brute fact that its parts compose something, while some slightly different parts do not.

Second, perhaps the substance dualist will say that there is only one soul where we are normally inclined to think that there is one soul, and it is a vague matter which objects are paired with that soul. We can give a similar response to the problem of the many for our being composite physical objects: There is just one brain or body or organism in my vicinity, and it is a vague matter which objects compose it. It might be objected that vague composition is more problematic than vague pairing of souls with physical objects, as vague composition will lead to an objectionable vague existence – that is, it will be vague whether some objects compose something, and so it will be vague whether that composite object exists.[57] In response, I would note that in this case vague composition does not lead to vague existence: It is a determinate matter that the composite person exists, and it is just vague which objects are among its parts. We may even go so far as to make room for the possibility that it can be a determinate matter that some person exists, while it is vague whether that person is composite.[58] The idea is that an object can determinately exist, and it can be vague whether it is a composite object if it is vague whether some parts compose it. The move here parallels a move which can be made by the substance dualist. The substance dualist can say that a soul can determinately exist, and it can be

---

[56] The parody I have presented is similar to the parody argument presented by Gasparov (2015) in response to Zimmerman's (2010, 2011) variant of the problem of the many argument for substance dualism. Rickabaugh (2018: §5.2.2) also argues that Unger's problem of the many argument for substance dualism can be transformed into an analogous argument against so-called emergent substance dualism.

[57] Cf. Lewis 1986: 212–213; van Inwagen 1990: §19. Thanks to Eric Olson for suggesting that I address this concern.

[58] See Carmichael 2011.

vague whether the soul is embodied if it is vague whether some physical parts, or some body, are/is paired with that soul.

Here is a third response. As we saw in Chapter 3, §3.6, some substance dualists think that God pairs souls with bodies.[59] If that's right, then presumably God could ensure that *these* objects, the xs, are paired with a soul, while some slightly different objects, the ys, are not. In response, I would note that those who think that we are composite physical objects are free to make a parallel move in response to the problem of the many: God ensures that *these* objects, the xs, compose someone, while some slightly different objects, the ys, do not.[60]

Here is a fourth and final response. Perhaps, for any given soul, that soul is paired with some physical objects the xs, but it is also paired with some other objects the ys, as well as some other objects the zs, and so on, where $xs \neq ys \neq zs$ (although perhaps some objects are included in the xs as well as the ys or the zs). If the xs compose a body, then perhaps we should say that the soul is paired with that body, and if the ys compose a body we should say something similar, and so on. In this case, a soul would be paired with multiple bodies.[61]

As Gasparov[62] notes, if this sort of response can be given to the parody argument against substance dualism, then an analogous response can be given to the original argument for substance dualism from the problem of the many. So, rather than saying that some parts, the xs, compose a composite person, and some slightly different parts, the ys, compose a different composite person, we should rather say that all of the parts in question compose that single composite person. One way of putting this: The composite person is composed of multiple pluralities (where a "plurality" is a disguised plural term – i.e., despite the fact that "plurality" seems to be a singular term, it really refers to multiple objects), just as, in the analogous proposal regarding souls, the soul has multiple bodies.

The parody I've been discussing contends that, for the parts of my brain (or body, or organism, or whatever), the xs, there are some slightly different objects, the ys, which we might also expect to be paired with a soul. A substance dualist might object that if we are immaterial souls, then we are paired with *brains* (or bodies, organisms, etc.), not *parts* of brains.

---

[59] Pope Pius XII 1950: §36; Swinburne 1986: 198–199; Eccles 1994: 180; Foster 2001: 29; Plantinga 2007: 132–133.

[60] Cf. Yang and Davis (2017), Bailey (2021: Ch. 5), and Brenner (2022), who argue that God might pair composite persons with their parts.

[61] Thanks to an anonymous referee for this suggestion. A similar proposal is made in Zimmerman 2011: 195.

[62] Gasparov 2015: 436.

4.8 The Argument from the Problem of the Many

In other words, it is *brains* (or bodies, organisms, etc.) which are ensouled, or which causally interact with souls, rather than the *parts* of those brains. So, we should not say that if I am an immaterial soul, then I am paired with the *x*s, but we should rather say that I am paired with my brain, which is *composed* of the *x*s. As Hudson[63] notes, however, the substance dualist will have to face the problem of the many with respect to their brains (or bodies, organisms, etc.). So, if the problem of the many forces us to say that there are many brains where I am inclined to think that there is only one brain, then, if we are substance dualists, we may be forced to say that each of these brains is paired with an immaterial soul, and we end up with a problem of many *souls* as well as a problem of many *brains*. So, once again, the substance dualist faces a parody, even if souls are paired with brains, rather than parts of brains.

---

[63] Hudson 2001: 20–21.

5

Interlude: What Exactly Is the Difference between Our Being Immaterial Souls and Our Being Composite Physical Objects?

Chapters 2–4 were largely negative. They tried to show that various arguments for or against the thesis that we are immaterial souls do not work, at least in part because they can be parodied and transformed into arguments for theses which are incompatible with the conclusions of the original arguments. These largely negative chapters are nevertheless noteworthy, since they support one of the main theses regarding the metaphysics of personal identity that I aim to defend over the course of this book, that it is surprisingly difficult to decide between substance dualism and the view that we are composite physical objects. Here, I would like to pause to briefly consider whether there are any other lessons to be learned from Chapters 2–4. In particular, are there any positive lessons to be learned regarding our understanding of the competing theses – that is, the thesis that we are composite physical objects and the thesis that we are immaterial souls?

It is surprising that so many of the arguments on both sides of this debate can be parodied. Sometimes this happens in philosophy. For example, ontological arguments for theism can often be parodied – or, at any rate, opponents of those arguments often claim that the arguments can be parodied.[1] But in that case what we have are only a certain class of arguments for a certain thesis (theism) being parodied. I have never seen anyone claim that *all* of the main arguments for or against theism can be parodied. More generally, I am not aware of any other philosophical debate where the arguments for the main competing views in the debate can be parodied so systematically. So, what's going on here? What explains this odd situation?

Here is one potential explanation of the odd dialectical situation we find ourselves in, one which I want to explore, but which I cannot confidently endorse or reject. The explanation is this: Perhaps the fact that the main arguments for the thesis that we are composite physical objects can be

---

[1] See, e.g., Oppy 1995: Ch. 11.

parodied, and that this is the case for the main competing thesis that we are immaterial souls, shows that these competing theses are more similar to one another than we might initially think. If this is correct, it would help account for the epistemic impasse we find ourselves in, and why it turns out to be surprisingly difficult to find compelling grounds which favor one of the competing theses over the other: Arguments for the competing theses fail to distinguish between them (because they can be parodied), because there are few or relatively insubstantial differences between the theses that might allow us to decide between them.

So, the question to ask now is, what exactly is the difference between the thesis that we are immaterial souls and its main rival, the thesis that we are composite physical objects? Philosophers commonly regard these competing theses as being very different from one another. Usually, substance dualism is seen as a much more metaphysically extravagant thesis. This seems to me to be a mistake. The discussion in Chapters 2–4 has brought out some interesting and perhaps surprising similarities between the two theses. For example:

- The differences between the two theses might be thought to consist in, or be revealed by, those considerations that are commonly cited in favor of one or the other thesis. But as we have seen over the course of Chapters 2–4, the most commonly cited such considerations can be parodied, and so fail to distinguish between the two theses.
- There is a sense in which both souls and composite physical objects like brains or bodies "float above" the parts with which they are paired, in the sense that they are not numerically identical with those parts,[2] but they nevertheless are closely related to, and arguably dependent upon, the parts for their existence and many of their properties. Composite physical persons, for example, have their physical properties (e.g., their size, mass) determined by the physical properties of and relations among their parts, and their mental properties determined by the configuration of the physical parts in the brain. This last point is true even if some sort of property dualism is correct. That is, even if mental properties are not reducible to physical properties, it is nevertheless true that mental properties are determined by the configuration of the physical *parts* of the brain. Similarly, immaterial souls' mental states are determined by the configuration of the physical parts of the brain. Even if mental properties are strictly

---

[2] This is assuming that composition as identity is false. This issue was discussed in Chapter 1, §1.3.

speaking properties of souls, rather than bodies or brains, the mental properties of souls are nevertheless causally dependent on the configuration of the physical parts of the brain.
- As we saw in Chapter 3, there are pairing problem concerns for both views.
- It is sometimes thought that our being composite physical objects makes more accurate empirical predictions than the thesis that we are immaterial souls, insofar as the former thesis fits better with the observed close correlation between mental properties and properties of the brain. But, as I noted in Chapter 2, §2.5, on either view, there will be a strong correlation between our mental properties and the properties of the parts of the body or brain, and in both cases, we will need laws to account for the correlation – either mereological laws (if we are composite physical objects) or psycho-physical laws (if we are immaterial souls).
- It might be thought that a composite physical object like a brain or body would have a location, while an immaterial soul would not. But, in Chapter 3, §3.3, I noted that there are prominent proponents of substance dualism who contend that immaterial souls are located.
- It might be thought that composite physical persons cause empirically detectable effects in the physical world that immaterial souls could not cause. But, as I noted in Chapter 2, §2.3, composite physical persons may only have causal effects that are overdetermined by the causal effects of their parts, and, as I noted in Chapter 2, §2.4, this point may receive support from considerations regarding energy conservation. If that's right, we may not be able to tell, on the basis of empirical observation, whether some effect is produced by a composite physical person, or it is only produced by that composite physical person's parts. And we can make similar points about immaterial souls: that souls' causal effects in the physical world may be overdetermined by the causal effects of the parts of the body, and that this point may receive support from considerations regarding energy conservation. Any considerations meant to show that composite physical persons could have empirically detectable effects on the physical world that are not overdetermined by the causal effects of their parts could presumably be appropriated by the substance dualist on behalf of the thesis that immaterial souls can have empirically detectable effects on the physical world that are not overdetermined by the causal effects of the parts of their bodies.

- Perhaps there is a *modal* difference between composite physical persons and immaterial souls: It might be thought that souls can survive without the parts of the body, but bodies cannot survive without the parts of the body. But now we should ask: (1) Why think that bodies cannot survive without their parts? That is, why think that some particular body requires its *actual* parts in order to exist, or indeed any parts at all? And (2) does this sort of modal difference allow us to discriminate between our being composite physical persons and our being immaterial souls? Plausibly it would only if it supports a modal argument for our being composite physical objects or for our being immaterial souls. But, as I argued in Chapter 4, §4.2, there appear to be parallel modal arguments both for and against our being immaterial souls, and no obvious grounds for endorsing one sort of modal argument but not the other.

I'm not trying to suggest that there are *no* real differences between the thesis that we are composite physical objects and the thesis that we are immaterial souls. My point is that there are fewer such differences than many philosophers seem to think. What's more, the genuine differences between the two theses are such that they do not allow us to decide in favor of one thesis rather than the other.

For example, here are two uncontroversial differences between a composite physical object and a *simple* immaterial soul: one is physical, the other is not; one is composite, the other is not. But these are differences between the two sorts of objects that are simply built into our definitions of objects of these sorts – for example, to be a simple immaterial soul *just is* (in part) to be both simple and nonphysical. We might doubt that these sorts of bare metaphysical differences between composite physical persons and simple immaterial souls – without other corresponding substantive differences – will allow us to discriminate between a situation where one of these objects exists and the other does not. What's more, on reflection it is surprisingly difficult to spell out what it is for an object to be physical or for an object to be nonphysical. One problem is that "physical" is usually characterized by reference to modern physics – that is, the physical is that which is studied by modern physics. But modern physics is almost certainly false in some details. To instead characterize "physical" in terms of ideal future physics would be to rob the predicate "physical" of much or all of its content, since we do not now know what an ideal future physics will look like.[3]

---

[3] For discussions of this and other concerns regarding the attempt to characterize the predicate "physical" see, among others, Montero 1999; Wilson 2006; Goff 2017: Ch. 2; Bailey 2020b.

And we can make some of the same points regarding another plausible difference between a composite physical object and an immaterial soul: composite physical objects – or at least the sorts of composite physical objects we might be (e.g., bodies, brains) – can be seen, touched, and smelled, while immaterial souls cannot.[4] This might very well be a real difference between composite physical objects and immaterial souls. But it is not the sort of difference that could allow us to decide between our being composite physical objects and our being immaterial souls. Take vision as an example. We may be able to see various composite physical objects (such as brains or bodies) if they exist. But, as we saw in Chapter 1, §1.2, we cannot tell on the basis of sense experience that composite physical objects *do* exist, since arguably our sense experiences would be the same whether or not these composite physical objects exist, as long as there are things appropriately arranged composite object-wise. What's more, we cannot tell on the basis of vision which composite physical objects, if any, *we* are. Think, for example, of the debate between those who think that we are brains, and those who think that we are organisms. How can our visual experiences decide between these two views? Take a good look at a brain, and then take a good look at a whole organism. Are you any step closer to deciding between the view that we are brains and the view that we are organisms? What visually detectable features of brains or organisms should we expect to find if we are brains, or if we are organisms?

Perhaps the idea is this: We see ourselves when, say, we look in mirrors. But we cannot see souls. So, this shows that we are not souls.[5] And *that's* why the fact that composite physical objects can be perceived but souls cannot, can help us decide between the view that we are composite physical objects and the view that we are immaterial souls. But this is not a very compelling argument. The substance dualist can ask why we should be so confident that we can see ourselves in mirrors, at least in a sense that would conflict with substance dualism. No substance dualist denies that there is *some* sense in which you can see yourself in the mirror. But, to refute substance dualism, you must be able to see yourself in a mirror in a much stronger sense – that is, in the sense that the light by which you see something reflected in the mirror is reflected by *you yourself*, rather than merely by some object paired with you (e.g., a body with which you are paired but with which you are not identical). But why should we think that we can see ourselves in mirrors in this very strong sense? To suppose

---

[4] Thanks here to Andrew M. Bailey.
[5] Cf. Merricks 2003: 85–87.

that we do seems to be question-begging against the substance dualist, since it simply assumes the point at issue, namely that the composite physical object I see in the mirror is *me*, rather than, say, a body paired with me.

So, again, it is surprisingly difficult to identify any appreciable difference between composite physical objects and souls that would allow us to decide between the view that we are composite physical objects and the view that we are immaterial souls. It's possible that you endorse some idiosyncratic argument for or against our being composite physical objects or immaterial souls, and *that's* why you think that we are composite physical objects, or why you think that we are immaterial souls. And I'm certainly aware of arguments of this sort that I don't have the space to discuss in this book. So, it's possible that some such argument is successful and cannot be parodied. But consider two points. First, it is surprising, at least to me, that all of the main arguments involved in this debate – that is, all of the arguments discussed over the course of Chapters 2–4 – can be parodied. This is something that is generally overlooked. Perhaps this provides some reason to think that the argument you endorse which I have not discussed can be parodied as well, even if cursory reflection on the matter leads you to think otherwise. Second, even if there is some argument which I have not considered that is successful and cannot be parodied, I may have nevertheless established an interesting conclusion: that our being souls and our being composite physical objects are more similar to one another than we might initially think, since there are all these parody arguments which until now have mostly been overlooked.

6
Nonself, Part 1: Arguments against Our Existence

6.1 Introduction

In response to the question "What are we?" a surprising number of thinkers have said "nothing" – that is, we aren't anything because we don't exist. My arguments in previous chapters were directed against the idea that we are composite objects, as well as the idea that we are simple (partless) objects. But I didn't address the question of whether we are anything at all. So, in this and the following chapter, I will address a number of considerations that have been thought to count against, or in favor of, our existence. The overall argument in this book is that we are unable to answer some of the central questions regarding the metaphysics of personal identity, since we are either simple, composite, or nothing, and yet each option seems to be problematic. In this and the following chapter, I will argue that the third option is problematic. I ultimately conclude, then, that we exist.

Here is a methodological point to keep in mind: In this and the following chapter, I do not take the success of any of the arguments discussed in the previous chapters for granted. In this chapter, I will examine some arguments against our existence, and I will sometimes ask whether those arguments are successful on the assumption that we are composite or on the assumption that we are simple. The point is to show that, given some possible assumptions about what we are (i.e., composite, simple), the arguments against our existence do not succeed. In §6.4, I will turn to the question of whether the arguments discussed in previous chapters can be marshaled in support of the thesis that we do not exist, by showing, for example, that we are not composite, and we are not simple, so perhaps we aren't anything.

In this and the following chapter, I will talk a great deal about the "self," and the question of whether the "self" exists. For most of this book, I deliberately avoid using the term "self." Philosophers tend to use the term "self" in very different ways, and for some philosophers, the term "self" carries metaphysical baggage that is not contained in other philosophers'

6.1 Introduction

use of the term "self." As a result, use of the term "self" tends to introduce needless obscurity and imprecision into discussions of personal ontology and often results in philosophers talking past one another.[1] In this and the following chapter, however, I make an exception, and I talk about the "self." I do this primarily because the main arguments against our own existence are arguments in favor of what is generally called the "nonself" or "no-self" or "not-self" thesis. The arguments in question generally aim to show that the "self" does not exist. I take the conclusion of these arguments to be that *we* do not exist (although in §6.2.2 I address the idea that some of the arguments I discuss are really directed against the existence of a particular sort of ontological posit, which may or may not be numerically identical to any of *us*). To avoid any confusion, throughout this and the following chapter, I use the term "self" to denote a kind that each of us belongs to. So, for example, "my self" would denote *me*, "your self" would denote *you*, and so on. If I exist, then at least one self exists. So, I'm working with a very minimal conception of what it takes for there to be selves. Given my use of the term "self," it is incoherent to say that I am anything other than a self, and confused to ask whether I am anything other than a self, confused to ask whether *we* are selves. I'm either a self, or I don't exist.

Westerhoff argues that selves would have to have various properties if they existed, but nothing has all of those properties, so selves do not exist.[2] Note that Westerhoff takes "self" to be a term whose referent is picked out descriptively, as whatever thing, if any, has such-and-such characteristics. My more minimal concept of the "self," by contrast, is such that the "self" is not picked out by way of a description. Rather, I just directly refer to my "self" – that is, me. Given this nondescriptivist way of picking out the referent of the term "self," if my "self" turned out to have very different properties than those properties which I thought I had, I would not, pace Westerhoff, conclude that my "self" (=me) does not exist. I would rather simply conclude that I have very different properties than I thought I had.[3]

---

[1] Cf. Olson 1998, who recommends that philosophers stop using the term "self," largely for these reasons. Zahavi (2005: 103–104) expresses similar concerns, but they don't stop him from using the term "self." Note also the following observation from van Inwagen, which is particularly apt in the present chapter. Van Inwagen (2002: 175–176) complains that when philosophers and scientists say that the self is a myth, it is often not clear to him what they mean by the word "self." If my "self" is just *me*, then these philosophers' and scientists' arguments against the existence of the self are quite weak. But if my "self" is something numerically distinct from me, then it isn't clear what the "self" is supposed to be.

[2] Westerhoff 2020: 141–142.

[3] Compare Kripke's famous refutation of the descriptivist theory of reference, as applied to names like "Aristotle" (Kripke 1980).

I have characterized the nonself thesis as the thesis that selves do not exist. But this claim should be qualified. Many of the arguments against the existence of the self which I discuss in this chapter are derived from the Indian Buddhist philosophical tradition. And it is important to note that within the Indian Buddhist philosophical tradition, the nonself thesis is often characterized as the thesis that the self does not *ultimately* exist (or that it is not *ultimately* true that the self exists), although the self does *conventionally* exist (or it is *conventionally* true that the self exists). This distinction fits within a broader distinction often made within the Buddhist philosophical tradition between "ultimate truths" and "conventional truths." This distinction was understood in different ways by different philosophers throughout the history of Buddhist thought.[4] I don't want to take a firm stance regarding how we should understand this distinction.[5] But for illustrative purposes, here is one plausible way to understand the distinction: To say that the self does not ultimately exist is to say that there aren't any such things as selves. But to say that it is nevertheless conventionally true that selves exist is to say that we can still *talk* as if selves exist because there is some useful convention according to which selves exist.[6] To borrow an example from Siderits,[7] it is also true that there is no college student referred to by the expression "the average college student." Nevertheless, there are contexts in which it is useful to speak of "the average college student," and so we might say that it is *conventionally* true (but not ultimately true) that there is such a thing as "the average college student." So, for something to "exist" merely conventionally is not, on this view, to exist. In other words, if something "exists" merely conventionally, it does not exist. It is just that it is useful to *talk* as if the thing in question exists.[8]

---

[4] For a helpful introduction to the issue, see Newland and Tillemans 2011.
[5] However, see Brenner 2020a and 2020b, where I argue, contra McDaniel 2019, that within the Abhidharma strain of Indian Buddhist thought the two truths should not be understood in ontological pluralists terms, according to which the difference between things which ultimately exist and things which merely conventionally exist is that the things which ultimately exist enjoy a different *mode of being* or *way of existing* than those things which merely conventionally exist. See also Brenner MS-d, where I suggest that the Buddhist notion of (mere) conventional truth is helpfully interpreted in terms of a certain sort of truth despite (ontological) presupposition failure.
[6] Monima Chadha (2021b: §2, 2021a) argues that for the Buddhist the notion that there are selves or persons is not part of a useful convention, since employing this convention undermines Buddhist soteriological and ethical goals. In response I would note that a convention can be useful for some purposes but not for others. The self or person convention can be useful for everyday talk, even if it might get in the way of some other distinctively Buddhist soteriological or ethical goals.
[7] Siderits 2007: 56.
[8] One way of fleshing out this idea is in terms of its being useful to employ a self fiction. See Sauchelli 2016.

6.1 Introduction

Why is it important to make this distinction between the thesis that the self "ultimately" exists and the thesis that the self merely "conventionally" exists? Well, first, as I note above, this is how the nonself thesis is often understood in the Indian Buddhist philosophical tradition, and I do not want to seriously misrepresent that tradition. But the distinction also helps us accommodate the very plausible idea that even if there are no selves, there *does* seem to be something correct about various statements which seem to be about selves. As Olson[9] notes, there is something obviously correct about the statement "there are many people in London," while there is something obviously wrong about the statement "there are many dragons in London," and even if we believe that neither people nor dragons exist, we should preserve the idea that the former statement is correct in a way in which the latter statement is not correct. The concern here is similar to a concern faced by the mereological nihilist, who denies that there are any composite objects. Even if one does not believe in composite objects such as tables, one must maintain that there is *something* correct about statements such as "I have a table in my office," while there isn't something similarly correct about statements such as "I have a dragon in my office." (In light of this concern, some mereological nihilists (or near-nihilists, who believe in very few composite objects) maintain that sentences such as "I have a table in my office" are true, at least in certain conversational contexts, even if strictly speaking, or "in the ontology room," we would truly say "there are no tables."[10] Others say that sentences such as "there is a table in my office" are simply false, although there is some sense in which they are "correct" or "almost as good as true."[11])

For ease of expression, in this and the following chapter, when I discuss the nonself thesis, I will generally simply describe it as the view that selves do not exist. This should be read with the tacit qualification that, according to much of the Indian Buddhist philosophical tradition, while selves do not ultimately exist, they *do* conventionally exist – it is still useful to *talk* as if there are such things as selves.

In Chapter 1, §1.2, I noted that the mereological nihilist might maintain that there are "simples arranged composite object-wise," even if there are no composite objects. The proponent of the nonself thesis might say something similar about the self: There are no selves, but there are things "arranged self-wise." So, for example, the influential Abhidharma Buddhist philosopher Vasubandhu says that "There is no sentient being here, nor

---

[9] Olson 2007: 183.
[10] van Inwagen 1990: Ch. 10, 2014; Horgan and Potrč 2008.
[11] Merricks 2003.

is there a self, but simple entities, each with a cause."¹² Similarly, Sider, a contemporary mereological nihilist, claims that while there are no persons, there are simple objects arranged person-wise which collectively think the thoughts we normally ascribe to persons.¹³

The proponent of the nonself thesis might naturally maintain that our assertions about selves are conventionally true in (but perhaps not *only* in) those situations in which there are things arranged self-wise. For example, in the influential Indian Buddhist work *The Questions of King Milinda*, the monk Nagasena compares talk of selves to talk of chariots: Just as it is correct in some sense to speak of chariots when there are things arranged chariot-wise (even if there are no chariots), it is correct in some sense to speak of selves when there are things arranged self-wise (even if there are no selves).¹⁴ Here "correctness" might be understood in the sense I described earlier when I talked about the idea that selves exist "merely conventionally": There is some useful convention or manner of speaking according to which the statement in question can be regarded as true, and so it is to that extent appropriate to talk as if it is true. (But why should we think there are no such things as chariots? It should be born in mind here that the Indian Buddhist philosophical tradition frequently defends or presupposes mereological nihilism, according to which, on one natural way of thinking of the matter, there are no such things as chariots, since chariots would be composite objects if they existed.¹⁵)

This same point is made succinctly in the following well-known passage from the Bhikkhunīsaṃyutta (part of the Pāli Canon's Sutta Piṭaka, an important early collection of texts containing discourses of the Buddha):

> Just as, with an assemblage of parts,
> The word 'chariot' is used,
> So, when the aggregates exist,
> There is the convention 'a being.'¹⁶

One way of reading this passage: Just as, when there are things arranged chariot-wise, it is correct in some sense to say that there are chariots (even if, strictly or "ultimately" speaking, there are no such things as chariots), when there are things arranged self-wise, then it is correct in some sense (i.e., it is "conventionally true") to say that there are selves. The term in this passage

---

¹² Quoted in Goodman 2009: 165.
¹³ Sider 2013: 268–269.
¹⁴ Davids 1890: 40–45.
¹⁵ Cf. Siderits 2007: 54; Buddhaghosa 2010: 617.
¹⁶ Bodhi 2000: 230.

for "things arranged self-wise" is "the aggregates." (Here, "the aggregates" (Pāli: khandhas) refers to those physical and mental constituents of reality which we are normally inclined to think make up selves. I'll say a bit more about this below.)

With this preliminary stage setting out of the way, I hope it is clear what thesis I denote with the term "nonself thesis." This stage setting will help us appreciate what's at stake in the arguments for and against the existence of the self which will occupy our attention for the remainder of this chapter, and in the following chapter. For the remainder of this chapter, I examine arguments for the conclusion that we do not exist. The arguments discussed in this chapter are generally associated with the Indian Buddhist philosophical tradition. In Chapter 7, I will discuss the positive case that might be made in favor of our existing. I will ultimately conclude that we have good grounds for thinking that selves exist, but these grounds are not decisive.

6.2 The Argument from Impermanence

The first argument we will consider is the argument from impermanence. This argument is attributed to the Buddha himself. In fact, according to Collins, "Statistically, a very high proportion of the discussions of not-self in the Suttas [i.e., discourses attributed to the Buddha in the Pāli Canon] consists in various versions of this argument."[17] Given the prominence of this argument in many of the earliest recorded teachings of the Buddha, it is unsurprising to find that it has exerted an enormous influence on the subsequent history of Buddhist thought.

One influential presentation of the argument from impermanence is contained in the Anattalakkhaṇa Sutta.[18] In the following passage, the Buddha is speaking with some of his male followers (bhikkhus):

> "What do you think, bhikkhus, is form permanent or impermanent?" – "Impermanent, venerable sir." – "Is what is impermanent suffering or happiness?" – "Suffering, venerable sir." – "Is what is impermanent, suffering, and subject to change fit to be regarded thus: 'This is mine, this I am, this is my self'?" – "No, venerable sir."
>
> [...]

---

[17] Collins 1982: 98.
[18] Although very similar, or even identical, presentations of the argument are also contained in a number of other places in the Suttas contained in the Pāli Canon.

"Therefore, bhikkhus, any kind of form whatsoever, whether past, future, or present, internal or external, gross or subtle, inferior or superior, far or near, all form should be seen as it really is with correct wisdom thus: 'This is not mine, this I am not, this is not my self.'"[19]

"Form" in this passage refers to one of the five aggregates. As I noted earlier, the aggregates are those physical and mental constituents of reality that we normally take to make up selves. The other aggregates are: feeling, perception, volitional formations, consciousness. How exactly we should understand the aggregates need not concern us here.[20] For our purposes, the important point to note is that the five aggregates are meant to give an exhaustive specification of where to find the self, if the self exists. And since the five aggregates are meant to be exhaustive, if the self cannot be found among them, then the self does not exist.[21] In the passage quoted above, the Buddha argues that one of the aggregates, form, should not be identified with the self, insofar as form is "impermanent, suffering, and subject to change." In subsequent parts of the Anattalakkhaṇa Sutta, the Buddha goes on to deny that the self should be identified with any of the other aggregates, since each of the aggregates is "impermanent, suffering, and subject to change." The idea is that the self, if it existed, would *not* be "impermanent, suffering, and subject to change." But since none of the five aggregates can be identified with the self, and the self must be identified with one or more of the aggregates if the self exists, the self does not exist.

I take the conclusion of the argument to be that *we* do not exist. In §6.2.2, I will consider the objection that the Buddha's argument is not meant to show that we do not exist but is only meant to show that "the self" does not exist, where "the self" is some metaphysical posit which may or may not be identical to any of *us*.

Assuming that the argument is meant to show that we do not exist, there are two points that deserve special scrutiny: (1) Is it really true that the self, if it exists, must be identified with one or more of these five aggregates? (2) Is it really true that the self, if it exists, will not be "impermanent, suffering, and subject to change"?

---

[19] Bodhi 2000: 902.
[20] Although for some discussion, see Gethin 1986; Gowans 2003: 34; Siderits 2007: 35–36.
[21] This step of the argument is not explicitly stated. Nevertheless, it seems plausible that this step is implicitly included in the argument (Collins 1982: 98; Siderits 2007: 37; Adam 2010: 246–247; Thompson 2020: 94). What's more, as Smith 2021: 9 notes, this step of the argument may be more or less explicitly stated in a nearby discourse included in the collection of Suttas from which the Sutta discussed in the main body of the text is taken. See Bodhi 2000: 885.

6.2 The Argument from Impermanence

For the sake of the argument, I will grant that the self must be found among the aggregates if it exists, either in the sense that the self must be identified with one or more of the five aggregates, or, more weakly, in the sense that the self must in some sense be *made up of* or *composed of* one or more of the five aggregates. This point can be granted for the following reason. Even if the self would not be found among the five precise aggregates identified by the Buddha, it seems plausible that whatever else we might try to identify with the self would be "impermanent, suffering, and subject to change," just as the five aggregates are. If, for example, we were to identify the self with a human animal, as animalists suggest we should, and even if human animals cannot be found among the five aggregates, the Buddha might still insist that the self does not exist, insofar as human animals are "impermanent, suffering, and subject to change." This is why I take it that, for our purposes, it doesn't matter how we should understand terms meant to refer to the aggregates in the Buddha's presentation of the argument from impermanence (e.g., the term "form"). Regardless of how we understand the five aggregates, and regardless of whether we are identified with one or more of the five aggregates or are rather identified with something else, the argument will proceed the same way: The thing with which we would be identical if we existed would be "impermanent, suffering, and subject to change," and this shows that we do not exist, since the self would *not* be "impermanent, suffering, and subject to change" if it existed.

The crucial question, then, is whether we have any grounds for thinking that the self would not be "impermanent, suffering, and subject to change" if it existed. And it is difficult to see why we should accept this assumption. For example, it certainly does not seem to be built into the *concept* of a self that it is permanent, or not subject to suffering or change.

Perhaps the cultural and religious context in which the Buddha presented the argument from impermanence is one that was more receptive to the assumption that the self would not be "impermanent, suffering, and subject to change" if it existed. Gowans comments:

> it may seem obvious to [Westerners] that a self can suffer. However, this aspect of the Buddha's argument is addressed to those in his culture who held that our true self is identical with the ultimate ground of reality (brahman). As such, the self was thought to be both permanent and beyond suffering. According to this view, expressed in the Upaniṣads, what appears to be our self may suffer, but our true self cannot suffer. By showing that each of the aggregates is impermanent, and hence suffers, the Buddha thinks he establishes that this alleged true self cannot be found in connection with any of the aggregates.[22]

[22] Gowans 2003: 88.

Passages in the Upaniṣads which teach that the self is permanent and/or not subject to suffering are not hard to come by. Here are a few examples:

> The self is 'not this, not this'. Unseizable, it is not seized; indestructible, it is not destroyed; without clinging, it is not clung to; unbound, it does not suffer, does not come to harm.[23]

> Maitreyī said, 'Blessed one, you have brought me to extreme confusion: I do not understand this.'
> He said, 'I do not speak to confuse you: this self is imperishable, of a nature (dharma) that cannot be destroyed.'[24]

> Ghora Āṅgirasa, having taught this to Kṛṣṇa son of Devakī, said – for he had become free from thirst – 'At the time of death one should take refuge in these three recollections: "You are the unperishing. You are the unfallen. You are the subtlest part of the breath."'[25]

> The self is free from evil, ageless, deathless, sorrowless, without hunger, without thirst, of true desire, of true resolve.[26]

While the argument from impermanence may have made the most sense in its original cultural and religious context, its influence extends far beyond cultures heavily influenced by the concept of the self contained in the Upaniṣads, and it continues to be the most popular argument for the nonself thesis among contemporary Buddhists. We might wonder, then, whether the argument can be salvaged, even if we reject the assumptions made about the self by the Buddha's original audience. The most obvious changes we might make to the argument involve dropping or modifying one or more of the following assumptions: (1) that the self would be permanent if it were to exist; (2) that the self would not suffer if it were to exist; (3) that the self would not be subject to change if it were to exist. I see no way of salvaging the assumption that the self would not suffer if it existed (although see the discussion below of the argument from control). What's more, in some presentations of or allusions to the argument from impermanence, the Buddha makes no reference to the aggregates' impermanence leading to suffering but rather seems to go directly from the impermanent or changing character of the aggregates to the nonself thesis.[27] So, the Buddha did not seem to think that the reference to suffering is an essential component of the argument. It makes sense, then,

---

[23] Bṛhadāraṇyaka Upaniṣad III.9.26; Roebuck 2003: 58. This formula is repeated several times in this Upaniṣad.
[24] Bṛhadāraṇyaka Upaniṣad IV.6.14; Roebuck 2003: 79.
[25] Chāndogya Upaniṣad III.17.6; Roebuck 2003: 142.
[26] Chāndogya Upaniṣad VIII.1.5; Roebuck 2003: 194.
[27] See, e.g., Ñāṇamoli and Bodhi 1995: 324.

6.2 The Argument from Impermanence

to ask whether the fact that the aggregates are impermanent or changing should lead us to affirm the nonself thesis, aside from any concerns about whether the aggregates' suffering should lead us to affirm the nonself thesis.

Begin with the first assumption that the self would be permanent if it were to exist. Siderits[28] suggests that in the argument from impermanence we interpret the claim that the self would be permanent if it existed to mean that the self would persist over the course of an entire lifetime if it existed. And in support of the claim that none of the aggregates persist over the course of an entire lifetime Siderits notes the fact that each of our physical and mental components (i.e., those physical and mental components meant to be included in the five aggregates) is either transitory and short-lived or not essential for our continued existence (assuming, for reductio, that we do exist). For example, the cells which make up our bodies are constantly being replaced. While certain parts of our bodies might persist over the course of an entire lifetime, no parts of our bodies are essential for our continued existence. For example, while the typical human being has the same heart over the course of an entire lifetime, we each can, in principle, survive a heart transplant. Similarly, while each of us has the same brain over the course of an entire lifetime, we can, in principle, imagine the replacement of one's brain with a suitably programmed substitute.

I have several responses to this line of argument.

First, note that there is nothing incoherent in the idea that each of us is short-lived, or does not persist over the course of an entire human lifetime. So, even if we grant that the self would not persist over the course of a human lifetime if the self existed, this would not show that none of us exists, since we might simply be short-lived.

Now turn to Siderits's observation that each of our physical and mental components is transitory – that, for example, our cells are constantly being replaced. This would not show that the self does not persist over the course of a lifetime. First, we will see why this is the case on the supposition that we are composite objects, and then we will see why it is the case on the supposition that we are simple objects.

Supposing the self is a composite object, then it may survive the replacement of each of its parts, especially if the replacement of the parts is gradual. Siderits hasn't given us any reason to think that this couldn't be the case. What about Siderits's observation that none of our physical or mental components is essential for our continued existence? Far from showing that the self does not exist, this observation would undercut the

---

[28] Siderits 2007: 40.

motivation for the nonself thesis contained in Siderits's observation that our parts are constantly being replaced – if none of those parts is essential for our continued existence, why should we be concerned that they are constantly being replaced? Siderits thinks that the observation that none of our parts is essential to our continued existence supports the nonself thesis by showing that we cannot identify anything which is essential for our continued existence. This might show that the self does not exist, since Siderits identifies the self with "some one part of the person that accounts for the identity of that person over time."[29] So, the idea is that the self is some part of me which survives for as long as I survive. But, Siderits observes, none of my parts survive for the course of a human lifetime, since my parts are constantly being replaced. So, since my self would have to survive the course of a human lifetime in order for me to exist, I do not exist. Here is what is wrong with this argument. There is no reason to think that in order to exist we must have some part that exists so long as we exist. It may be the case that all of our parts are replaceable. It also seems odd to say that the self is "part" of the person, or "accounts for the identity of [the] person over time." On my way of understanding these terms, the self *is* the person. This is, I take it, a standard way of understanding terms like "self" and "person," at least in modern vernacular English.[30] If Siderits does not take the "self" to be identical to the "person," then his arguments against the existence of the "self" might not be arguments against the existence of anyone reading this book, as anyone reading this book is presumably a person.

Now suppose that the self is not a composite object – suppose, for example, that it is a simple immaterial soul. In that case, Siderits's rendition of the argument from impermanence would still not show that the self does not exist. A simple immaterial soul has no parts. So, Siderits has not identified some part of a simple immaterial soul whose loss it could survive, since there is no such part. And the fact that our physical and mental components are transitory would not show that a simple immaterial soul is transitory. If, for example, my cells are constantly being replaced, this

---

[29] Siderits 2007: 33.
[30] Some proponents of the nonself thesis claim that we are "persons," but not "selves," but what they mean by this is that we do not ultimately exist, but there is some useful convention or manner of speaking according to which we exist, and so we exist conventionally. See, e.g., Flanagan 2011: 124, 135; Garfield 2022. This way of using the term "person" seems to me to be confusing and misleading. I suggest, then, that we think of ourselves as persons only if we think that we (ultimately) exist. If we do not (ultimately) exist, then we aren't anything – at most there is some useful *convention* or *fiction* according to which we are something – and so of course we are not persons. (But this is not to suggest that we must be persons if we exist. Perhaps we sometimes exist as nonpersons – e.g., as embryos, or in comatose states, assuming embryos and the comatose are not "persons.")

6.2 *The Argument from Impermanence*

would not show that the soul paired with the body composed of those cells cannot survive the constant replacement of those cells. And we can say something similar about any of our mental characteristics: The loss of any of our mental characteristics (including those mental characteristics which we know are not retained over the course of an entire lifetime) would not obviously cause any simple immaterial soul which has those mental characteristics to cease to exist.

I've just examined Siderits's rendition of the argument from impermanence, one which does not require that the self would be permanent if it existed but rather only requires that the self would persist over the course of a lifetime if it existed. I have argued that, even so modified, the argument from impermanence is not successful: The self need not persist over the course of a lifetime, and anyway the fact that none of our physical or mental characteristics persist over the course of a lifetime would not show that the self does not persist over the course of a lifetime.

But another component of the argument from impermanence does not appeal to the impermanence of each of the aggregates but rather appeals to the *changing nature* of the aggregates.

The notion that the self would be unchanging if it existed has some superficial plausibility if we conflate it with the distinct thesis that the self would *persist* if it existed. Commentators on the argument from impermanence sometimes conflate these distinct theses, perhaps because in some contexts they use "change" to mean "change from one self to another numerically distinct self" or "change from existing to nonexisting." To give one example, Rupert Gethin writes that

> Our everyday linguistic usage of terms such as 'I' amounts in practice to an understanding of self as precisely an unchanging constant behind experiences. Thus when someone declares, 'I was feeling sad, but now I am feeling happy,' he or she implies by the term 'I' that there is a constant, unchanging thing that underlies and links the quite different experiences of happiness and sadness.[31]

What is odd about this statement is that, contra Gethin, when one asserts "I was feeling sad, but now I am feeling happy," one is *explicitly* saying that one has changed. So, what that statement implies is not that there is an unchanging self which "underlies" the experiences, but at most that there is a *persisting* self which "underlies" the experiences, since something must persist in order to change (perhaps this is what Gethin has in mind

---

[31] Gethin 1998: 135.

by his use of the term "constant"). The only sense in which this self is "unchanging" is insofar as it does not change from one self to another numerically distinct self (although perhaps here we should really talk of a self being *replaced* by another self, rather than "changing" into that self), or from existing to nonexisting.

So, let's not conflate the idea that the self would be unchanging if it existed with the distinct thesis that the self would persist if it existed.

It seems very implausible that the self would have to be entirely unchanging if it were to exist. But a more plausible version of the argument contends, not that the self would be *entirely* unchanging if it existed, but rather that the self would be unchanging in *some* respects if it existed. This observation serves as the foundation of Gowans's[32] rendition of the argument from impermanence. Gowans contends that the self must have certain substantive properties in order for it to continue to exist. The problem, Gowans claims, is that the aggregates are constantly changing in all respects, so that they do not instantiate any substantive traits for any appreciable length of time – for example, they do not exercise any psychological capacities for an appreciable length of time. So, the self cannot be found among the aggregates. But if the self exists, then it will be found among the aggregates. So, the self does not exist.

Of course, it is uncontroversial that the self would have *some* essential properties if it existed – for example, the property of being self-identical, or the property of being such that 2 + 2 = 4. When Gowan says that the self would have certain essential properties if it existed, I take it that he has in mind properties which are not trivially and automatically instantiated by any objects whatsoever. The idea is that the self must have certain *substantive* (nontrivial) properties if it exists. And, similarly, when Gowans says that the aggregates are constantly changing in all respects, this should be taken to mean all *substantive* respects, since of course the aggregates are not constantly losing properties which all objects trivially and automatically instantiate (e.g., the property of being such that 2 + 2 = 4).

So, what sorts of substantive essential properties does Gowans think that the self would instantiate, if the self existed? One such essential property may be the self's ability to exercise certain psychological capacities. Gowans seems to endorse this idea when he writes that

> A self is a being that is ontologically distinct from other beings and has as its identity some essential properties that do not change. These properties include the regularly exercised capacities to experience, remember, imagine, feel, desire, think, decide, act, and so on. The self is in control of the exercise

---

[32] Gowans 2003: 34, 78.

6.2 *The Argument from Impermanence*

of some of these capacities. Finally, a self is capable of being aware of itself as a self.[33]

Gowans claims here that the self would have among its essential properties the "regularly exercised capacities to experience, remember, imagine, feel, desire, think, decide, act, and so on." But I doubt that these are essential properties of the self, and so I doubt that the self must exercise these sorts of psychological capacities in order for it to exist. For example, it seems plausible that I was once a fetus or young infant which did not exercise all of the psychological capacities in question. It also seems plausible that I would not cease to exist if I entered a lengthy coma in which I did not regularly exercise the various psychological capacities cited by Gowans.

There seems to me to be an even more serious problem with Gowans's rendition of the argument from impermanence. Even granting Gowans's contention that the self must maintain certain substantive traits in order to continue to exist, I think that we should question the other main component of Gowans's rendition of the argument from impermanence, namely the claim that each of the aggregates is constantly changing in every (substantive) respect. This seems to me to be simply false. The body is not constantly changing in every respect – my body was not seven meters tall yesterday, and it is not seven meters tall today. Similarly, I have various psychological capacities which I have continued to exercise for many years, and which I will (hopefully) continue to exercise many years into the future. So, the aggregates, which encompass my physical and psychological characteristics, are simply not constantly changing in every (substantive) respect, and Gowans's rendition of the argument from impermanence fails.

Perhaps this is a needlessly strong reading of Gowans's claim that the self is constantly changing in every (substantive) respect. Perhaps Gowans only means to endorse the weaker claim that, in every (substantive) respect in which we might change, we are constantly changing to some degree. So, for example, he would not claim that, if I was not seven meters tall yesterday, then I will be seven meters tall today. Rather, the idea is that, if my body had a certain height yesterday, then it has a slightly different height today. And that's true. But this weaker way of interpreting the claim that we are constantly changing in every respect does not seem to me to support the nonself thesis. It does not support the nonself thesis because it does not show that we fail to retain any substantive traits for any appreciable period of time. It is compatible with my having a certain substantive trait for an

---

[33] Gowans 2003: 33.

appreciable period of time and that there is slight variation in that trait over time. For example, if I retain the capacity to remember a certain experience over the course of a year, this is compatible with frequent small changes in the precise manner in which I would remember the experience if I were to exercise my capacity and consciously recall the experience.

6.2.1 *Galen Strawson on the Self*

Galen Strawson argues that subjects of experience are very short-lived. He does not make this point in the context of a defense of the argument from impermanence. However, his arguments for the thesis that selves are very short-lived are worth considering here, as they may, in conjunction with the view that the self cannot be short-lived if it exists, support the Buddhist argument from impermanence. Unfortunately, Strawson's argument for the conclusion that the self is short-lived is not as clear as we might like. I will do my best to reconstruct it.[34]

Strawson contends that for each human life there are a number of short-lived subjects of experience, each one successively thinking the thoughts and having the experiences that we are normally inclined to attribute to a long-lived subject of experience. According to Strawson, these short-lived subjects of experience are selves. If Strawson is correct, then the self exists for a period of time that is far shorter than we are normally inclined to think it exists, as these short-lived subjects of experience each exist for several seconds at most (more on this in a moment). In addition to the short-lived selves, there are long-lived human beings, and the short-lived selves are, Strawson claims, parts of the long-lived human beings.[35] Sometimes our use of first-person pronouns such as "I" refer to a long-lived human being, and sometimes they refer to one or more of the short-lived selves that are parts of that human being. But Strawson claims that the long-lived human being is not a subject of experience (there is nothing it is like to be one of these long-lived human beings),[36] and that the "short-lived selves are what we are really talking about when we talk about the self."[37]

Why believe in these short-lived subjects of experiences? Why not believe instead in, say, long-lived subjects of experience who are not themselves composed of short-lived subjects of experience?

---

[34] Here I have in mind especially Strawson's defense of the view that the self is short-lived which he gives in Strawson 2009 and 2017.
[35] Strawson 2017: 74.
[36] Strawson 2017: 75–76.
[37] Strawson 2017: 75.

6.2 The Argument from Impermanence

The answers to these questions are connected with the circumstances under which objects compose other objects. (To say that some *x*s compose a *y* is to say that the *x*s are all parts of *y*, and *y* has no other parts not included in the *x*s.) Strawson claims that a primary criterion for whether some objects compose some other object is whether the former objects exhibit a sufficient degree of "unity." The more "unified" some objects are, the more plausible it is that they compose some further object. The short-lived subjects of experience that Strawson proposes we believe in each exist just as long as it takes for them to partake of an "experientially unitary period of experience."[38] Our conscious lives are not smooth and uninterrupted but are rather jumpy and discontinuous. The periods of time in which we have an "experientially unitary period of experience" are therefore very short, so that "in the normal course of events truly hiatus-free periods of thought or experience are invariably brief in human beings: a few seconds at the most, a fraction of a second at the least."[39] We might call the experiences had during these "experientially unitary periods of experience" "units of experience." Such units of experience might include, for example, "the grasping of a thought-content, the seeing of a bird and the seeing of it as a bird, and so on."[40]

Now, Strawson claims, in any unit of experience, that the objects involved in giving rise to that experience exhibit a great deal of the sort of unity relevant to composition:

> Certainly it seems that there is, in nature, as far as we know it, no higher grade of physical unity than the unity of the mental subject present and alive in what James calls the 'indecomposable' unity of a conscious thought.
>
> ...
>
> It is ... hard to see that there are any better candidates for the status of physical objects than [short-lived subjects of experience] or selves.[41]
>
> It's arguable, in fact, that there is no more indisputable unity in nature, and therefore no more indisputable physical unity or singularity, and therefore no better candidate for the title "physical object", than the unity that we come upon when we consider the phenomenon of the (thin) subject of experience as it exists in the living moment of experience, experiencing seeing books and chairs and seeing them as such, say, or consciously comprehending the thought that water is wet ....[42]

[38] Strawson 2017: 72.
[39] Strawson 2017: 26.
[40] Strawson 2017: 72.
[41] Strawson 2017: 71.
[42] Strawson 2017: 177.

Here, when Strawson talks about "physical objects," he has in mind *composite* physical objects. So, there are no better candidates for composite physical objects than these short-lived subjects of experience, insofar as they exhibit the requisite sort of unity to a greater degree than any other phenomena of which are aware. And that's why we should believe in these short-lived subjects of experience but need not believe in any long-lived subjects of experience, since the long-lived subjects of experience would not exhibit as great a degree of "unity" as the short-lived subjects of experience.

Earlier, I noted that, according to Strawson, long-lived human beings *do* exist, but they are not subjects of experience. I'm not sure how to make this fit with Strawson's apparent view that the (alleged) parts of the long-lived subjects of experience do not exhibit a sufficient degree of unity to compose a long-lived subject of experience. If they can compose a long-lived *human being*, why can they not compose a long-lived subject of experience? I'm not sure what the answer to this question is. Strawson does say that the subject of experience cannot have "long-term diachronic continuity," since to suppose that they can would be to suppose that "a many-membered set or series of [short-lived subjects of experience] in a certain relation can be a single subject of experience."[43] And, Strawson claims, "a many-membered set of [short-lived subjects of experience] in a certain relation is simply not the kind of thing that can itself be a subject of experience."[44] I agree that "a many-membered set or series of [short-lived subjects of experience] in a certain relation" cannot be a single subject of experience. But I still don't see why many short-lived subjects of experience could not work together to *compose* a long-lived subject of experience if they can compose a long-lived human being. This is my first objection to Strawson's account of the self. Perhaps the simplest way of solving the problem is to contend that long-lived human beings don't exist, whether or not they are subjects of experience. This view would fit naturally with the idea that short-lived subjects of experience (which are, on Strawson's view, parts of long-lived human beings) do not exhibit a sufficient degree of unity to compose any long-lived composite object.

I have several additional objections to Strawson's account of the self, objections that do not have such straightforward solutions.

Objection 1: Strawson thinks that the relevant sort of unity which results in composition is a *mental* or *experiential* unity. So, for example, he writes that

---

[43] Strawson 2017: 75.
[44] Strawson 2017: 75–76.

6.2 The Argument from Impermanence

> The total experiential field involves many things – rich interoceptive (somatosensory) and exteroceptive sensation, mood-and-affect-tone, deep conceptual animation, and so on. It has, standardly, a particular focus, and more or less dim peripheral areas, and it is, overall, extraordinarily complex in content. But it is for all that a unity, and essentially so. It is fundamentally unified, utterly indivisible, as the particular concrete phenomenon it is, simply in being, indeed, a total experiential field; or, equivalently, simply in being the content of the experience of a single subject at that moment.[45]

I'm not sure I understand everything that Strawson says here. But the important point for our purposes is that Strawson seems to think that the parts of short-lived subjects of experience compose those short-lived subjects of experience because the short-lived subjects of experience exhibit a sufficient degree of "unity," and that this unity is largely or entirely *experiential unity* – that is, unity with respect to the experiences had by the short-lived subjects of experience. Whatever this experiential unity is supposed to be, I see a problem. Strawson thinks that the parts compose the subjects of experience because the subjects of experience exhibit the experiential unity. So, Strawson is committed to thinking that the subjects of experience exist because they exhibit the experiential unity. But this seems to get the order of dependence backwards. A *precondition* for there being experiences is that there is a subject of experience (as Strawson, and many others, explicitly assume). So, the experiences, and so the experiential unity associated with those experiences, presuppose the subject of experience. In fact, this very point seems to be expressed when Strawson writes that experiential unity obtains "simply in being the content of the experience of a single subject at that moment" – the experiential unity obtains *because* the experiences are the experiences of a single subject at that moment. So, contra Strawson, one should not say that the subject of experience exists *because* the relevant experiential unity obtains. The order of dependence runs in the other direction, with the experiential unity obtaining (in part) because the subject of experience exists.

Objection 2: Strawson says that we should believe in the short-lived subjects of experience because the objects that compose those short-lived subjects of experience exhibit a relevant sort of unity to a greater degree than any other phenomena of which we are aware. But even if short-lived subjects of experience exhibit the relevant sort of unity *more* than any other phenomena of which we are aware, it does not follow that long-lived subjects of experience do not exist, since they may also exhibit whatever

---

[45] Strawson 2017: 179.

degree of unity is sufficient for composition to occur. To rule this out, Strawson must have some idea of what degree of "unity" is required for composition. But I'm not sure how Strawson could know this.

Objection 3: Strawson's argument for the existence of short-lived subjects of experience appeals to the alleged fact that the parts of those short-lived subjects of experience exhibit a great deal of "unity," which should lead us to think that the parts in question compose further objects, short-lived subjects of experience. But I don't think that we can take it for granted that composition occurs. Recall the discussion of mereological nihilism in Chapter 1, §1.2: Mereological nihilism, which says that composite objects do not exist, is not obviously false (it is not, e.g., obviously ruled out by our sense experiences).[46] What's more, some of the arguments discussed in previous chapters, which were directed against the thesis that we are composite physical objects, generalize and undermine belief in composite objects more generally. Strawson cannot take it for granted, then, that there are any such things as composite objects.

Objection 4: Even if there *are* composite objects, we need some reason to think that a good way to identify when and where composition occurs has something to do with objects exhibiting the sort of "unity" Strawson appeals to. In other words, we need some reason to endorse this particular theory of composition. The problem is compounded by the fact that the concept of "unity" employed here is very vague (which is why I have been putting the term in scare quotes).

Objection 5: In Chapter 2, §2.7, I discussed the question of whether, given substance dualism, we can ever know that the soul occupying some body now is identical to the soul that occupied the body at some point in the past (say, five minutes ago). One response I gave to this concern was that it is generally much simpler to suppose that there is one soul occupying a body over an extended period of time, rather than a series of souls successively occupying that body. I would offer basically the same response to Strawson's claim that where we think that there is a long-lived subject of experience there is really a series of short-lived subjects of experience. It is far more complex to suppose, for any given human life, there is a stream of successive short-lived subjects of experience associated with that life rather than a single long-lived subject of experience. So, it is more plausible to think what we are normally inclined to think: that in any given human life, there

---

[46] And, a point I did not mention in Chapter 1, §1.2, mereological nihilism is not obviously ruled out by the findings of science either (Dorr 2002: §1.4.2; Rosen and Dorr 2002: §7; Sider 2013: §11; Brenner 2018).

6.2 The Argument from Impermanence

is a single long-lived subject of experience, rather than a succession of short-lived subjects of experience.

So, I do not think that Strawson has shown that subjects of experience are all short-lived. Recall that the reason I have discussed Strawson's view is that it might indirectly support the argument from impermanence, a crucial step of which is that all of the things that might be seen as candidate selves are too short-lived to be selves.

I conclude, then, that the argument from impermanence is unsuccessful: it has not been shown that all of the candidate objects with which we might reasonably identify the self are all too short-lived to be the self.

6.2.2 Have I Attacked a Strawman?

Before I move on to consider other prominent arguments against the existence of the self, I would like to pause to consider an objection that might be made to my critique of the argument from impermanence. According to this objection, I have misunderstood what sort of "self" is targeted by the argument from impermanence – the argument from impermanence may successfully undermine belief in this sort of self, even if it does not undermine belief in a "self" as I'm using that term (i.e., even if it does not undermine belief in our own existence). If this objection is correct, then it might also undermine my critique of other arguments for the nonself thesis below, if those arguments are not intended to undermine belief in the existence of a "self," as I use the term "self."[47]

I took the argument from impermanence to be directed against belief in our own existence. If the argument from impermanence is not meant to undermine belief in our own existence, then what is it intended to accomplish? The objection is that the argument from impermanence, and some other early Buddhist arguments for the nonself thesis, are only meant to undermine belief in a certain very strong metaphysical posit, one which we might refer to with the term "self." Earlier I noted that the concept of the self contained in the Upaniṣads is one according to which the self is permanent and indestructible. This might lend support to the objection I have in mind here: The Buddha did not mean to refute our existence

---

[47] A similar objection would be that the "argument from impermanence," and other arguments contained in the early Buddhist Suttas, are not even meant to lead us to reject belief in the self, whether "self" is construed in the way I suggest, or some other way. Perhaps, for example, these arguments are not meant to lead us toward some metaphysical conclusion or other, but serve some other purpose. For discussion, see Harvey 1995: Ch. 1; Albahari 2002; Smith 2021. In the interest of brevity, I will not examine this objection in detail. But what I say in response to the other objection does, I think, go some way toward addressing this objection.

but rather merely meant to refute the existence of *permanent* or *long-lived* selves, or, more specifically, the sort of self posited by the Upaniṣads. In a similar vein, Harvey writes that

> It can thus be seen that the Self-ideal which early Buddhism worked with was of an unconditioned, permanent, totally happy 'I', which is self-aware, in total control of itself, a truly autonomous agent, with an inherent substantial essence, the true nature of an individual person. Of course, not all Self-views may explicitly say this, but the 'early Suttas' and the early Theravāda interpretative texts imply that such ideas are implicit in these views and in the more deep-rooted 'I am' attitude.[48]

And Gombrich writes that

> ... for the Buddha's audience *by definition* the word *ātman/attā* ["self"] referred to something unchanging; in that linguistic environment, to add a word meaning 'unchanging' [to the statement "there is no self"] would have been redundant.[49]

It is not enough to say that proponents of the argument from impermanence simply assumed that we would have all of these traits if we existed. That would not salvage the argument from impermanence but would simply burden that argument with implausible premises (e.g., the premise that we would be unchanging if we existed or that we would be totally happy if we existed). In order to salvage the argument from impermanence, we must say that "self" functions in that argument as a technical term meant to denote a metaphysical posit with various properties, including, for example, the properties of being permanent and unchanging. In this case, the "self" need not be what we refer to with first-person pronouns, since we might very well exist (and so terms like "we" might successfully denote) even if a "self" does not exist.

Early Buddhist arguments against the existence of an unchanging transcendent self might certainly tell us something about personal ontology if they tell us that we are not transcendent unchanging selves (since there aren't any such things). But it seems clear to me that early Buddhist advocates of the nonself thesis, as well as many subsequent Buddhist interpreters of that thesis, *do* take the word "self" to correspond to the referents of our first-person pronouns (if there are any such referents). The "self" at issue here is not simply a certain metaphysical posit the existence of which is a separate matter from whether *we* exist. Rather, if the arguments at issue show that the "self" does not exist, then they show that *we* do not exist. For example, recall from my presentation of the argument from

---

[48] Harvey 1995: 51.
[49] Gombrich 2009: 9. Cf. Gombrich 2006: 15–16.

6.2 The Argument from Impermanence

impermanence that the Buddha took this argument to establish that we cannot be found among any of the aggregates, that our personal pronouns are not correctly taken to refer to any of the aggregates: We should conclude, for each of these aggregates, "This is not mine, this I am not, this is not my self."[50] This point is reinforced when, elsewhere in the Pāli Canon, we see the Buddha argue that the nonexistence of the self should lead us to no longer cling to or appropriate personal characteristics, experiences, or possessions.[51] The idea he had in mind seems to be that if I do not exist, then these things are not and could not be *mine*, and so I lose my motivation to cling to or appropriate these things. This line of thought makes sense: If there does not exist anyone who might benefit from clinging to or appropriating something, then it wouldn't make much sense to cling to or appropriate that thing. But if the Buddha thought that we *do* exist, although we are not unchanging or transcendent, it is hard to see why that should lead us to no longer cling to or appropriate personal characteristics, experiences, or possessions.

Similarly, Buddhaghosa, an influential Theravāda Buddhist philosopher, wrote that "For there is suffering, but none who suffers; Doing exists although there is no doer. Extinction is but no extinguished person; Although there is a path, there is no goer."[52] Here, Buddhaghosa seems to say that *we* do not exist, not just that a transcendent and permanent personal being does not exist. Similarly, in *The Questions of King Milinda*, another influential early Buddhist work, the protagonist of the dialogue, Nâgasena, denies of each of the aggregates that he is identical with that aggregate, and he also denies that he is a composite made up of the aggregates or that he is identical with anything outside of the aggregates.[53] Note that he does not simply deny that a "self" is identical with any of the aggregates, or identical with a composite made up of the aggregates, or identical with anything outside of the aggregates, but rather he denies that *he himself* is identical with any of these things. The conclusion we are meant to draw from this argument is that Nâgasena is not identical with anything, and so does not exist.[54] So too, the influential Mahayana Buddhist philosopher Nāgārjuna, after alluding to the argument from impermanence, writes that "The self not existing, how will there be 'what

---

[50] Bodhi 2000: 902.
[51] See, e.g., Nāṇamoli and Bodhi 1995: 279–282, 329–330, 528–529, 891, 1089–1091.
[52] Buddhaghosa 2010: 529. Cf. 575, 627.
[53] Davids 1890: 40–45.
[54] Notably, however, in keeping with the common Buddhist idea that the self "conventionally" exists, Nâgasena does maintain that it is appropriate to use the word "Nâgasena" when we talk of the activities of the aggregates associated with the name "Nâgasena" (Davids 1890: 44–45).

belongs to the self'? / There is no 'mine' and no 'I' because of the cessation of self and that which pertains to the self. / And who is without 'mine' and 'I'-sense, he is not found. / One who sees that which is without 'mine' and 'I'-sense does not see."[55] Nāgārjuna's point here is that if there is no self, then there is no one to engage in appropriation – no one to say that something is "I" or "mine." But then Nāgārjuna's seems to assume that if the self does not exist, then *we* do not exist, since if we existed then we would presumably engage in the relevant sort of appropriation. (Bear in mind that the idea I am attributing to Nāgārjuna is a *conditional* claim: that *if* there is no self, then we do not exist. A classic controversy concerning Nāgārjuna and other Mādhyamika thinkers is whether they endorse any positive philosophical theses. My attribution of a conditional thesis to Nāgārjuna will, hopefully, be less controversial than an attribution of a categorical or nonconditional thesis to Nāgārjuna.)

Similarly, the hugely influential Mahayana Diamond Sutra seems to reject belief in our own existence in passages such as this one:

> "Subhūti, what do you think? Let no one say the Tathāgata cherishes the idea 'I must liberate all living beings.' Allow no such thought, Subhūti. Wherefore? Because in reality there are no living beings to be liberated by the Tathāgata. If there were living beings for the Tathāgata to liberate, he would partake in the idea of selfhood, personality, ego entity, and separate individuality. Subhūti, though the common people accept egoity as real, the Tathāgata declares that ego is not different from nonego. Subhūti, those whom the Tathāgata referred to as 'common people' are not really common people; such is merely a name."[56]

Or consider Śāntideva, another influential Mahayana Buddhist philosopher. Śāntideva is celebrated for, among other things, arguing that the nonself thesis should lead us away from egoism and toward universal altruism. The core of the argument is contained in the following passage:

> The continuum of consciousnesses, like a queue, and the combination of constituents, like an army, are not real. The person who experiences suffering does not exist. To whom will that suffering belong? Without exception, no sufferings belong to anyone. They must be warded off simply because they are suffering. Why is any limitation put on this? If one asks why suffering should be prevented, no one disputes that! If it must be prevented, then all of it must be. If not, then this goes for oneself as for everyone.[57]

[55] Siderits and Katsura 2013: 196.
[56] Price and Mou-Lam 2012: §25.
[57] Śāntideva 1995: Ch. 8, §§101–103.

6.2 The Argument from Impermanence

For present purposes, it is useful to make two points about this passage. First, Śāntideva seems to imply that we do not exist. If we did exist, then suffering would certainly "belong" to many of us, in the sense that many of us would suffer. So, the fact that "no sufferings belong to anyone" implies that we do not exist. Second, Śāntideva's inference from the nonself thesis to universal altruism only makes sense on the assumption that we do not exist. If Śāntideva interpreted the nonself thesis to mean simply that certain changeless beings do not exist (beings who may or may not be *us*), then we might very well object to the argument by noting that we should feel special concern for our own suffering because it is *our* suffering. Śāntideva aims to block such a move by contending that we do not exist, and so there isn't any sense in which any of us "owns" our own suffering, to the exclusion of the suffering of others.

Let me be clear that the Buddhist philosophers I have just cited were very different from one another, and surely did not think about the nonself thesis and its purported implications in precisely the same way. The point I am making here simply concerns the fact that they all seemed to think that the nonself thesis entails that we do not exist. Despite their other differences, this is one idea they seemed to have in common.

So, I think that we should conclude that in the Buddha's original presentation of the argument from impermanence, as well as in much of the subsequent Buddhist tradition, when the existence of the "self" is refuted this is meant to refute *our* existence – what is under dispute is not just the existence of some very strong metaphysical posit, but our own existence. So, the notion that refutation of the existence of the self should lead us to think that *we* do not exist is not foreign to the Buddhist intellectual tradition. I do not claim that this way of thinking of the nonself thesis is universally endorsed in the Buddhist intellectual tradition or even the Indian Buddhist intellectual tradition specifically. For one thing, there is the vexed question of how to interpret the Buddhist "personalists" (Pudgalavādins) who, on a common interpretation, accepted belief in some sort of person (pudgala) even as they claimed to follow Buddhist orthodoxy in rejecting belief in a self (ātman). I don't know how to interpret the views of the personalists, but it is worth noting that their Buddhist opponents frequently accused them of rejecting the nonself thesis.[58] There is also the controversial question of

---

[58] For some discussion, see Harvey 1995: 34–38. For the view that the personalists have been generally misunderstood, and that they endorsed a fictionalist account of the person compatible with the nonself thesis, see Lusthaus 2009. Chadha (2021a) notes that standard Buddhist arguments against the existence of the self (ātman) will also undermine belief in persons (pudgala). If that's right,

132   6 Arguments Against Our Existence

whether the Mahayana "Buddha-nature" doctrine conflicts with the nonself thesis.[59]

This section has been something of a detour, and I don't plan to devote any more space to these interpretive matters. Even bracketing these interpretive questions, we can wonder whether classical Buddhist arguments for the nonself thesis (such as the argument from impermanence) would show that we don't exist. It is this latter question which mainly interests me. So, for the remainder of this chapter, I will simply assume that classical Buddhist arguments are directed against our own existence, and I will ask whether these arguments, interpreted in this manner, are sound. We have seen one such argument, the argument from impermanence, which is, I claim, not sound. This argument is probably the most influential argument for the nonself thesis contained in the Buddhist intellectual tradition. I turn now to another influential argument within that tradition: the argument from lack of control.

6.3   The Argument from Lack of Control

The argument from lack of control is also contained in some early discourses of the Buddha. Here, I discuss the presentation of the argument in the Anattalakkhaṇa Sutta. Once again, the Buddha is addressing some of his male followers (bhikkhus):

> "Bhikkhus, form is nonself. For if, bhikkhus, form were self, this form would not lead to affliction, and it would be possible to have it of form: 'Let my form be thus; let my form not be thus.'
>
> "Feeling is nonself …. Perception is nonself …. Volitional formations are nonself …. Consciousness is nonself. For if, bhikkhus, consciousness were self, this consciousness would not lead to affliction, and it would be possible to have it of consciousness: 'Let my consciousness be thus; let my consciousness not be thus.' But because consciousness is nonself, consciousness leads to affliction, and it is not possible to have it of consciousness: 'Let my consciousness be thus; let my consciousness not be thus.'"[60]

In this passage, the terms "form," "feeling," "perception," "volitional formations," and "consciousness" refer, once again, to each of the five aggregates. If the self exists, it will be found among one or more of these

---

then even if the personalist view is not incompatible with the nonself thesis, it may still be false if the standard arguments for the nonself thesis are sound.

[59] Williams 2009: Ch. 5.
[60] Bodhi 2000: 901–902.

6.3 The Argument from Lack of Control

aggregates. But none of these candidates fits the bill for being the self. This is because if something is a self, then it must be such that the self can exert a great deal of control over that thing, to say of it "let it be thus" and "let it not be thus." And in particular, one would be able to ensure of one's self that it would not suffer from afflictions. But clearly enough we do not exert this sort of control over any of the aggregates. So, none of the aggregates is the self, and, since the self would be among the aggregates if it existed, we can conclude that the self does not exist.

This seems to me to be an even less promising argument for the nonself thesis than the argument from impermanence. The most obvious problem with the argument is the premise that the self would have a great deal of control over itself if it existed, and in particular enough control that one can prevent any affliction which one encounters. I see no reason at all to accept this premise. Perhaps this premise would have seemed more compelling to people immersed in the cultural and religious context in which the Buddha lived and taught. In that context, it very well may have been widely taken for granted that the self, if it existed, would have this large degree of control over itself. Collins makes some relevant comments:

> ... a major motive for world-renouncing asceticism in Brahmanical thought was the desire for universal power, attained through knowledge of, and control over, the self (atman) as microcosmic reflection of the macrocosmic force of the universe (brahman). The first way in which the Buddha attempted to deny the existence of such a self was, accordingly, to claim that no such control existed.[61]

And just as I noted, in my discussion of the argument from impermanence, that the Upaniṣads teach that the self is permanent and not subject to suffering, so too we can note here that the Upaniṣads emphasize the idea that the self is a "controller." For example, Bṛhadāraṇyaka Upaniṣad[62] repeatedly identifies the self as a "controller" and stresses all the things over which it has control. The following passage is representative: "'That which, resting in the earth, is other than the earth; which the earth does not know; of which the earth is the body; which controls the earth from within: this is your self, the inner controller, the immortal.'"[63]

If we lack these cultural and religious presuppositions, which emphasize the idea that the self has a great deal of control over itself, can the argument from lack of control be salvaged?

---

[61] Collins 1982: 97.
[62] Book III, Chapter 7.
[63] Bṛhadāraṇyaka Upaniṣad III.7.3; Roebuck 2003: 49.

Sometimes, the Buddha suggests that the principle that a self would have a great deal of control over itself is justified by analogy with the principle that a king would have total control over his kingdom – for example, able to execute who he wants to execute, fine who he wants to fine, and banish who he wants to banish.[64] But this argument by analogy is not very compelling. For one thing, kings do not always have a great deal of control over their kingdoms. And even if many kings *do* have a great deal of control over their kingdoms, that seems to me to provide no support at all for the idea that selves would have a great deal of control over themselves.

Here is another way in which we might try to salvage the argument. Siderits[65] suggests that the argument from lack of control[66] be interpreted in terms which make use of the "antireflexivity principle," according to which nothing can operate on itself. I take it that for something to "operate" on itself is for that thing to change itself, or at the very least causally interact with itself in an attempt to change itself. Interpreted in this way, the argument from lack of control claims that, for each of the aggregates, we can operate on that aggregate, since we can causally interact with that aggregate in an attempt to change it. This shows, for each of the aggregates, that the self is not that aggregate, since nothing can operate on itself. But if the self exists, then it would be found among the aggregates. So, the self does not exist. I doubt that this is the sort of argument the Buddha has in mind in the passage cited above (the Buddha says nothing which seems to indicate that he has the antireflexivity principle in mind), but we can nevertheless evaluate this modified version of the argument from lack of control.

Note that this argument makes use of the premise that for each of the aggregates "we can operate on that aggregate." But if *we* do anything, then we exist, and so the self exists. It would be best if we can understand this premise in terms that do not conflict with the nonself thesis. In response to this concern, Siderits suggests that in cases where we seem to operate on some aggregate, it is better to say that some aggregates operate on some other aggregates.[67] For example, on some occasion where my hand moves my hair, we should not say that I use my hand to move my hair, since this would imply that I exist. The proponent of the nonself thesis would

---

[64] Ñāṇamoli and Bodhi 1995: 325.
[65] Siderits 2007: 46–50, 2022: 21.
[66] Incidentally, Siderits calls it the "argument from control." This seems to me to be an odd title for the argument, since the argument emphasizes the *absence*, not the presence, of control over the aggregates.
[67] Siderits 2007: 49.

6.3 The Argument from Lack of Control

say that in this case we should say that the aggregates associated with my hand move the aggregates associated with my hair. This way we describe the causal interactions involving the aggregates without presupposing that the nonself thesis is false.

I'll grant Siderits's reply to this concern. A much more pressing concern with the argument is that I see no reason to accept the antireflexivity principle. What is our motivation for accepting this principle? Siderits notes that the principle is widely accepted among Indian philosophers. But he provides no motivation for the principle other than its apparent immunity to counterexamples. Apparent counterexamples to the principle can, he says, be explained away. For example, when presented with the apparent counterexample of the doctor who treats themself, Siderits replies that in such cases one part of the doctor treats some other part of the doctor (when, e.g., a doctor's hand removes an ingrown toenail from the doctor's foot). Siderits continues: "Those who support the [antireflexivity principle] claim that all seeming counter-examples will turn out to involve one part of a complex system operating on another part. So there are no counter-examples, and the principle is valid."[68]

What should we make of this argument? Are there really no counterexamples to the antireflexivity principle, and if so, would that show that we should accept the antireflexivity principle?

It's true that if the antireflexivity principle really has no counterexamples, then the antireflexivity principle is true. But from the fact that we are not *aware* of any counterexamples, it does not follow that the principle is true. We are generally not justified in believing a principle simply on the basis of the fact that we are not aware of any counterexample to the principle. We are not aware of any counterexamples to Goldbach's conjecture,[69] but that does not mean that we are justified in believing that it is true. Perhaps Siderits would reply that we *would* be aware of counterexamples to the antireflexivity principle if the principle was false. By contrast, perhaps Goldbach's conjecture is such that, given the present state of our knowledge, we should not expect to be aware of counterexamples to the conjecture even if there are such counterexamples. I'm not sure what to make of this. Why think that we would be aware of counterexamples to the antireflexivity principle if the principle was false?

---

[68] Siderits 2007: 47.
[69] Goldbach's conjecture is a famous unproved conjecture in mathematics. It claims that every even natural number greater than 2 is the sum of two prime numbers. While the conjecture remains unproven, it also has no known counterexamples.

An additional worry is that, while we may be aware of no counterexamples to the antireflexivity principle that do not involve the self, the principle may nevertheless not apply in the case of the self. In that case, we should not generalize from the fact that the antireflexivity principle holds true of nonselves to the conclusion that it therefore holds true of selves. It might seem *ad hoc* to suppose that the antireflexivity principle was true of all objects, with selves being the only exception. But perhaps there is some crucial difference between selves and nonselves, such as the fact that selves generally have mental states. As Strawson notes: "There is no insuperable difficulty in the matter of present or immediate self-awareness .... The case is just not like the case of the eye that cannot see itself, or a fingertip that cannot touch itself. A mind is, rather dramatically, more than an eye."[70]

In any case, I think that we *are* aware of counterexamples to the antireflexivity principle. Some such counterexamples involve the self: I can think about myself, write about myself, vote for myself, look at myself in a mirror, destroy myself, and so on. The advocate of the argument from lack of control might contend that these purported counterexamples simply beg the question against the nonself thesis. I have three responses. First, the counterexamples may be more plausible than the nonself thesis and serve to legitimately undermine the nonself thesis. Second, in this dialectical context, the counterexamples are meant to undermine the *antireflexivity principle*, and they are not presented as direct counterexamples to the nonself thesis. And the cogency of these counterexamples strikes me as far more plausible than the antireflexivity principle, even if (perhaps contrary to fact) it *would* be question-begging to present the counterexamples in order to directly refute the nonself thesis. Third, the counterexamples can be reframed in terms acceptable to the proponent of the nonself thesis, even as they continue to violate the antireflexivity principle: Some aggregates think about themselves, write about themselves, vote for themselves (as when the aggregates arranged Obama-wise vote for themselves), look at themselves in a mirror, destroy themselves, and so on.

These counterexamples don't seem to succumb to the objection that they "turn out to involve one part of a complex system operating on another part." For example, when some aggregates write about themselves, this doesn't seem to be a case where some aggregates write about some other aggregates. This is because the aggregates doing the writing can write about one set of aggregates, then another, and so on, until they have written about

---

[70] Strawson 2017: 59.

6.3 The Argument from Lack of Control

all of the aggregates in which they themselves are included. If they follow that procedure, they will at some point write about themselves.

We can even see that apparent counterexamples to the antireflexivity principle involving doctors treating themselves also need not succumb to the objection that they "turn out to involve one part of a complex system operating on another part." Perhaps it is true of the doctor who removes an ingrown toenail on their foot that really one of their parts removes the toenail from some other part. But consider a surgeon who performs brain surgery on themself (say, by way of a complex series of mirrors or a video feed). In this case, the surgeon operates on themself, assuming that the surgeon is some composite physical object that either is their brain or which includes their brain as a part. In this case, we should not say that one part of the surgeon, their hand, operates on another part, their brain. The brain ultimately directs the movements of the hand. So, if the operation should be attributed to any *part* of the surgeon (rather than the surgeon themself), it should presumably be attributed to the brain or some part of the brain. But then there is nothing stopping us from saying that the brain operates on itself, or that the relevant part of the brain operates on itself. So, either the surgeon operates on themself, or their brain does (or both, if they are their brain).

Some stock examples of the antireflexivity principle at work also do not seem to work. It is sometimes claimed, for example, that we see the antireflexivity principle at work in the fact that my fingertip cannot touch itself, knives cannot cut themselves,[71] scissors cannot cut themselves, and eyes cannot see themselves. But all of these examples trade on contingent features of our space-time. In a sufficiently curved or compactified space-time, a fingertip may be able to touch itself, knives may be able to cut themselves, scissors may be able to cut themselves, and eyes may be able to see themselves (think very strong gravitational lensing, which turns photons back on their source and functions as a mirror). Or, to take an easier-to-visualize possibility, imagine a world in which there are spatial portals, of the sort contained in the video game Portal. Whatever enters one portal immediately exits another spatially separated portal. Portals of this sort would allow fingertips to touch themselves, knives to cut themselves, scissor to cut themselves, and eyes to see themselves, without any sort of physical intermediary (e.g., a mirror). So, it is just a contingent feature of the geometry of our space-time that we can't do these sorts of things. And

---

[71] Siderits 2007: 46.

we may not even need exotic space-time geometries for some of these things – for example, a sufficiently long and flexible knife may be able to cut itself.

But there is a further problem with the antireflexivity principle, beyond the fact that it is unmotivated and seems to suffer from counterexamples. It seems natural to ask *why* the antireflexivity principle is true (where this question is distinct from the question of why we should *think* that the principle is true). The mere fact that it allegedly lacks counterexamples is not very illuminating. The principle seems to me to be an oddly arbitrary metaphysical principle. Is there some deeper reason why the principle is true, or is it simply a brute fact? Perhaps we should be unalarmed at its being true if it is a *necessary* truth, but it simply doesn't look like it *is* a necessary truth, a point underwritten by the counterexamples to the principle discussed above, especially those involving portals or very curved space-times which are, if not physically possible, very likely metaphysically possible.

So, I do not think that the argument from lack of control is very compelling, in either its original formulation or reformulated in terms that refer to the antireflexivity principle.

6.4 The Neither One nor Many Argument

Another argument for the nonself thesis is the "neither one nor many" argument. The neither one nor many argument is prominently associated with the Buddhist philosopher Śāntarakṣita,[72] although he used the argument to attack a wider range of theses than just the thesis that the self exists. The basic form of the neither one nor many argument, as adapted in support of the nonself thesis, looks like this: If the self exists, it is either simple (without parts) or composite (with parts); the self could not be simple; the self could not be composite; so, the self does not exist. Some modern advocates of the nonself thesis basically defend an argument of this sort, even if they do not call it the "neither one nor many argument." For example, Unger's arguments against his own existence are really arguments against his being a composite object.[73] An important component of his argument, then, whether or not it is made explicit, is that he is not a simple object. Similarly, Westerhoff defends a "mereological argument against the existence of the self," which consists of two premises: (1) There are no wholes, only simples; (2) The self is a complex whole.[74] The first premise entails that the self is

---

[72] See especially his *Madhyamakālaṃkāra* (Ichigo 1985).
[73] Unger 1979a, 1979b.
[74] Westerhoff 2020: 114–120.

not a composite, and the second premise entails that the self is not a simple, and from these two premises Westerhoff derives the conclusion that the self does not exist.[75]

The neither one nor many argument might find support from the arguments presented in earlier parts of this book since I have argued that the view that we are simple faces many of the same difficulties as the view that we are composite. I have, in effect, presented a number of arguments against our being simple and a number of parallel arguments against our being composite.

Is the neither one nor many argument sound? Well, I suppose that if we exist, then we must be either simple or composite, and so if we had conclusive grounds for thinking that we could be neither simple nor composite then we would have conclusive grounds for thinking that we do not exist. But I am not convinced that we have conclusive grounds for thinking that we are neither simple nor composite. It is one thing to argue, as I have in previous chapters of this book, that the thesis that we are simple and the thesis that we are composite face many of the same difficulties. But it is another matter to show that these difficulties are insurmountable. And if we had good reasons to believe that we exist, then we would presumably have good reason to think that one or more of the objections to our being simple or composite must be surmountable. I think that the lesson that we should draw from the objections to our being simple and the objections to our being composite is not that we do not exist but rather just that we cannot tell whether we are simple or composite. And the reason I think this is because I think that we have good grounds for thinking that we exist, or at any rate that the disjunction of the arguments against our being simple or composite is less plausible than the thesis that we exist. My justification for this latter claim must wait until Chapter 7, where I discuss the positive case for the existence of the self.

6.5 The Argument from Simplicity or Parsimony

Another argument against the existence of the self is based on simplicity or parsimony considerations. The basic thought is: It is simpler to suppose that the self does not exist. Simpler theories are, other things being equal, more likely to be true. So, simplicity considerations give us some reason to think that the self does not exist.[76]

---

[75] See Goodman 2009: 101–105 for a similar argument.
[76] Simplicity-based arguments against the existence of the self are defended in Albahari 2006: Ch. 8; Siderits 2015: 43; Benovsky 2018: 65–66.

Vasubandhu argues that we should think that the self does not exist because we can neither perceive the self nor infer that it exists.[77] The idea is that if the self *did* exist, then we *would* be able to perceive it or infer that it exists from other things we know: "for of all phenomena [that exist] there is direct perception [that establishes their existence], as there is of the six objects and the mental organ unless [direct] perception of them is impeded, or there is correct inference [that establishes their existence], as there is of the five [sense] organs."[78] This line of thought might naturally be fleshed out by an appeal to simplicity as a criterion of theory choice. Absent *perceptual* or *inferential* grounds for believing that the self exists, we lack *any* grounds for thinking that the self exists. Absent any grounds for believing in the self, we should think that the self does *not* exist since this simplifies our total theory, and simpler theories are, other things being equal, more likely to be true.

I'll take this to be the canonical formulation of a simplicity-based argument against the existence of the self (whether or not Vasubandhu himself meant to put forward a simplicity-based argument). Is it a sound argument? In Chapter 2, §2.2, I discussed simplicity-based arguments against the existence of composite objects. There I noted that I think that it is plausible that simpler theories are, other things being equal, more likely to be true. So, at this point, we should ask two questions: (1) Is it really simpler to believe that the self does not exist? (2) Are "other things" equal? In other words, do we have reason to believe in the existence of the self that would override simplicity-based considerations against the existence of the self?

Start with the first question.

Is it really simpler to suppose that there is no self? Well, that depends on what the proposed alternative is. After all, if the thesis that there is a self is contrasted with some very complex thesis that entails that there are no selves, that latter thesis will be more complex than the bare thesis that there is a self. So, what is the salient alternative to there being a self, whose complexity we wish to compare to the complexity of the thesis that there is a self? There seem to me to be two main options here: (1) There is no self, but there are thoughts, experiences, etc., despite the fact that there is nothing to have those thoughts and experiences; (2) there is no self, but there are things that collectively have the thoughts and experiences which

---

[77] Vasubandhu 2003: 71–72.
[78] Vasubandhu 2003: 71. Material in brackets is inserted by the English translator of Vasubandhu's text (James Duerlinger), to indicate ideas implicit in the text. Note that the idea I attribute to Vasubandhu with this quote is present even if one ignores the material in brackets.

6.5 The Argument from Simplicity or Parsimony

we erroneously attribute to a self. I will discuss both of these possibilities further in Chapter 7. For now, the question which concerns us is whether each of these two options enjoys a boost in plausibility in light of its greater parsimony when compared to the thesis that the self exists.

Option 1: There is no self, but there are thoughts, experiences, etc. Here when I talk of "thoughts, experiences, etc." I mean that there are certain *objects* to which these terms correspond. There is no one who thinks, but there are, say, thoughts, and these are objects which are just as real as electrons, phones, and books. In other words, on the view in question we are not ontologically committed to the existence of thinkers, but we are ontologically committed to these mental particulars (e.g., thoughts, experiences). Leave aside the concern that this view is just incoherent. This option is much less simple than supposing that there is a self. It is much simpler to suppose that there is a self who thinks, experiences, and so on, but without the existence of any mental particulars, than it is to believe in various mental particulars without a self. If we believed in selves as well as thoughts and experiences – that is, if we included selves as well as thoughts and experiences in our ontology – then it might be simpler to get rid of the self while retaining thoughts and experiences in our ontology. But we should not believe in selves *in addition* to thoughts and experiences. Again, it is enough just to believe in selves who think and experience.

Option 2: There is no self, but there are things that collectively have the thoughts and experiences which we erroneously attribute to a self. This is the option which would be endorsed by many proponents of the nonself thesis. For example, as I noted above, many Indian Buddhist philosophers do not believe in the self, but they do believe in the aggregates, which at least in some phases of the Buddhist philosophical tradition (e.g., among Abhidharma philosophers) were interpreted as certain sorts of simple constituents of reality (dharmas). Jiri Benovsky, a contemporary proponent of the nonself thesis, puts the point very clearly: "an allegedly single entity, the Self, can be eliminated because there is a plurality of other entities which satisfy all our theoretical and practical needs, namely, successive impermanent psychological states/experiences arranged 'Self-Wise'."[79]

It seems to me that if there are things collectively thinking the thoughts and having the experiences I normally attribute to myself, then that probably would be simpler than the alternative view according to which *I* think those thoughts and have those experiences. This is because if I exist and think those thoughts and have those experiences, then I am likely either

---

[79] Benovsky 2018: 65–66.

a composite object or an immaterial soul conjoined somehow with a body (or with some things arranged body-wise). The proponent of the nonself thesis simply gets rid of the composite self, or the immaterial soul, while keeping the things that were erroneously thought to compose that self or to compose the body associated with that soul. This simplifies our ontology without obviously introducing new complexity to our total theory.[80]

So I grant that on one way of developing the nonself thesis, according to which my thoughts and experiences are had by some things collectively, the nonself thesis is probably simpler than the view that I exist. That's a point in favor of the nonself thesis. But there are other difficulties associated with the view that my thoughts and experiences are collectively had by many things. This is an issue I return to in Chapter 7, §7.3.

So, I think that the proponent of the nonself thesis can plausibly claim that, in at least one way of developing the nonself thesis, the nonself thesis is simpler than its denial. But this brings us to the second question I said we should ask about the argument from simplicity or parsimony: Do we have reasons to believe in the existence of the self that would override simplicity-based considerations against the existence of the self? This question takes us away from arguments against the existence of the self, which have occupied our attention in this chapter, toward positive grounds we might have for believing in the self.

---

[80] This point is supported by arguments I have given elsewhere to the effect that mereological nihilism, the view that objects never compose other objects (although there may be things arranged composite object-wise), simplifies our total theory a great deal, without thereby introducing any new complexity into our total theory. See Brenner 2015a, 2015b, 2021, MS-b.

7
Nonself, Part 2: The Self Exists

7.1 Introduction

Many people suppose that it is just obvious that they exist. I share this sentiment: it just seems *obvious* that I exist. But on reflection, it turns out to be surprisingly difficult to articulate exactly what grounds I have for thinking that I exist. Do I form this belief on the basis of introspection, some sense modality, some sort of rational intuition, or in some other manner? And how does the cognitive faculty which informs me that I exist "know" that I exist? How does it track that portion of reality? In other words, how does it know that this particular thing exists, and that this particular thing is *me*?

I don't have answers to all of these questions. I'm still confident that I exist. But I also don't think that it is reasonable to say that it is obvious that the self exists, and to leave it at that. As we have seen, many intelligent and thoughtful people have claimed that the self does not exist, and so it is not obvious to *them* that the self exists.

Recall that Vasubandhu argues that we should think that the self does not exist because we can neither perceive the self nor infer that it exists. I think that this way of breaking down the issue is helpful, so in the next two sections I address each of these questions in turn: (1) Can we perceive that the self exists? (2) Can we infer the existence of the self from other things we know?

7.2 Can We Perceive That the Self Exists?

The question posed by the section heading asks if we can perceive that the self exists. Here we might also add similar purported noninferential sources of justification for belief in the self: introspection, or direct acquaintance (assuming that such acquaintance wouldn't simply involve perception or introspection). What I have to say about alleged perceptual justification for belief in the self will also apply to these other alleged noninferential sources of justification for belief in the self.

Hume famously claims that

> For my part, when I enter most intimately into what I call *myself*, I always stumble on some particular perception or other, of heat or cold, light or shade, love or hatred, pain or pleasure. I never can catch *myself* at any time without a perception, and never can observe anything but the perception.[1]

It is controversial how exactly we should interpret Hume's views on personal identity.[2] But many philosophers seem to agree that the remark of Hume's, which I have just cited, is correct and that we never come into contact with the self by way of perception or introspection. These philosophers think that we come into contact with particular *thoughts or perceptions*, but we never come into contact with a *self* having those thoughts or perceptions. So, for example, Chisholm complains that

> The two great traditions of contemporary western philosophy – 'phenomenology' and 'logical analysis' – seem to meet, unfortunately, at the extremes. The point of contact is the thesis according to which one is never aware of a subject of experience [... when] as Hume put it, we enter most intimately into what we call ourselves. Thus Sartre seems to say that, although we may apprehend things that are *pour-soi*, things that are manifested or presented to the self, we cannot apprehend the self to which, or to whom, they are manifested – we cannot apprehend the self as it is in itself, as it is *en-soi*. And Russell has frequently said that the self or subject is not 'empirically discoverable'; Carnap expressed what I take to be the same view by saying that 'the given is subjectless'.[3]

Similarly, Dennett claims that "Since the dawn of modern science in the seventeenth century, there has been nearly unanimous agreement that the self, whatever it is, would be invisible under a microscope, and invisible to introspection, too."[4]

But is it really true that we never come into contact with the self by way of perception? And is it really true that we never come into contact with the self by way of introspection? Let's look at each of these questions in turn.

On some ways of thinking of personal ontology, it is just obviously false that we cannot come into contact with the self by way of perception. If I'm a composite physical object such as a human organism, then I perceive myself all the time (no microscope required). If I'm a brain, then no one has

---

[1] Hume 2000: 165.
[2] See Butler 2015 for an overview of some of the interpretive difficulties.
[3] Chisholm 1994: 94; quoted in Albahari 2006: 146.
[4] Dennett 1991: 412.

ever perceived me, but there are no great obstacles standing in the way of someone perceiving me – just cut open my head! Matters are more tricky if I am an immaterial soul, since we plausibly can't perceive immaterial souls. But our inability to perceive ourselves if we are immaterial souls doesn't stem from the fact that we don't exist. Rather, it just stems from the fact that we lack the ability to perceive immaterial objects.

Are we unable to come into contact with the self by way of introspection? Again, this just seems to be clearly false. It seems that I can know a lot about myself by way of introspection. For example, I know by way of introspection that I want to eat, so I know at least one property of the self by way of introspection. Swinburne makes a similar point:

> In a famous passage the enormously influential eighteenth-century Scottish philosopher David Hume wrote, 'When I enter most intimately into what I call myself, I always stumble on some perception or other [in my terminology, some conscious event], of heat or cold, light or shade, love or hatred, pain or pleasure. I never catch myself at any time without a perception'. But no one is ever aware of any substance except by being aware of some property of that substance. We never observe a house without being aware of some property of the house, such as its colour, shape, or such like. So the mere fact that Hume is never aware of himself without being aware of some property of himself, such as his having some thought or feeling some pain, doesn't mean that he is not aware of himself. And what he is aware of is not merely that some conscious event is happening in someone, but that it is happening in himself; that is, in the person who is aware of it. He is aware of himself by being aware of some property of himself.[5]

Some philosophers have recently argued that certain psychological disorders provide evidence that in typical cases (i.e., cases in which the psychological disorders are not present), the self is represented in experience. If they are right, then that would provide further support for the idea that we can come into contact with the self by way of perception, introspection, or some similar mechanism.

Matt Duncan[6] argues that the phenomenon of thought insertion provides evidence that in typical cases the self shows up in experience. Thought insertion, which is common among those suffering from schizophrenia, involves the impression that some of one's thoughts are not produced by the subject of those thoughts but are rather "inserted" from the outside (e.g., the thoughts in question may feel as if they are someone else's thoughts). What this indicates is that in typical cases, where we have

[5] Swinburne 2019: 106.
[6] Duncan 2019.

thoughts that are not cases of thought insertion, our thoughts feel as if we *are* their authors. This would imply that the self is present in the experience of our having those thoughts, insofar as the self is presented as the author of those thoughts.

Alexandre Billon[7] gives an argument similar to that given by Duncan, although Billon focuses on those suffering from certain sorts of depersonalization disorders and Cotard's syndrome, who claim (among other things) that they do not exist. It is difficult for those suffering from the disorders in question to articulate their experiences, and it is difficult for those of us who do not suffer from the disorders in question to grasp the phenomenology associated with those experiences. Nevertheless, based on a detailed examination of self-reports made by those suffering from the disorders in question, Billon concludes that the best explanation for why they feel as if they do not exist is because they suffer from an experiential deficit, insofar as their experiences fail to represent or include the existence of the self having those experiences. Billon argues that this interpretation of the disorders in question lends support to the idea that in typical cases our existence *is* represented in some manner in our experiences.[8] Perhaps we could construct a similar argument with reference to cases in which, under the influence of drugs such as LSD and psilocybin, people report having experiences as of their own nonexistence.[9]

So, on the most straightforward readings of such claims as "we never come into contact with the self by way of perception" and "we never come into contact with the self by way of introspection," both of these claims are very dubious. But there are subtler ways of understanding these claims which are less dubious. I'll go through a few of these.

First, perhaps the idea is not that we cannot detect the self by way of perception or introspection, but rather that perceptual or introspective evidence cannot tell us whether the self *exists*. Compare: If composite objects exist, then we can know a lot about them by way of empirical observation. But empirical observation will not tell us *whether* composite objects exist, since our perceptual experiences would arguably be the same whether or not composite objects exist, as long as there are simples arranged

---

[7] Billon 2015, 2023.
[8] That being said, we should interpret the self-reports of those suffering from Cotard's syndrome with a grain of salt. As Zahavi (2005: 144–145) notes, the behavior and expressed beliefs of those suffering from Cotard's syndrome will often conflict with their professed belief in their own nonexistence – they frequently claim, e.g., that they are immortal, which conflicts with their self-professed belief that they are dead or nonexistent.
[9] For discussion of these cases, see Millière and Newen in press, especially §4.

7.2 Can We Perceive That the Self Exists?

in the appropriate manner.[10] So, for example, if I have some simples arranged couch-wise which compose a couch, my perceptual experiences can tell me what color the couch is, how large it is, etc. But arguably my perceptual experiences cannot tell me that the simples arranged couch-wise compose a couch, since my perceptual experiences cannot distinguish between a situation in which there is a couch and a situation in which there are merely simples arranged couch-wise. Perhaps we should say something similar about the self: If the self exists, then perception and introspection might tell us a lot about the self (that it is hungry, or whatever), but we cannot tell on the basis of perception or introspection whether there is a self in the first place.

I'm not sure what to make of this idea. After all, I seem to be able to tell by way of introspection not just that there is a desire to eat, but that *I* desire to eat, which would seem to entail that I exist. But proponents of the nonself thesis will generally claim that this line of thought is erroneous. They may claim, for example, that some simples arranged self-wise can collectively desire to eat, collectively instantiate the phenomenal states associated with having that desire, and collectively instantiate the thought "I want to eat." How could we tell whether the thought "I want to eat" occurs because some single subject wants to eat, rather than because some simples arranged self-wise collectively want to eat? Below I will return to this idea that our thoughts and experiences are had collectively by many things. I will argue that if our mental states are collectively instantiated in the manner suggested here then this would undermine, rather than vindicate, the nonself thesis.

Yet another less obviously false way of rendering the thesis that we cannot come into contact with the self by way of perception or introspection goes like this: We do not come into contact with the self qua-subject when we come into contact with it qua-object. In other words, to come into direct contact with the self by perception or introspection is to view it as an object (a thing being seen, or encountered in introspection), rather than a subject (the one *doing* the seeing/encountering), and so to view it as something other than the self. There is a sense, then, in which we cannot come into direct contact with the self by way of perception or introspection, since to come into contact with it in this manner is to falsify its status as the self. To encounter the self in perception or introspection is to see it as something *other* than the self. This is a not uncommon claim among proponents of the nonself thesis. For example, Albahari seems to have something like this idea in mind when she writes that the self is "elusive" in the sense that

---

[10] Cf. Rosen and Dorr 2002: 158; Merricks 2003: 9; Sider 2013: 258–263; Brenner forthcoming-a.

"one is never aware of a subject of experience, or more accurately, to the fact that the subject cannot observe itself as an observing subject that is simultaneously its own object of experience. The subject is systematically elusive to its own attentive purview."[11]

But this line of thought seems to me to be mistaken. First, simply because one has perceptual or introspective awareness of the self, and so views the self as an *object* of awareness, it doesn't follow that one does not also view it as the *subject* of that very act of awareness. Compare: A sentence may refer to itself, in which case the sentence is both the thing being referred to, as well as the thing doing the referring.[12] A mirror sitting in front of another mirror can reflect an image of itself, and so serve both as the thing reflecting the image and the thing whose image is being reflected. What's more, even if it were true that one could not simultaneously view the self in perception or introspection as both subject and object, it would not follow that one could not come into contact with the self by way of perception or introspection. Why could one not come into direct contact with oneself by way of perception or introspection simply because in doing so one would view oneself as an object and not a subject? Why would one's not viewing oneself as a subject entail that one *isn't* a subject (i.e., a subject perceiving or introspecting oneself)? More generally, why would the fact that we can't perceive ourselves as subjects support the view that there are no subjects?

Perhaps the antireflexivity principle prevents one from coming into direct contact with oneself by way of perception or introspection.[13] But we have already seen (in Chapter 6, §6.3) grounds for doubting the antireflexivity principle.

I conclude that it isn't clear whether we have perceptual or introspective grounds for believing in the existence of the self. It is very plausible that if the self exists, then we can come into contact with the self by way of perception or introspection. But it doesn't obviously follow that perception or introspection would allow us to learn that the self exists. Perhaps the strongest perceptual or introspective grounds for believing in the self would be the apparent fact that in introspection I am aware, not just that something or other has certain properties (e.g., the property of wanting to eat), but that *I* have that property. But the proponent of the nonself thesis can respond that some things arranged self-wise can collectively have these same introspective grounds for believing in the self.

---

[11] Albahari 2006: 146. Cf. Klein 2014: 46–47.
[12] Thanks to Peter Finocchiaro for this analogy.
[13] See, e.g., Albahari 2006: 146; Siderits 2015: 31–32.

I turn now to a discussion of whether we have inferential grounds for believing in the existence of the self. As we will see, I eventually conclude that even if some things collectively have my thoughts or experiences, this would vindicate, rather than undermine, belief in the existence of the self.

7.3 Can We Infer That the Self Exists?

Start with Descartes's *cogito*: I know that I exist because I'm pondering the question of whether I exist, and in order to ponder anything I must exist. It is sometimes claimed that this argument is defective for the following reason: Perhaps we are justified in believing that there is thinking (or "pondering" specifically), but we cannot assume, without begging the question, that *I* am thinking. In order to avoid begging the question, we must suppose at the start of our argument, not that I think, but that there is thinking.[14] If there can be thoughts without a thinker, then it might very well be true that this thinking occurs even though I do not exist. (In what follows I frequently use terms like "thoughts" and "thinking." I take these terms to include both propositional attitudes or cognitive processes (e.g., the thought "I wonder if I exist"), as well as phenomenal states (e.g., the experience of seeing the color blue).)

It is true that we should not assume at the outset that I think, or I ponder my own existence. But I will now argue that if thinking occurs, and in particular, if the pondering of my own existence occurs, then I exist. The basic thought is this: Something thinks my thoughts. (In order to avoid assuming at the outset that I exist, we should specify that the phrase "my thoughts" does not simply mean "thoughts had by me," but rather means something like "the thoughts which are such that, absent a commitment to the nonself thesis, we are normally inclined to think are thought by me.") But if something thinks my thought, then I am that thing. And if I think my thoughts, then I exist. As we will see, my defense of this sort of argument is rather elaborate, and while the basic motivation behind the argument is present in the *cogito*, the overall course of the argument is not nearly so straightforward as the *cogito* is normally presented. What's more, the *cogito* is normally thought to justify *certainty* regarding the existence of the self. But my argument does not provide this sort of certainty. But it may be the best we can do.

---

[14] Cf. Lichtenberg 1971: 412.

So, return to the idea that if something thinks my thoughts, then I am that thing. Why think *that's* true? Well, it seems pretty obvious to me.[15] If it requires an argument, here is one: "I" is self-reflexive; it refers to whatever utters/employs it.[16] So, consider my thought expressed by the words "I wonder if I exist." The referent of "I" in that thought (or in the sentence which expresses that thought) is the thinker of that thought, since "I" refers to whatever employs it. It follow that if "I wonder if I exist" is thought by anything, then *I* am the one who thinks it. So, that's at least one thought which is thought by me. That doesn't actually establish the conclusion that *all* of my thoughts are thought by me. But one thought is enough to establish that I think, and so that I exist.

There are a few different ways to reject this argument. A less common way to reject the argument is to deny that anything thinks my thoughts. For example, we might be eliminative materialists, who think (!) that there is some sense in which nothing thinks, or at any rate that nothing has *phenomenal* states, where something has phenomenal states if there is something it is like to be that thing. Another way to deny that anything thinks would be to contend that nothing at all exists.[17] Neither eliminative materialism nor ontological nihilism is very plausible (they are certainly less plausible than the nonself thesis), and so I won't discuss them further here.

Here is another way of developing the idea that nothing thinks my thoughts: There can be thoughts without anything to do the thinking. Is it plausible to suppose that there are entities of this sort, thoughts, without anything doing the thinking? I think that many readers would sympathize with Shoemaker when he says that it is "an obvious conceptual truth that an experiencing is necessarily an experiencing by a subject of experience, and involves that subject as intimately as a branch-bending involves a branch."[18] I am sympathetic to the idea that there are not any such things as thoughts, thinkings, or experiences – we should rather say that there are merely beings who think and have experiences. As Noonan puts it: "for an experience to occur just is for a person to be in a certain state, just as for a dent to exist is just for a surface to be dented. In short, experiences are 'adjectives of their subjects and not independent entities in their own right'."[19] Similarly, Salje

---

[15] It has seemed pretty obvious to other philosophers working on personal identity as well. For example, it is the linchpin of the "thinking animals" argument for animalism: There is an animal thinking my thoughts, and I am identical to whatever thinks my thoughts, so I am an animal (Olson 1997, 2007: 29–30).

[16] Cf. Kaplan 1989.

[17] Perhaps this is what Mādhyamika Buddhists did, although that's controversial (Westerhoff 2016).

[18] Shoemaker 1996: 10. See also Strawson 2009: 268–277.

[19] Noonan 2003: 97.

7.3 Can We Infer That the Self Exists?

writes that "… there really isn't any daylight between the occurrence of an episode of thinking and the presence of a thinker in whom the thinking occurs; to be aware of a given conscious state *just is* to be aware of a way that the subject is with respect to its conscious properties."[20] That all sounds very plausible to me. But I am also sympathetic to the idea that even if there *are* such things as thoughts and experiences, they are ontologically dependent on things having the thoughts and experiences – that is, a thought is ontologically dependent on a thinker, and an experience is ontologically dependent on an experiencer.[21] But perhaps I can't take any of this for granted, since some intelligent, reflective, and sincere philosophers have thought that there can be experiences without subjects of experience. So here are some arguments.

First, positive grounds sometimes cited in favor of the idea that there can be thoughts without thinkers do not hold up under scrutiny. For example, there are cases where individuals have experiences, and yet seem to lack a sense of ownership over those experiences, in the sense that they do not seem to themselves to be the ones having the experiences in question.[22] It is sometimes claimed that this sort of phenomenon supports the idea that there can be thoughts without thinkers, or experiences without experiencers. For example, Metzinger[23] says that cases of Cotard's syndrome show that conscious experience does not require a self. But this inference seems to me to be confused: Just because someone claims they do not exist, it does not follow that they actually don't exist, and just because someone's experiences do not represent or include the existence of the subject having those experiences, it doesn't follow that the experiences in question are not had by a subject of experience. Similarly, Albahari[24] notes that in cases of epileptic automatism, there is awareness without a sense of a self engaging in that act of awareness. Albahari claims that this provides some support for the idea that there can be acts of awareness which are not had by selves. But again, this inference seems to me to be dubious: Just because it is possible for us to have awareness without a *sense* of self, it does not follow that there can be acts of awareness without a self.

Second, as Swinburne[25] notes, if there are such things as "thinkings," then they are properties – for example, the property of having such-and-such

---

[20] Salje 2020: 6.
[21] Cf. Foster 1991: 212.
[22] In addition to the examples mentioned in the main body of the text, see the cases described in Zahn et al. 2008; Klein and Nichols 2012; Klein 2014: Ch. 5.
[23] Metzinger 2009: 63–64.
[24] Albahari 2006: 172.
[25] Swinburne 2019: 73.

thought. To suppose that there are thoughts is to suppose that the properties in question are instantiated. But the properties cannot be instantiated unless there exist things to instantiate those properties. So, there cannot be thinkings unless there are thinkers having the thoughts corresponding to the "thinkings."[26] This argument will not appeal to trope theorists. Given trope theory, there can be properties (such as the property of having such-and-such a thought or experience) without there being anything which has those properties, since according to trope theory we should think of properties as particular property instances (e.g., the property instance of this particular instance of blueness).[27] My response would be to reject trope theory, something I obviously can't hope to defend in detail here. But one point worth noting here is that the adverbial account of the property of having a thought, according to which "a thought exists" should be interpreted as "there is a thinking subject," is much simpler than trope theory, primarily because it eschews ontological commitment to innumerable property instances. So, if the proponent of the nonself thesis must commit themselves to trope theory, that would undermine the argument for the nonself thesis from simplicity or parsimony. And the argument from simplicity or parsimony is, I think, perhaps the most promising argument for the nonself thesis.[28]

Third, even leaving aside concerns about trope theory specifically, it is ontologically extravagant to posit these *sui generis* thoughts or experiences, thoughts or experiences which are not thoughts or experiences *of* anyone or anything, nor are such that they can be paraphrased away in terms of there being beings who think or experience.[29] But the best argument for the nonself thesis is on the basis of parsimony. So the view that there are thoughts without thinkers is unparsimonious, which undercuts one of the main motivations for the nonself thesis.

Fourth, what we know about the brain (or, more carefully, what we know about things arranged brain-wise) supports the idea that the brain is in mental states, and so mental states are states *of* the brain (or, more carefully, some part(s) of the brain, or some things arranged brain-wise).

---

[26] The same point is made by some Naiyayikas in their attacks on the Buddhist nonself thesis (Chakrabarti 1982: 214–216).

[27] Notably, Abhidharma Buddhist philosophers were trope theorists (see Siderits 2007: §§6.2–6.3).

[28] Perhaps the nonself theorist can claim that they only accept trope theory with respect to selves, but do not endorse a more general trope theory. This would make their commitment to tropes less ontologically extravagant. But Chakrabarti (1992: 109) notes that it is implausibly arbitrary to suppose that external physical objects are correctly described in terms of objects or substances instantiating properties, if we are not similarly willing to say the same thing about the self.

[29] Cf. Gert 2021.

7.3 Can We Infer That the Self Exists?

Why overturn the default and seemingly plausible conclusion to be drawn from what we know of the brain and its connection to mental states, namely that the brain (or part(s) of the brain, or things arranged brain-wise) is in mental states? The positive arguments for the nonself thesis? But we have seen that those arguments are rather weak. Perhaps we should overturn the idea that the brain (or part(s) of the brain, etc.) is in mental states on the basis of arguments for substance dualism, so that brain states *cause* or otherwise bring about mental states in a soul, but those mental states are not had by the brain. But arguments for the conclusion that mental states are not had by the brain (or some part(s) of the brain, etc.) because they are had by *something else*, a soul, will not support the idea that mental states can occur even if they are not had by anything. Ditto for arguments to the effect that some physical object other than my brain (or some part(s) of my brain, etc.) thinks my thoughts.

Fifth, and much more tentatively, perhaps if there are mental states which are not mental states *of* something, then we should say that there is some sense in which I *am* just one of these free-floating mental states, or I am wholly composed of these free-floating mental states. This view seems to have been endorsed by William James.[30] Perhaps it is the view which is meant to be endorsed by some of those who endorse a "bundle" view of the self, according to which the self is a "bundle" of mental states. I don't endorse this view. But if this view is coherent, then even if there are mental states not had by some ontologically distinct subject, the nonself thesis may still be false, if the mental states themselves are, or wholly compose, thinkers or selves.

Let's recap the argument I've presented up to this point in this section. If something thinks my thoughts, then I am that thing. But something *does* think my thoughts. So, I am that thing. But then I'm *something*, and so I exist. I have discussed some objections to this argument which don't seem to me to be very promising. These objections turn on the idea that nothing thinks my thoughts, either because the thoughts in question don't occur (eliminative materialism, ontological nihilism) or because those thoughts do occur but they are not had by any thinker. I now discuss a more promising objection.

The proponent of the nonself thesis might say that there is no self, not because nothing at all thinks my thoughts, but rather because no *individual thing* thinks my thoughts. Rather, many things *collectively* think my thoughts. This is what many proponents of the nonself thesis, both ancient

---

[30] James 1890: 400–401.

and modern, have tended to say. For example, Abhidharma Buddhist philosophers said that while there is no self, there are *dharmas*, simple constituents of reality, and that our psychological states should be analysed in terms of those dharmas. So, for example, the influential Abhidharma Buddhist philosopher Vasubandhu says that where we normally think there is a subject of experience there are really just many simple objects:

> There is no sentient being here, nor is there a self, but simple entities …. There are twelve categories of being, the spheres, and there are aggregates, and components; having thought about all these, one still doesn't perceive any person. Everything that belongs to you is empty. Perceive it as empty; perceive it as external. He who meditates on emptiness does not exist.[31]

Here Vasubandhu does not deny that experiences occur, and in fact seems to assume that they occur when he refers to thought, perception, and meditation. Since he contends that where we normally think there is a subject of experience there are really just many simple objects, he seems to be implying that it is the simple objects which experience (which, e.g., think, perceive, and meditate).

More recently, mereological nihilists (who contend that composite objects do not exist) often contend that the self does not exist, and that our thoughts are collectively thought by many simples (perhaps, say, those simples which are arranged brain-wise).[32]

Collective property instantiation is the sort of phenomenon we talk about when we say that some dogs collectively surround a cat, even if none of the dogs *individually* surrounds the cat.[33] Note that what is not being suggested is that there are multiple individuals, each of which thinks the thoughts in question. We might have that sort of situation if, say, I am a composite object, but I am colocated with another composite object which thinks all of the thoughts which I think. Or we might have this sort of situation if I am an immaterial soul, and my thoughts supervene on the physical processes going on in my brain, but my brain is paired with two

---

[31] Quoted in Goodman 2009: 165.
[32] Rosen and Dorr 2002: 159–160; Sider 2013: 268–269; Benovsky 2018: 65–66. Garfield (2022: Ch. 2) also claims that our thoughts and experiences are had collectively by many things together, rather than by some single self, but he does not make this point in terms of "simples." Kant similarly suggests that many parts may work together to collectively think my thoughts, although he makes this point in response to the suggestion that my thoughts must be thought by a *simple*, rather than a composite, subject. He writes, "the unity of a thought consisting of many representations is collective, and, as far as mere concepts are concerned, it can be related to the collective unity of the substances cooperating in it (as the movement of a body is the composite movement of all its parts) just as easily as to the absolute unity of the subject" (*Critique of Pure Reason* A353; Kant 1998: 418).
[33] Cf. Yi 2002.

souls, and the other soul's thoughts also supervene on the same physical processes in the brain on which my thoughts supervene. In both of these cases there is a sense in which I think the same thoughts as someone else. But these are not cases of *collective* instantiation of those thoughts, since me and the other individual thinking my thoughts do not *work together* to think those thoughts, in the manner in which the dogs which surround the cat *work together* to surround the cat, since none of them individually can surround the cat.

There are two questions we should ask at this point: (1) Is it plausible that my thoughts could be collectively thought by many objects working together, rather than individually thought by one or more objects? (2) If my thoughts *are* collectively thought by many objects working together, would that support, or would it undermine, the nonself thesis?

Start with the first question. Here, you might be reminded of the combination problem for panpsychism, and you might think that a solution to the combination problem would also help make sense of the idea that some things could collectively think something which none of them individually thinks. According to panpsychism, our microscopic constituents have phenomenal or "proto-phenomena" states. The combination problem is the problem of accounting for how a bunch of little minds (the minds in our microphysical constituents) can add up to a single big mind (each of us).[34] But when we wonder whether some objects might collectively think something which none of them individually thinks, there *is* no big mind, in the sense of a single mind associated with the objects working together to produce a thought. Rather, the objects work together to collectively have a thought despite the fact that there is no single mind having that thought, and despite the fact that none of the objects individually has that thought. So, a solution to the combination problem for panpsychism would not obviously help us make sense of the idea that some objects might collectively think something which none of them individually thinks.

Several philosophers have challenged the idea that my thoughts could be collectively thought by many things working together.[35] For example, van Inwagen writes that

> I do not see how we can regard thinking as a mere cooperative activity … things cannot work together to think – or, at least, things can work together to think only in the sense that they can compose, in the strict and mereological understanding of the word, an object that thinks …. Now,

---

[34] Goff 2017: Ch. 7; Roelofs 2019.
[35] Van Inwagen 1990: §12; Madden 2015: 59; Bailey 2016; Dowland 2016; maybe Goff 2017: 265.

surely, planning for tomorrow or feeling pain cannot be activities that a lot of simples can perform collectively, as simples can collectively shine or collectively support a weight?[36]

Unfortunately, van Inwagen doesn't provide any arguments for this idea. Olson[37] also examines the question of whether thoughts can be collectively thought, without being thought by any individuals, and he seems like he might be sympathetic to the idea that they can't be, but after examining some arguments he thinks up for this thesis he concludes that they are unconvincing. I too lack any knockdown arguments for the idea that thoughts cannot be collectively thought by many things working together, and yet that idea seems plausible to me. It seems particularly plausible with respect to phenomenal states. Consider the qualitative experience associated with seeing the color blue. It just seems implausible that some objects could somehow collectively have that experience, even though none of the objects individually has the experience, and the objects do not compose something which has the experience. An experience is from an individual perspective. Even when multiple subjects are having qualitatively identical experiences, we should say that there are two individual perspectives which are qualitatively identical, not that there is one perspective which is somehow shared by the two individuals. That an experience is from an individual perspective is implicit in a common way of characterizing phenomenal episodes, that there is *something it is like* to experience that phenomenal episode[38] – that is, something it is like *for some subject*. But in the scenario in which there is collective experience, but no individual experience, no individual has the experience, and so it is hard to see how the experience could be from an individual perspective.

In any case, however, I think that even if thoughts *can* be collectively thought in the manner advocated by many proponents of the nonself thesis, this would not help salvage the nonself thesis – it would, rather, undermine the nonself thesis. This brings us to the second question I said I would address: If my thoughts *are* collectively thought by many objects working together, would that support, or would it undermine, the nonself thesis? I'm inclined to say that if some things collectively think my thought, then this would undermine the nonself thesis, for two reasons.

First, the fact that some objects arranged me-wise are collectively thinking my thoughts would not prevent their use of first-person pronouns (as

---

[36] Van Inwagen 1990: 118.
[37] Olson 2007: 188–193.
[38] Nagel 1974.

7.3 Can We Infer That the Self Exists?   157

in the thought "I exist") from referring to some or all of them. If all of these things collectively think my thought, but there is no single entity (e.g., a composite person) who thinks these thoughts, then my use of pronouns such as "I" may just refer to *multiple* things, rather than just one thing. But that's compatible with my "I" thoughts having referents. In fact, it would seem to support the idea that "I" has not just one referent, but *many* referents. And since my first-person pronouns refer to these objects, I am plausibly among these objects.

Second, it seems plausible that each of the things collectively thinking my thoughts is a self. If they collectively think my thoughts, then there is a sense in which they are each thinkers. But they are each thinkers not in the sense that they each individually think. Rather, they are each thinkers in a weaker sense. Compare: Suppose that some soldiers collectively conquer a country. None of the soldiers individually conquers the country, since none of them is capable of doing that individually. But they work together to conquer the country. There is a clear sense in which each of the soldiers is a conqueror. After all, the country was conquered by soldiers, and these are the soldiers who did that. But while each of the soldiers is in some sense a conqueror, this does not mean that each of the soldiers is *individually* a conqueror. Analogously, if some objects collectively instantiate phenomenal states, then they are subjects of experience, at least in the weak sense in which the soldiers are all conquerors. After all, the phenomenal states are instantiated, and they are instantiated by *these* objects. There is something it is like to be *these* objects, at least in the sense that there is something it is like collectively to be these objects. *They* are the subjects of experience, albeit in a strange sense, since none of them is individually the subject of any experience. And since *these* are the objects which think *my* thoughts and have *my* experiences, I am plausibly among these objects. Having admitted subjects of experience of a sort into our ontology, and having admitted that those subjects of experience have the experiences which I seem to have, why deny that any of those subjects of experience are *me*?

It may be objected that the self must be a single thing, rather than many things.[39] But the view I have in mind is one in which the self *is* a single thing, rather than many things, and there are just a lot of selves collectively thinking my thoughts.

I should clarify that I am not suggesting that one thing, me, is identical with many things (namely, those things which collectively think my thoughts). On the view I am suggesting, it is not the case that one self is

---

[39] Cf. Strawson 2017: Ch. 2.3.

identical with many selves. (Recall the discussion of composition as identity in Chapter 1, §1.3, where we saw that there are good reasons to think that one thing could not be identical with many things.) Rather, there are just the many selves, namely those selves which collectively think thoughts.

I should also clarify that the view I am discussing is not the view which may have once been held by Chisholm,[40] according to which we are each a physical simple. The view I'm discussing does not have some privileged physical simple which, among all of the simples making up my body, is the real self. Rather, according to the view I have in mind, all of the physical objects arranged me-wise are selves. This view does not require a mysterious physical monad currently unknown to science. Rather, it just requires that we believe in physical objects we already believe in (particles, strings, fields, whatever) and acknowledge that these objects would be selves if they collectively instantiate my mental states. Note that the main problem with a view like Chisholm's is that it is unmotivated – why should we believe in this mysterious physical simple? But the view I'm discussing is not unmotivated, but rather is motivated by the idea that there are things which collectively instantiate my mental states.

So, I suggest, if there are many things collectively thinking my thoughts, then those things are all selves, and one of those things is me. But remember, I am inclined to *reject* the idea that my thoughts could be collectively thought by many things working together. So, I endorse a conditional claim: *If* we can make sense of the idea that some objects can collectively think even if none of them individually thinks, then it seems plausible that the objects in question are all thinkers in some sense, they collectively refer to themselves via first-personal thoughts and pronouns, and so they are all selves.

To recap, my overall argument is this: It is plausible that something thinks my thoughts, or some things think my thoughts. If some single thing thinks my thoughts, then I am that thing, and I exist. If some things collectively think my thoughts, then I am among those things. Regardless, I exist, and since none of my arguments are applicable to me but not to you, you exist as well. Congratulations!

---

[40] Chisholm 1978.

8

Personal Ontology and Life after Death, Part 1: Resurrection, Reincarnation

8.1 Introduction

One reason people care about personal ontology, and the philosophy of personal identity more generally, is because they are interested in life after death. It is natural to wonder how my arguments regarding personal ontology, which I have developed over the course of this book, might affect what we think about the possibility of life after death. This is one topic which is of general concern, inside and outside philosophy, where our beliefs regarding personal ontology might make a crucial difference.

There is much to be said against certain afterlife scenarios. For example, the thesis that we exist and have fairly complex mental lives without our bodies after death, without the aid of divine intervention, may be ruled out by what we know about the dependence of the mind on the brain.[1] Admittedly, this objection to our having mental lives without our bodies is not *completely* decisive. William James[2] notes that the observed correlations between brain states and mental states does not entail that those mental states are *produced* by the correlated brain states. James suggests that this correlation may be the result of the brain transmitting and filtering the mental states of an immaterial person, rather than producing those mental states, just as the keys of a pipe organ simply filter and control the air passing through the organ, and it is the air (rather than the keys) which produces the sound coming out of the organ. If that's right, then the observed correlations between brain states and mental states does not preclude the possibility that those mental states can occur without the brain. It might be objected that, if James's proposal were correct, then brain damage or general anesthesia would not cause us to cease having conscious experiences, as it evidently does.[3] But I think this objection can be overcome. It may well be that we continue to have conscious experiences when, say, general

---

[1] This point is emphasized *ad nauseam* in Martin and Augustine 2015: Part I.
[2] James 1898.
[3] Thanks to Eric Olson for suggesting this objection.

anesthesia puts us into a state in which we are asleep, and in which we do not later remember having any conscious experiences. We would have no way of knowing whether we have these experiences as long as the anesthesia prevents our brains from forming memories of the experiences in question. I have a different objection to James's proposal: While the observed correlations between brain states and mental states does not strictly *entail* that our mental states are produced by our brain states, it does provide significant evidence that they are. And it strikes me as significantly simpler to think that mental states are produced by our brain states rather than produced in some other way and then merely filtered by the brain.

In this chapter, I will focus on two other prominent conceptions of the afterlife: the general resurrection of the dead and reincarnation. These two conceptions of the afterlife have the distinction of being widely endorsed, and they both largely avoid the concern noted above that after death we should not have any conscious experiences without a body, since on both of these conceptions of the afterlife we *do* have bodies after death, at least eventually. In Chapter 9, I will go on to discuss another prominent approach to life after death, "mind uploading."

8.2 Resurrection

The Bible and Qur'an both teach that there will be a general resurrection of the dead – that is, some point in the future where many people (perhaps everyone) will be resurrected.[4] This sort of afterlife is a corporeal one, in which we will have physical bodies,[5] perhaps bodies that are numerically identical with the bodies we had prior to death.

It is sometimes thought that the plausibility of the resurrection turns on the plausibility of certain views regarding personal ontology. For example, Olson writes that

> The Biological Approach [to personal identity] ... bears on some religious doctrines. On that view, you are an animal, and an animal ceases to exist when it dies – when its vital functions cease and its tissues decay beyond the point where they can be reanimated. So existence after death seems to be ruled out. Once biological death has occurred, not even God can call you back into being, at least if I am right about what it takes for an animal to persist through time ....[6]

---

[4] See, e.g., Daniel 12: 1–3; Luke 20: 27–40; 1 Corinthians 15; Qur'an 2: 259–260, 64: 7.
[5] Paul's reference in 1 Corinthians 15: 44 to the resurrected body being "*soma pneumatikon*" (what the NRSV translates as "spiritual body"), in contrast to "*soma psychikon*" (NRSV: "physical body"), has led some to infer that Paul did not regard the resurrection as being a physical resurrection. But this interpretation of Paul seems dubious. For discussion, see Wright 2003: 347–356.
[6] Olson 1997: 71.

8.2 Resurrection

I've argued that it is surprisingly difficult to decide between substance dualism and the view that we are composite physical objects. If that's right, then it is going to be difficult to decide whether we are animals in the sense Olson has in mind here since animals would presumably be composite physical objects. So, if Olson is correct that we could not be resurrected (even by God) if we are animals, then the arguments developed over the course of this book might lead you to be agnostic about whether such a resurrection is possible.[7]

In fact, however, I do not think that this is the conclusion we should draw. It seems to me that a general resurrection is possible regardless of which of the accounts of personal ontology discussed in this book we adopt, with one obvious exception: If the nonself thesis is correct, then we will not be resurrected, since we do not exist even now.

It is easy enough to see how we might be resurrected if we are immaterial souls: God simply inserts our souls (=us) into new bodies. If the resurrection involves the resurrection of numerically the same bodies we had prior to death, as many believers in the resurrection maintain,[8] then matters become more complicated. It might be thought that God cannot bring back numerically the same bodies we had prior to death. So, for many philosophers, the sticking point for whether or not resurrection is possible will lie in the question of whether it would be possible for God to resurrect numerically the same bodies we had prior to death, either because we are those bodies or because we are souls paired with those bodies.[9]

Philosophers have identified a number of materialist-friendly ways in which God could pull this off.[10] I would be surprised if none of the proposals works.

---

[7] See also Johnston 2010: Ch. 1, which argues that the Christian doctrine of resurrection requires substance dualism.
[8] See, e.g., Aquinas, *Summa theologica*, IIIa Suppl., q. 79, a. 1, as well as citations in Ratzinger 1988: 135–136.
[9] Of course, we might be some composite physical objects other than our bodies (e.g., our brains). But the difficulties involved in resurrecting numerically the same body are the same difficulties involved in resurrecting some other composite physical objects. So, for simplicity of exposition, let's assume that if we are composite physical objects then we are bodies.
[10] Whether the resurrection is metaphysically possible has been addressed throughout the history of Western religious thought, and some defenses of the resurrection are compatible with materialist views of personal ontology. For a history of debates regarding the resurrection of the body in patristic and medieval Christian thought, see Bynum 1995. In recent analytic philosophy, attempts to reconcile a materialist view of persons with the resurrection include: Mavrodes 1977; van Inwagen 1978; Baker 1995, 2001, 2007, 2011a; Corcoran 1998, 2001, 2006: Ch. 5, 2016; Merricks 1999b, 2001, 2009; Zimmerman 1999, 2013, 2016; Hudson 2001: Ch. 7, 2016; Murphy 2006: Ch. 4, §5; Jacobs and O'Connor 2010; Davis 2016; Yang and Davis 2017; Mooney 2018; Turner 2019; Bailey 2021: Ch. 5; Brenner 2022.

Here is an example. Baker[11] thinks that we are not our bodies, although we *are* physical objects *constituted* by our bodies. This is the same sort of relation which, Baker claims, holds between a statue and the hunk of marble from which the statue is made: The statue is *constituted by* the hunk of marble but is not identical with it. Strictly speaking, Baker does not give an account of how the body is resurrected since she does not think that persons (who are resurrected) are identical with their bodies. Nevertheless, she gives a straightforward account of how we are resurrected, despite the fact that we are physical objects: God can stipulate which bodies constitute which people, and so at the resurrection God can simply stipulate that some body constitutes someone who has died.[12]

There is a similar proposal, which does not require a constitution account of personal ontology. In many discussions of the resurrection, it is assumed that when God tries to resurrect someone God simply ensures that certain physical and/or psychological facts obtain – for example, God makes sure that some matter is configured as my body is configured at my death – and then God hopes for the best, so to speak, since there is nothing further that God could do to resurrect some specific person. So, for example, in a discussion of resurrection, van Inwagen asks rhetorically: "what can even omnipotence do but *reassemble* [one's parts]? What else is there *to* do?"[13] On the account I would now like to propose, there *is* something further God can do: In addition to assembling or reassembling some parts, God can *pair* some particular composite person with those parts. In other words, God can simply stipulate that some parts compose some specific individual who died at some point in the past, rather than some other individual.[14] Note that this account also provides a straightforward solution to the mereological pairing problem, which I explored in Chapter 3: Even prior to the resurrection, God can pair composite persons with their parts.

This proposal seems to me to be very promising. After all, it is widely accepted that if we are immaterial souls, then God could, by divine *fiat*, simply pair us with new bodies at the general resurrection. If God can pair souls and bodies in this way, why would God be unable to pair bodies and their parts? Does the problem stem from the idea that wholes depend on their parts for their existence? But on some views, souls depend on their bodies for their existence. If this sort of view is correct, it's hard to see why souls depending on their bodies for their existence would prevent God from

---

[11] Baker 2001, 2011a.
[12] Cf. Corcoran 2016: 202–203.
[13] Van Inwagen 1995: 486.
[14] Yang and Davis (2017) and Bailey (2021: Ch. 5) defend this sort of account of the resurrection, and I defend it myself at length in Brenner 2022.

being able to pair souls and bodies at will. And, similarly, it's hard to see why the fact that wholes depend on their parts should make it the case that God cannot pair bodies and parts at will. So where is the crucial difference between souls and bodies that would make the former easier to resurrect than the latter?

Perhaps the problem is that our bodies go out of existence for a while after death, while souls (let's assume) do not, and God cannot bring back something that went out of existence. But why could God not recreate the body after it has gone out of existence? God made us at one time, so what is preventing God from making us again? God is omnipotent, after all. I like the way that the Qur'an expresses more or less this same point:

> Can man not see that We created him from a drop of fluid? Yet – lo and behold! – he disputes openly, producing arguments against Us, forgetting his own creation. He says, 'Who can give life back to bones after they have decayed?' Say, 'He who created them in the first place will give them life again: He has full knowledge of every act of creation. It is He who produces fire for you out of the green tree – lo and behold! – and from this you kindle fire. Is He who created the heavens and earth not able to create the likes of these people? Of course He is! He is the All Knowing Creator: when He wills something to be, His way is to say, "Be" – and it is!'[15]

There is an influential thought experiment which is supposed to support the idea that in the resurrection we cannot come back into existence after an interval during which we did not exist. Van Inwagen[16] asks us to imagine a scenario in which some monks claim to have in their possession a manuscript produced by Augustine, despite the fact that the manuscript was incinerated in the year 457. The monks claim that the manuscript was miraculously recreated by God in the year 458. Van Inwagen thinks that not even an omnipotent God could pull this off – at most God would be able to create a *perfect duplicate* of the manuscript, but not the manuscript itself.

Well, why couldn't God recreate the original manuscript? Van Inwagen tells us that

> The manuscript God creates in the story is not the manuscript that was destroyed, since the various atoms that compose the tracings of ink on its surface occupy their present positions not as a result of Augustine's activity but of God's. Thus what we have is not a manuscript in Augustine's hand. (Strictly speaking, it is not even a *manuscript*.)[17]

---

[15] Qur'an 36: 77–82; Abdel Haleem 2005: 284. Cf. Al-Ghazālī's *The Incoherence of the Philosophers*, 20.49 (Al-Ghazālī 2000: 223).
[16] Van Inwagen 1978: 116–118.
[17] Van Inwagen 1978: 118.

Van Inwagen makes this point in response to the suggestion that the original manuscript has been recreated because the matter which originally composed the manuscript has been imprinted with the "form" it had prior to its incineration. I have no interest in defending an account of the resurrection in terms of "forms" being "imprinted" onto matter. But my impression is that the point van Inwagen makes here is meant to be very general and meant to motivate the idea that not even God could recreate the original manuscript, regardless of whether God attempts to do so by way of imprinting a "form" onto some matter.

I do not find van Inwagen's argument here compelling. The ink on the document may not be there as a direct causal result of Augustine's handwriting, but it simply does not follow that the document is not numerically identical with the object on which Augustine wrote. I concede that there is a *sense* in which this object is not an Augustine manuscript. For something to be a manuscript is for it to be a document which is such that the token words currently written on it were written by hand. This is why, van Inwagen claims, after God's alleged recreation of the object in question it is not really a manuscript – the token words currently written on it were not written by hand, since God did not put those words there using a hand. For the object to be an *Augustine* manuscript would be for it to have writing that is on the document as a direct causal result of Augustine's handwriting. Understood in this way, I agree that the document in question is not an Augustine manuscript, as the token words currently on the document are not there as a direct causal result of Augustine's writing but are rather there as a direct causal result of God's arranging the microscopic parts of the manuscript. But we cannot infer from the fact that this document is not an Augustine manuscript that it is therefore not numerically identical with the object which once was an Augustine manuscript. To suppose otherwise we would have to assume that the Augustine manuscript is *essentially* an Augustine manuscript, in the sense that in order to exist it must be such that the writing on it is a direct causal result of Augustine's handwriting. Van Inwagen seems to be making this assumption regarding the essential properties of the manuscript in question.

So, the question of whether the document is numerically identical with the object which was once an Augustine manuscript, and the question of whether the document is *now* an Augustine manuscript are two separate questions. Our conflating these two issues can lend some specious plausibility to the idea that the document is not the object which was once an Augustine manuscript, and, by extension, lends some specious plausibility

8.2 Resurrection

to the more general idea that God cannot recreate an object after it has gone out of existence.

Perhaps the question of whether the document is really an *Augustine manuscript* is a distraction. Perhaps what van Inwagen's concern really amounts to is this: A resurrected person could not be identical with some person who died and then went out of existence because they could not be causally related in the right way to the person who died. In particular, and assuming that you go out of existence after death, any person which God might create at the resurrection would at most be a duplicate of you, since they would not be *immanently* causally related to you. Olson expresses this "immanent causation requirement" when he writes that

> When a thing causes itself to continue existing, or to have a certain property, in a way that doesn't go entirely outside that thing, we call it "immanent" causation – as opposed to the "transeunt" causation of a thing's affecting something else. If I continue to believe that 5 is odd, my believing it earlier immanently causes me to believe it later. If I convince you that 5 is odd, my believing it transeuntly causes you to do so. If I convince you that 5 is odd, then forget that fact completely and you teach me it afresh, then my earlier belief might be a cause of my later one; but because the causal chain passes outside me, it is not immanent causation. For a thing that exists now to exist in the future, then, it must cause itself to exist then, and the way it is now must to some extent cause it to be the way it is then. Or at least the existence and state of a thing in the future has to relate to its existence and state now by a chain of causal connections. And these connections must be immanent. This *immanent-causation requirement* constrains our persistence.[18]

The immanent causation requirement does not rule out all forms of resurrection. For example, if the soul or body exists at every point in time between death and resurrection, then the immanent causation requirement could be satisfied, as the soul or body at resurrection could be immanently causally related to itself at every time between death and resurrection. (Could bodies continue to exist between death and the resurrection? Below we will see at least one way this might happen.) The immanent causation requirement is meant to rule out intermittent existence, where a person goes out of existence at death, or at some point after death, and then comes back into existence at the resurrection. The immanent causation requirement is supposed to rule this out because if there is a temporal gap between a person's existence at death and the person's existence at the resurrection, then the person's existence at the resurrection could not be

---

[18] Olson 2016: 56. Cf. Hasker 2011: 83–84.

immanently causally related to itself prior to the resurrection – at most, the resurrected person could exist as a result of *God's* creative activities, and this would not be a case of *immanent* causation. Perhaps the immanent causation requirement could be satisfied if the immanent causation could occur *across* the temporal gap during which the person does not exist.[19] But the proponent of the objection to resurrection from the immanent causation requirement will think that it is implausible that that gap could be bridged.[20]

I don't want to adjudicate the issue of whether immanent causation could be maintained across a temporal gap. I have a more basic concern with the objection to resurrection from the immanent causation requirement: I don't see why we are supposed to accept the immanent causation requirement. Olson seems to think that the requirement is obviously correct,[21] but it does not seem obvious to me – in fact, the requirement seems very arbitrary. One way of seeing that it is arbitrary is to note that the requirement only applies to things which have existed at some point in the past. Nobody would think that the immanent causation requirement would apply to things which have never existed before, since then nothing would come into existence, as nothing would be able to be immanently causally related to itself at some prior time at which it did not exist. But while we can see *that* the immanent causation requirement could not apply to things which have not existed in the past, it is hard to see *why* the requirement would apply to things which have existed in the past, but not to things which have not existed in the past. If there is *no* previous time at which the object exists, then its existing at the time in question need not even partially result from an immanent causal connection with itself at a previous time, while if there *is* a previous time at which the object exists, then its existing at that time must at least partially result from an immanent causal connection to itself at a previous time. The existence of this object at *this* later time requires the immanent causal relations, while the existence of this object at *that* earlier time does not. This is arbitrary. If you are antecedently committed to the immanent causation requirement, then you may see nothing arbitrary about this. But those who are not antecedently committed to the immanent causation requirement will, like me, see the obtaining of the immanent causation requirement in the one case but not the other as arbitrary.

---

[19] See Zimmerman (1999) and Mooney (2018) for a couple of ways this might work.
[20] See Olson 2016: 60–65 for a response to Zimmerman's (1999) proposal regarding immanent causation across a temporal gap, and see Zimmerman 2016: 48–50 for a response to Olson.
[21] Olson 2016: 59.

8.2 Resurrection

There is an additional problem regarding arbitrariness. The immanent causation requirement is not supposed to apply to things at the earliest moment at which they exist but *is* supposed to apply to things at any later times at which they exist. But time might very well be continuous rather than discrete – in other words, such that time does not have smallest intervals, and any period of time can be subdivided into smaller intervals of time. If time is continuous, then there will be no earliest moment of time at which a person exists, just as, since the real numbers are continuous rather than discrete, there is no first real number immediately greater than 0. So, if time is continuous, then we cannot say that the immanent causation requirement does not apply to things at the earliest moment of time at which they exist, but does apply to things at any later times at which they exist. Instead, we will have to say something like: The immanent causation requirement does not apply during some *initial temporal interval* of an object's existence, but does apply during any later temporal interval. But which temporal interval should count as the "initial temporal interval" – the first second, the first two seconds, or what? Whatever answer we give to this question will seemingly be very arbitrary.

An additional problem is that the obtaining of the immanent causation requirement in the one case but not the other – that is, at later times but not some earlier time – makes the existence of the person at the later time dependent on extrinsic factors, that is, regarding what happens at some earlier time, something many philosophers will find objectionable.[22] The extrinsic factor is, minimally, that there exists some earlier time for the person to exist at.

Here is an additional potential difficulty for the resurrection of our bodies. It is often suggested that at the resurrection our bodies must have some or even many of the parts which they had prior to death in order to be successfully resurrected.[23] Cannibalism has often been thought to pose a special problem here.[24] After all, if I eat you, and then I die, then part of my body would have once been part of your body. So, if we are both

---

[22] This is a common objection to the closest continuer theory of personal identity (as in Nozick 1981: Ch. 1), that on that theory personal identity depends on extrinsic factors. As we will see below, this is also a major objection to resurrection by reassembly, that whether resurrection by reassembly will preserve personal identity will depend on extrinsic factors, like whether the parts of one's body are reassembled once, or more than once.

[23] This point is made by, e.g., the Church Fathers Tertullian, Gregory of Nyssa, Jerome, and Augustine (Bynum 1995: 63, 96). The idea has been expressed more recently in, e.g., Hershenov 2002; Sorabji 2006: 70.

[24] See, e.g., the discussion in Al-Ghazālī's *The Incoherence of the Philosophers*, 20.36 (Al-Ghazālī 2000: 217); Aquinas, *Summa Contra Gentiles*, 4.81.12–13. More recently, see Olson 2015. A similar, but less fun, concern involves organ transplantation – see Merricks 2001; Rice 2022: 32.

resurrected at the general resurrection, and we each require many or even all of the parts we had at death, who gets those parts which were parts of each of us at our deaths? In response to this concern, Augustine supposed that God would simply return the parts to whoever had them originally.[25] On this view, presumably, our bodies cannot have in the resurrection all of the parts which they had at death, but this does not strike me as a problem – after all, does my body really need to have every molecule of my fingernails in order to be successfully resurrected? You might be tempted to think that Augustine's solution to the cannibalism problem does not help us avoid one particular variant of the problem, though: What about cannibals who only eat human flesh for their entire lives? It seems that at the resurrection these cannibals will have no parts which can be used to form their resurrected bodies, as all of their parts will be assigned to the bodies of the people they ate. But this scenario wouldn't pose a problem for Augustine. First, our bodies are not entirely made up of the food we eat – there's also, for example, the water we drink, the air we breathe, the parts we derive from our parents. So, the bodies of the cannibals in question would include parts that were not derived from the humans they ate.[26] Second, there simply are no cannibals of the sort described in the problem, whose only sources of food for their entire lives are the bodies of other human beings. Real-world cannibals' diets mainly consist of things other than other human beings. So, this is not something God will have to worry about at the resurrection.

But all of these concerns only arise because, it is claimed, at the resurrection, our bodies must have many of the parts they had at death. And frankly, I see no reason to think that this is true, especially if, as I've claimed, God can just stipulate at the resurrection which bodies some things arrange body-wise compose.

Here is an additional concern, which is similar to the cannibalism concern: At the resurrection, God might recreate your body *twice*. Perhaps, for example, God reassembles the parts you had when you were a child, and simultaneously reassembles the parts you had when you were very old. Which resulting person will be numerically identical with you?[27] A natural response to this concern is to contend that God would not let themself be put into this sort of bind. In other words, God would not reassemble the parts of your body twice over at the resurrection. Van Inwagen gives

---

[25] Augustine, *City of God*, Book 22, Chapter 20.
[26] Thanks here to Peter Finocchiaro.
[27] For discussion of this problem, see van Inwagen 1978: 120, 1995: 486; Baker 2005; Davis 2016: 26–27; Mooney 2018.

8.2 Resurrection

the following retort: "if He [God] were to reassemble either set of atoms, the resulting man would be who he was, and it is absurd, it is utterly incoherent, to suppose that his identity could depend on what might happen to some atoms other than the atoms that compose him."[28] In other words, the fact that personal identity could not be maintained if your parts were reassembled twice over at the resurrection is itself problematic, whether or not your parts actually *are* reassembled twice over at the resurrection. Personal identity should not depend on these sorts of extrinsic factors. For example, whether some parts at the resurrection compose *you* should not depend on whether some other parts (say, the parts you had when you were three years old) are also reassembled.

Here is my response to this concern: this is not a problem for resurrection *per se*, but only for particular ways of thinking of the resurrection. For example, it is a problem for the view that a sufficient condition for your resurrection is the reassembly of the parts that composed your body at some point during your lifetime. This is the "God reassembles the parts and hopes for the best" view again. But if God pairs composite persons and their parts, then the problem does not arise. Even if God decided to simultaneously reassemble the parts you had when you were a child and the parts you had when you were very old, God can simply stipulate which, if either, collection of parts composes *you*.

We have been discussing the question of whether God could bring back into existence bodies that have gone out of existence. But we might deny that our bodies *do* go out of existence between the time of our deaths and the time of our resurrection. One proposal along these lines, which has received much attention, is van Inwagen's proposal that, at death, God might snatch our bodies away for preservation while leaving behind an indistinguishable duplicate to rot in its place.[29]

In some ways, this is the proponent of resurrection's ace in the hole since pretty clearly this proposal faces no insuperable *metaphysical* difficulties. The main problem for this view is not metaphysical but moral: It might be thought that on this proposal God engages in an objectionable sort of widespread deception, since, if God snatches bodies away when they die, then God will have to replace them with perfect duplicates, duplicates that we are tricked into thinking are the originals. This is the worry Dean Zimmerman may have in mind when he writes:

---

[28] Van Inwagen 1995: 486.
[29] Van Inwagen 1978.

Of course it is in some sense possible that God takes our brains when we die and replaces them with stuff that looks for all the world like dead brains, just as it is possible that God created the world 6000 years ago and put dinosaur bones in the ground to test our faith in a slavishly literal reading of Genesis. But neither is particularly satisfying as a picture of how God actually does business.[30]

I would like to make a few remarks regarding this worry. I think that the worry is most compelling when directed against a scenario in which God snatches the corpse for safekeeping along with its part and then replaces the corpse with a simulacrum, that is, some particles arranged corpse-wise (perhaps composing a corpse, perhaps not) which are qualitatively indistinguishable from the corpse which was snatched away for safekeeping. When God replaces the corpse with qualitatively indistinguishable particles arranged corpse-wise, it seems that God's intention is to deceive, and make it look like the corpse has *not* been snatched away for safekeeping. You might wonder whether this sort of deception is really so bad.[31] But I don't have anything interesting to say about that subject.

Here is something I can say. There is another way God could snatch away the corpse for safekeeping which would (1) be empirically undetectable (and so such that, for all we could know on the basis of our empirical evidence, it regularly occurs), and (2) does not involve any objectionable deception that I can see. The proposal is that God snatches away the corpse *while leaving behind its parts*. That God might do this is a natural corollary of my earlier suggestion that God might stipulate how parts and wholes are paired. The suggestion now is that at death God might simply de-pair the corpse from its parts and have the corpse either continue to exist as a partless object or have its parts replaced with new parts.

Compare: If we are souls, then God might "snatch" away the soul at death while leaving behind the body. If God does snatch away souls at death, de-pairing them from their bodies (and, if souls are located, removing them from the location of their decaying bodies), it doesn't seem as if God would thereby be engaged in an objectionable sort of deception. But the proposal that at death God snatches away the soul while leaving the body seems very similar to the scenario in which God snatches away the corpse while leaving its parts. So, it seems like the latter scenario would also not involve any objectionable deception on God's part. We could not complain that it still *looks* like the composite person, and not merely their parts, is

---

[30] Zimmerman 1999: 197.
[31] Qur'an 8: 43–44 suggests that God sometimes deceives us in order to achieve some greater good. That really doesn't sound so implausible to me.

8.2 Resurrection

there in their grave, since of course things would look the same whether or not the parts compose anything.³² We might as well complain that the configuration of the solar system deceives us, since it "looks" like the Sun revolves around the Earth, rather than the other way around. In response to this accusation, God might reasonably reply that casual observation cannot distinguish between the Sun's revolving around the Earth and the Earth's revolving around the Sun. (As Leibniz says, in a different context: "The external senses, properly speaking, do not deceive us. It is our inner sense which often makes us go too fast .... Now when the understanding uses and follows the false decision of the inner sense (as when the famous Galileo thought that Saturn had two handles) it is deceived by the judgement it makes upon the effect of appearances, and it infers from them more than they imply."³³)

It is instructive to note that, entirely separated from debates regarding the possibility of resurrection, there is a debate regarding whether we are ever identical to corpses.³⁴ One component of this debate is whether corpses exist. Some philosophers claim that we are our bodies, but that at death we cease to exist, and that those parts we had at death cease to compose anything (from which it follows that they do not compose a corpse). Suppose that this thesis is true and that at death our parts cease to compose anything. I do not think that, if it turned out that corpses do not exist, then anyone would claim that God deceives us about this – God never made any promises about the metaphysical status of composite objects such as corpses! But if we should not complain of deception in the case where, at death, a composite physical person ceases to exist, but their parts remain, why should we complain of deception if, at death, a composite person is removed for safekeeping, while their parts remain? What deception would occur in the latter case which would not also occur in the former case? None that I can see.

Perhaps it will be objected that what makes the scenario in which God snatches the body but leaves the parts a scenario in which God intends to deceive us is because God chose to leave the parts. The reason God leaves the parts, so the objection goes, is because God wanted to give the impression that the corpse was still there, rather than stashed away somewhere else for safekeeping. And that's deception. Here is my response

---

³² Recall the discussion of this issue in Chapter 1, §1.2: Empirical observation does not seem able to directly inform us of whether there are composite objects, or rather whether there are merely things "arranged composite object-wise."
³³ Leibniz 2001: 109–110.
³⁴ See, e.g., Feldman 1992: Ch. 6; Carter 1999; Hershenov 2005; Olson 2013; Francescotti 2017.

to this concern: There are other conceivable reasons why God might leave the parts, beside God's having an intention to make us think that a corpse is still there. For example, God might have reason to leave the parts because if God removes the parts, then this would result in a dramatic impact on the causal sequence of events in the physical world. By contrast, if the corpse is causally inert, or such that anything it causes is overdetermined by the causal activities of its parts, then God can safely remove the corpse without disrupting the causal sequence of events in the physical world.[35] This is not to deny that God might sometimes have reason to introduce miracles and disrupt the causal sequence of events in the physical world. But, in order to ensure that the sequence of physical events is orderly, law-like, and predictable, God might not want to introduce those sorts of miracles too often, or at least not as often as every time a human dies. And if God wants to resurrect any *non*human animals, then God would have to introduce these miracles even more often: any time any of these animals dies. The disappearance of every corpse, and every corpse part, after death would also have a profound historical and cultural impact: there would be nothing to bury or cremate; paleoanthropology would be impossible; autopsies, or even any very basic postmortem examination, would be impossible; organ transplantation would be impossible; unless the death/disappearance is witnessed it will be entirely unclear whether someone has died or has simply gone missing. (In *Return of the Jedi* Luke Skywalker witnesses Yoda's death, and the disappearance of Yoda's body (and the parts of that body) at death. Can you imagine how confused Luke would have been if he had not been present at Yoda's death?) It is not at all clear that God would prefer a world so radically different from our own in these ways. (Incidentally, these considerations also support van Inwagen's proposal that God might snatch away the corpse and its parts, and replace them with qualitatively indistinguishable duplicates. Or, more specifically, it supports the idea that after snatching away the corpse and its parts God would have reason to replace them with qualitatively indistinguishable duplicates.)

Above I said that the main concern with the view that God snatches our bodies away at death for safekeeping is not metaphysical, but rather moral. But then my defense against the accusation that God would be engaged

---

[35] Recall the discussion of causal overdetermination and composite objects in Chapter 2, §2.3. Note that Merricks, who presses these overdetermination concerns against the existence of most composite objects, thinks that we cause things which are not causally overdetermined by our parts because we have certain sorts of conscious mental properties (Merricks 2003: 88–89). But *corpses* would not have these conscious mental properties. So, Merricks's argument for the conclusion that we sometimes cause things which are not causally overdetermined by our parts would not establish that *corpses* cause things which are not causally overdetermined by their parts.

in an objectionable deception if God snatched away our bodies relied on a metaphysical thesis which many readers will find dubious: that God might snatch away the corpse, while leaving behind the parts which composed the corpse immediately prior to death. I said that if God did *that* then God would not be engaged in an objectionable form of deception. But *could* God do that? Maybe not – or, at least, many readers will think that not even God could do this. Fair enough, the points I make in the previous few paragraphs will not convince those who think that God could not snatch away a body while leaving behind its parts. But you should probably not be so skeptical of the idea that God could snatch away the body while leaving behind the parts. After all, you will probably agree that our bodies could have different parts from the parts which they actually have. This point is supported by the observation that most of the parts of our bodies are replaced several times over the course of our lives. So, why could God not replace all of your parts at once at death, by snatching away the body, giving it new parts, and leaving behind the parts it had immediately prior to death? God might not even need to give the body new parts in order to keep it in existence. God might simply keep the body in existence, even if nothing composes it.

You might complain that a composite object is "nothing over and above its parts," and so a body could not go separate ways from its parts, or have its parts replaced so quickly. My response is that there is no way of understanding the phrase "nothing over and above its parts" which is such that a composite object really is "nothing over and above its parts," and which would make it impossible for God to snatch away a body while leaving behind its parts. "Nothing over and above its parts" is a phrase one often finds in discussions of composition, but those who use the phrase rarely bother to say what it means, and its meaning is frustratingly obscure. But the most natural interpretation of the phrase is that it is saying that a composite object is numerically identical with its parts. This is composition as identity, a view I discussed and rejected in Chapter 1, §1.3. Another natural way of interpreting the phrase is that it is saying that a composite object overlaps with its parts, and does not overlap with anything else (except perhaps itself). This is true, but uninteresting, and would not support the idea that God could not snatch away a body while leaving behind its parts.[36]

---

[36] For more discussion of what the phrase "nothing over and above its parts" might mean, see Smid 2017.

So, all in all, I don't think that agnosticism regarding the metaphysics of personal ontology should lead us toward agnosticism regarding whether it is possible for the general resurrection to occur. There seem to be ways in which God could achieve a general resurrection regardless of which account of personal ontology is correct (with the exception of the nonself thesis). I don't claim to have offered an exhaustive defense of this view, or examined all of the possible ways God could bring about the resurrection. The ideas I have explored in relatively greater detail – God can pair bodies with parts, God can snatch away bodies while leaving behind their parts, etc. – are somewhat idiosyncratic. But that is precisely why I have explored those particular ideas: I think they are underappreciated.

Among those who believe in a general resurrection, it is sometimes thought that we will also exist and have conscious mental states in an intermediate state between death and resurrection. Since my primary focus is on resurrection, I will only briefly comment on the intermediate state. The first point to note is that in Judaism, Christianity, and Islam, the intermediate state is theologically less important, and more controversial, than the resurrection. Still, we might wonder whether uncertainty about which account of personal ontology to adopt should lead us to be uncertain about whether such an intermediate state is possible. I don't think it should. It is sometimes argued that an intermediate state requires substance dualism.[37] An intermediate state certainly seems to be *compatible* with substance dualism, but I do not think that it *requires* substance dualism. First, God may give us bodies or body parts in an intermediate state,[38] or preserve our present bodies in that state.[39] Second, as I discussed in Chapter 4, §4.2, we need not assume that if we are currently physical, then we are essentially physical.[40] Perhaps we are physical objects now, but exist as nonphysical objects in an intermediate state between death and resurrection.

8.3 Reincarnation

So much for resurrection. What about reincarnation? Some philosophers reject reincarnation because of an antecedent belief in materialism

---

[37] See, e.g., Cooper 1989, 2018.
[38] Baker 1995: 498–499.
[39] Corcoran 1998: 335.
[40] Cf. Hooker 1978; Merricks 1994; Thornton 2019; Bailey 2021: Ch. 2.

regarding human persons.[41] These philosophers think that reincarnation only makes sense on the assumption that we are immaterial souls. Presumably, the idea is that reincarnation could only work by way of an immaterial soul moving from one body to another. But I do not think that materialism with respect to human persons is the primary difficulty for reincarnation. Reincarnation might very well work by way of an immaterial soul moving from one body to another. But it might also work by way of a composite physical object such as a body moving from some parts (i.e., the parts that compose the body in the first life) to some other parts (i.e., the parts that compose the body in the second life). So, reincarnation is compatible with substance dualism, but it also seems to be compatible with the view that we are composite physical objects.

Reincarnation of a sort may also be compatible with the nonself thesis. The Buddhist philosophical tradition generally endorses the nonself thesis as well as the thesis that reincarnation occurs. This might seem puzzling at first: If we think that reincarnation involves the transfer of a person from one life to the next, how could that happen if there are no people? I would be inclined to reject the possibility of reincarnation given the nonself view for this very reason if it were not for the long history within Buddhist thought of using the word "reincarnation" to describe a process that is compatible with the nonself thesis. Through this long history of use, the term "reincarnation" has come to take on a broader meaning according to which "reincarnation" is compatible with the nonself thesis.[42] The idea is that while no *person* or *self* literally moves from one life to the next, various mental or physical characteristics in one life cause similar mental or physical characteristics in the next life, and it is in virtue of this causal series of mental or physical characteristics that it is conventionally true to say that some individual is the reincarnation of some individual from a previous life.[43] A useful analogy here is that of an image in a reflection. As Buddhaghosa puts it: "while the arrangement of the ornaments on the face does not pass over to the reflection of the face in the looking glass, yet the arrangement of the ornaments does not because of that fail to appear."[44] In other words: When the ornaments on my face are reflected in a mirror, they do not literally move to the location of the mirror. But there is nevertheless

---

[41] See, e.g., Hales 2001: 338–339; van Inwagen 2015: 259. Matthew Owen, who is not himself a materialist, nevertheless claims that reincarnation is "obviously impossible" if we are identical with our bodies (Owen 2021: 56).
[42] Of course, typical lay Buddhists may believe in both reincarnation and selves, and so may believe in an account of reincarnation where selves move from one life to the next.
[43] Cf. Anālayo 2018: Ch. 1.
[44] Buddhaghosa 2010: 628.

an *image* of those ornaments in the mirror, an image that resembles the ornaments themselves because it is caused by those ornaments.

So, reincarnation is compatible with all of the main views regarding personal ontology which I have discussed in this book. But I think that there are at least three other difficulties facing belief in reincarnation. These three difficulties are interrelated. The difficulties are interesting in their own right, but reflecting on these difficulties will also eventually allow us to reach a somewhat surprising conclusion: Not only does reincarnation not *require* substance dualism, but the main evidence generally cited in support of reincarnation – alleged cases where mental states (such as memories) have been transferred from one life to a subsequent life – does not *support* substance dualism.

First difficulty for belief in reincarnation: For reincarnation to occur, there must be some mechanism which accounts for the movement of the person from one life to the next. If we are souls, for example, there must be some mechanism which ensures that after death we move from the body we had prior to death to some other body. And if we are bodies (or other composite physical objects), then there must be some mechanism which ensures that after death we cease to be composed of the parts which composed us prior to death, and we come to be composed of some parts in a new incarnation (i.e., in some parts arranged fetus-wise). Proponents of reincarnation often endorse just such a mechanism. They generally contend, for example, that karma explains why people are reincarnated as they are – for example, if someone has performed good actions, then they earn karmic merit, and this results in their being reincarnated into a better life. Or, proponents of reincarnation sometimes contend, God moves a person from one incarnation to the next.[45] The problem is that these mechanisms complicate our total theory, especially if we lack independent grounds for believing in either karma or God, or lack independent grounds for thinking that karma or God would operate in this manner (moving a person from one life to the next). More complex theories are, other things being equal, less likely to be true, and so we should generally avoid complicating our total theory if we can help it.[46] I'm inclined to think that impersonal karmic laws would be particularly gratuitous, for two reasons. First, we lack independent grounds for thinking there are laws of

---

[45] Some of those who believe in karma think that karma operates by way of God's activities. In this case, karma and God would not be competing explanations for why people are reincarnated as they are. For discussion, see Reichenbach 1990: 96–100.

[46] Cf. Paul 2012; Brenner 2017b, forthcoming-b, MS-a; Bradley 2018.

this sort, whereas we have independent grounds for believing in God.[47] Second, karmic laws would be particularly complex, since the nonmoral facts governed by the laws would be wildly heterogeneous. For example, karmic laws would have to take the form: If someone performs bad actions (where an action's being bad supervenes on a complex heterogeneous and disjunctive supervenience base), then they are more likely to be reborn into a bad life (where a *life's* being bad is very different from an action's being bad, and a life's being bad also supervenes on a complex heterogeneous and disjunctive supervenience base). Matters are complicated further by the interplay of different actions on one's karmic desert – for example, I might perform a bad action, and so deserve some bad consequence as a result, but my degree of desert will be increased or diminished by other actions I perform. In contrast with impersonal karmic laws, God's actions may track the moral facts (e.g., God may perform good actions) by way of a simple mechanism: God is morally good, and God knows which actions are morally good/best, and so God performs good actions. Alternatively: God has a very simple motivational structure, according to which God acts on the basis of the reasons for action which God believes God has (including moral reasons). Moral reasons provide overriding reasons for action, or are grounded in or supervene upon overriding reasons for action. Being omniscient, God is aware of all of the relevant moral reasons for action applicable to God. So, God performs the morally good actions corresponding to God's moral reasons for action.[48]

The second difficulty for the notion of reincarnation is similar to the first: that of providing some mechanism for how *mental and physical states* are transferred from one life to another. Focus in particular on transfer of mental states. The mind depends on the brain. We have certain experiences and memories primarily because of what happens in our brains. So, if my brain is destroyed at death, how is it that some of my mental states (such as memories from my present life) are transferred to a new life? Strictly speaking, with the possible exception of Buddhist nonself accounts of reincarnation, reincarnation does not *require* any such transfer of mental states from one life to another. But as a matter of fact, the primary evidence cited in favor of reincarnation appeals to the fact that there are cases where mental states are allegedly transferred from one life to a subsequent life. Aside from appeals to scriptural authority, the most commonly cited evidence for reincarnation is the following:[49] There are

---

[47] See, e.g., Swinburne 2004; Craig and Moreland 2009; Walls and Dougherty 2018.
[48] For a similar line of thought, see Swinburne 2004: 103–105.
[49] See Stevenson 1974; Almeder 1992: Ch. 1; White et al. 2016; Anālayo 2018: Ch. 3–4.

people who have episodic memories apparently of past lives, which include details that are later verified; there are people who have knowledge of languages learned in past lives (xenoglossy), or who can recite material in a foreign language learned in a past life; there are people who recognize items owned by themselves in a previous life; there are people who have skills or personality traits associated with a prior life; there are people who have birthmarks corresponding to injuries received in a past life; there are people who have phobias corresponding to the cause of death in a previous life (e.g., being afraid of buses if one was killed by a bus in one's previous life). A full evaluation of the evidence for reincarnation is beyond the scope of this book.[50] The important point to note here is that the evidence for reincarnation primarily consists in mental states (e.g., memories) which have allegedly been transferred from one life to the next. And it is difficult to see how these mental states *could* be transferred from one life to the next, given what we know about the dependence of our mental states on our brains, brains which decay after death. Once again, we might appeal to God or karma to account for the transfer of mental states from one life to the next. But these mechanisms, especially karma, may insert gratuitous complexity into our total theory. So, this gives us good reason to doubt that mental states such as memories could genuinely be transferred from one life to the next, which gives us reason to think that cases where mental states purportedly *have* been transferred from one life to the next must have some alternative explanation.

Here is a third difficulty for belief in reincarnation. I have just said that the primary evidence for reincarnation is that there are cases where mental states such as memories have seemingly been transferred from one life to the next. On reflection, however, and given what we know about how our psychological states are encoded in the brain, someone's seeming to have memories or other psychological states from a previous life would not show that they are numerically identical with anyone from a previous life. And, perhaps surprisingly, this is true even if the psychological states correspond to the psychological states actually had by somebody who lived in the past — for example, even if someone has memories of such-and-such an experience, and someone in the past really had that experience. In fact, it's true even if the psychological states in question really have somehow been transferred or copied from one life to a subsequent life. We can see why this is the case by reflecting on why someone might think that their seeming to have memories or other psychological states from a previous life *would* show

---

[50] Although see Lester 2005: Part 3 for a critical evaluation of the evidence.

8.3 Reincarnation

that they are numerically identical with someone in a previous life. There are two possibilities here:

Possibility 1: The continuity of psychological states shows that numerical identity obtains because the numerical identity explains why the psychological continuity obtains – that is, the reason why the person has psychological states associated with a previous life is because they are numerically identical with the person who had those psychological states in a previous life. This is, I take it, the standard view among proponents of reincarnation for why apparent psychological continuity with a previous life is supposed to show that reincarnation has occurred. This account fails because we know that memories and other psychological states are encoded in processes in the brain. Simply being *numerically identical* with someone at a previous time would not by itself do anything to make you have the psychological states had by that earlier person. For example, being the same soul, or being the same composite physical object would not have any tendency to give you the same psychological states, since psychological states such as memories are not carried by sameness of soul or sameness of composite physical object, but are rather carried by certain physical structures in the brain. These physical structures are not carried over from one life to a subsequent life, as physical continuity is broken in reincarnation. In short, memory retention, and retention of psychological states more generally, just doesn't work the way it would have to work for numerical identity to explain why someone has psychological states associated with a previous life.

Possibility 2: Perhaps instead the continuity of psychological states is not explained by numerical identity, but rather numerical identity is explained by continuity of psychological states. This idea would pair naturally with a psychological continuity theory of diachronic personal identity, of the sort described in Chapter 1, §1.1. But this account of how psychological continuity is supposed to show that reincarnation has occurred also does not work. First, it is very hard to see why moving some psychological states (say, from one life to a subsequent life) would have any tendency to move a soul, or a composite physical object. This is a subject I will return to in Chapter 9, §9.3, when I discuss whether it is possible to "upload" ourselves into computers. But, second, psychological continuity theories of diachronic personal identity generally require a great deal of psychological continuity in order for numerical identity to obtain. The psychological connections which are alleged to obtain between subsequent lives in reincarnation are generally rather weak – for example, it might involve limited episodic memories from a previous life, and in any case, these memories generally fade after childhood. What's more, proponents of psychological continuity theories of diachronic personal identity sometimes maintain that a necessary condition for numerical identity over time is that the psychological connections are maintained in the way that they are *normally* maintained. If psychological continuity between subsequent lives is possible, it is certainly not maintained the way that psychological continuity is normally maintained. Psychological continuity is normally maintained by way of continuity of those brain structures which encode our psychological states, brain structures which are destroyed at death. All in all, then, there are obstacles to supposing that a psychological continuity theory of diachronic personal identity will enable us to infer that psychological continuity between lives, of the sort we allegedly find in real-world cases of reincarnation, would entail numerical identity.

Here is an interesting corollary of the fact that, contra what many people seem to think, a transfer of psychological states from one life to a subsequent life would not show that someone is numerically identical with someone in a subsequent life. It is sometimes thought that evidence for reincarnation would *ipso facto* be evidence for substance dualism. For example, Parfit writes that while we have no good evidence for substance dualism, such evidence *might* have been forthcoming. For example, it might have been the case that many people had accurate memories seemingly of previous lives, and these seemingly accurate memories would have led us to conclude that reincarnation occurs. In this case, Parfit claims, we would have been forced to postulate immaterial souls which carried the memories from one life to the next, and from there we may have reasonably concluded that we *are* those immaterial souls.[51] I don't think this is right. That is, I don't think that the evidence of the sort Parfit discusses should, if actual, reasonably lead us to conclude that each of us is an immaterial soul. First, it is unclear why we should think that, if there are immaterial objects that carry memories from one life to the next, *we* are those immaterial objects. Second, as I noted earlier, reincarnation does not require substance dualism. Reincarnation is compatible with our being composite physical objects because we may move from one life to the next by moving from some parts to some other parts – that is, from the physical parts associated with one life to the physical parts associated with a new life. If, following Parfit, we should infer from a transfer of memories from one life to the next that some *object* carrying those memories is transferred from one life to the next, there seems to be no reason to prefer postulating a soul to carry out this task when the composite physical person can also do the job. What's more, we know that within a

---

[51] Parfit 1984: 227.

8.3 Reincarnation

single lifetime memories are encoded in the brain and encoded by way of the physical properties of the brain's parts (e.g., the physical properties of the neurons that compose the brain). Since this is the case, and souls are not in general the sorts of things that seem to carry our memories, there is no particular reason to think that a soul is a better candidate than the composite physical person to carry the memories from one life to the next. It follows that, not only does the transfer of memories from one life to the next not *require* substance dualism, but substance dualism does not make such a transfer of memories any more probable. So, *pace* Parfit, even if this sort of transfer of memories really occurs that would not provide evidence for substance dualism. The principle regarding evidence appealed to here is a basic consequence of the probability calculus: Conditionalizing on some evidence (e.g., memory transfer) raises the probability of a hypothesis (e.g., substance dualism) only if the hypothesis's being true would render the evidence more probable than if the hypothesis were false.

9

Personal Ontology and Life after Death, Part 2: Mind Uploading

9.1 Introduction

Let's turn our attention to one final approach to life after death, *mind uploading*. Mind uploading involves the transfer or copying of one's mental states to a computer. Mind uploading can be gradual or fast. Gradual uploading might involve, for example, the gradual replacements of parts of the body or brain with artificial components, until every part of the body or brain has been replaced. The end result will be a man-made robot or computer, which, it is hoped, will have mental states that are psychologically continuous with the mental states the person had prior to having the parts of their body or brain replaced. Fast uploading instead would involve, for example, quickly constructing a simulation of someone's brain, perhaps by scanning a brain and simulating its activities in a computer (so-called whole-brain emulation).[1] Mind uploading can also be destructive or nondestructive. Destructive mind uploading involves the destruction of the original brain during the process of uploading. Some forms of mind uploading, for example, would involve slicing the brain into thin slices in order to scan each of them in detail. Needless to say, slicing the brain into a bunch of thin slices will destroy the brain and result in the (biological) death of the person whose brain is being scanned.

In discussions of mind uploading, two questions have received the most attention:

1. Would uploading preserve personal identity? In other words, if I were to attempt to upload myself, would the resulting simulated person (if there is any such person) be *me*?
2. If we were to simulate a brain in a computer, would the simulation, or the computer running the simulation, be conscious, in the sense that there is something it is like to be that simulation or computer?

---

[1] For details, see Koene 2013, 2014; Sandberg 2013.

9.1 Introduction

The two questions are related. For example, many proponents of mind uploading think that the uploaded person will be *me* only if it will be psychologically related to me in the right way, where the psychological relations involve conscious experiences. So, if the uploaded person has no conscious experiences, as a negative answer to the second question would entail, then it could not be me, since it could not be psychologically related to my preupload state in the right way.

There are two more questions regarding mind uploading which are sometimes discussed, though less frequently than the previous two questions:

3. What is the *personal ontology* of "uploaded" persons?
4. What sort of thing would we have to be now in order to be the sort of thing that could be uploaded?[2]

The third question is more closely related to the question I have discussed throughout this book: What are we? We can think of this new question as something like "What *would* we be if we were 'uploaded' to a computer, and this uploading process preserved personal identity?" The fourth question is also related to the question "What are we?" It asks, in effect, which answers to the question "What are we?" would be most amenable to uploading's preserving personal identity.

Since this book is about the metaphysics of personal identity, I am mainly interested in the first, third, and fourth questions.[3]

Is mind uploading a feasible strategy for thwarting death? I'll start addressing this question by noting a common objection to mind uploading's preserving personal identity, which I do not endorse. The concern is that mind uploading allows *duplication*, since the process which results in our simulating a person's mental states in a computer could be duplicated.[4] If, for example, we simulate the mental states in a computer, there is nothing stopping us from simultaneously simulating the mental states in a second computer. But if we have these two simultaneous uploaded persons, then it would be objectionably arbitrary for me to be identical with one of them rather than the other.[5] So, the objection goes, I am identical with neither of them.

---

[2] Thanks to an anonymous referee for suggesting that I clearly spell out this question.
[3] Although for a discussion of the second question, and more specifically for some concerns regarding the idea that whole-brain emulations would be conscious, see Mandelbaum 2022.
[4] See Mandik 2015: 146; Mercer 2015: 181; Olson 2017: 38–39, 2022: 388–390; Schneider 2019: Ch. 6; Liao 2020: 490; Goldwater 2021: 233.
[5] Presumably, this duplication concern would not apply to some forms of gradual uploading. If, e.g., I come to occupy a robotic body by gradually replacing the organic parts of my body with synthetic substitutes, it's not obvious to me how this process could be multiplied in a way that would result in two simultaneous synthetic duplicates, each of which has an equal claim to being identical with me preupload.

I do not think that this is a good objection to mind uploading's preserving personal identity. Note that the issue here concerns pairing relations: which computer, or which parts, or whatever, is one paired with after the duplication? Recall the discussion of pairing problems in Chapter 3. Some pairing relations are either brute, in the sense that there is no explanation for why the relata of those pairing relations are paired as they are, or they have some explanation. Supposing that pairing relations are brute, then we can just say that the pairing relations in cases of duplication are brute – that is, if we are souls, then it is brute which computer or simulation is paired with the preduplication soul, and if we are composite physical, objects then it is brute which parts are paired with the preduplication composite physical person. On the other hand, if pairing relations are not brute, and so pairing relations have explanations, then they will presumably have explanations in the cases of duplication. So, it will not be objectionably arbitrary that the one being uploaded ends up as one duplicate rather than the other. Here is an illustration of what I have in mind. In Chapter 3, §3.6, I discussed antirealist responses to pairing problems, which claim that we decide pairing facts, or God does. Suppose that this sort of antirealist response to the pairing problems is correct. Well, then there will be an explanation for pairing facts. And so we can give an antirealist response to the mind uploading duplication concern: We decide, or God decides, which duplicate is the original.[6] If we are souls, then we decide, or God decides, which computer or simulation is paired with the preduplication soul, and if we are composite physical objects, then we decide, or God decides, which parts are paired with the preduplication composite physical person.[7]

What's more, whether or not mind uploading occurs, each of us faces a concern analogous to the duplication concern: In principle, your brain hemispheres could be transplanted into separate bodies, in which case we might think that it would be objectionably arbitrary for you to be identical with one hemisphere recipient rather than the other. Of course, we might not be very concerned by split-brain fission if as a matter of fact our brain hemispheres have not been transplanted into separate bodies. But then, the proponent of mind uploading can make a similar point and say that they are not very concerned by the prospect of mind uploading duplication, as long as the duplication hasn't actually taken place.[8]

---

[6] Cf. Bamford and Danaher 2017.
[7] For a more detailed discussion of the issues raised in this paragraph, see Brenner MS-c.
[8] An alternative response to the duplication concern, which I do not endorse, is given by Cerullo (2015): In these duplication cases, the preupload person is identical with each of the uploads. This

So, I am not moved by the duplication concern for mind uploading. But I'll now describe what seems to me to be some serious difficulties in the notion that mind uploading would allow us to thwart death, in the sense that it allows us to exist in simulated form after our deaths. I have two main concerns. First, mind uploading has an obscure and problematic personal ontology: It is not at all clear what we would be, or *could* be, if we were to upload ourselves, and if uploading preserved personal identity. Second, it is problematic to suppose that someone could be *moved* into a computer, in the sense in which they would have to be moved into a computer if mind uploading preserves personal identity. After discussing these two concerns for most of this chapter, I'll turn to the question of how we should behave in light of these concerns. Would it be prudent to attempt to "upload" oneself, given the concerns I raise?

9.2 Obscure and Problematic Ontology

Discussions of mind uploading, and whether it would allow us to thwart death, generally discuss whether or not we should endorse a theory of personal identity over time which would accommodate the notion that mind uploading preserves personal identity.[9] But making sense of the *personal ontology* of uploaded persons matters as well, because we need to know if uploaded persons are the sorts of things we could become. Whether uploaded persons are the sorts of things we could become will presumably depend on both the correct personal ontology of uploaded persons and the correct personal ontology of non- or preuploaded persons, since we may need to know if we are now the sorts of things which could be uploaded. But when we turn our attention to personal ontology rather than criteria of personal identity over time, the notion that mind uploading preserves personal identity can come to seem particularly dubious. First, it is not clear if we are now the sorts of things which could be uploaded. One reason why this is the case should be clear from prior chapters of this book: Since it is not clear what sorts of things we *are*, it is not clear if we are the sorts of things which could be uploaded. Second, it is not clear what sorts of things we would be if we *did* manage to upload ourselves. And some of the most prominent proposed personal ontologies for uploaded persons face significant difficulties. In order to show that this is the case, in this section

---

response does not work for the very simple reason that the uploads are not identical with one another, and so the preupload person could not be identical with each of them.

[9] See, e.g., Chalmers 2010; Walker 2011; Pigliucci 2014: §5; Cerullo 2015; Bamford and Danaher 2017.

I will discuss the different proposals that have been made regarding the personal ontology of uploaded persons.[10]

9.2.1 Nonself

James Hughes[11] approaches mind uploading from the perspective of someone who thinks that the self does not exist. In other words, he advocates for mind uploading, despite the fact that he thinks that selves do not exist. This way of thinking of the ontology of uploaded persons can quickly be put aside. The question which primarily interests me here is whether mind uploading would preserve personal identity. If selves do not exist, then personal identity isn't preserved by *any* process, since persons do not exist. Of course, it may be *conventionally* true in some sense that mind uploading preserves personal identity if, say, a computer comes to mimic your behavior, or replicates many of your mental states, to such a degree that we might naturally talk as if you have been moved into a computer. But the question which interests me in this section is not whether it is natural or convenient to talk as if mind uploading preserves personal identity. What interests me is whether mind uploading really does preserve personal identity.

9.2.2 Immaterial Souls

It is sometimes claimed, usually by opponents of the notion that mind uploading preserves personal identity, that proponents of mind uploading are implicitly committed to some sort of substance dualism.[12] Is that right? Substance dualism *does* naturally pair with mind uploading, since it provides a natural account of how someone might swap bodies, in the sense that they leave behind their biological body in order to occupy a synthetic body or computer. After all, if you are a ghost in a machine, then there's no obvious barrier to your being housed in one machine (a computer) rather than another (a body). And proponents of mind uploading really

---

[10] See also Olson 2019, which also contains an overview of different possible personal ontologies which might be associated with simulated or virtual persons, and which also surveys some of the difficulties associated with these different personal ontologies.
[11] Hughes 2013.
[12] See Hauskeller 2012: 196; Hopkins 2012; Olson 2017. In a similar vein, van Inwagen (1996, 2002) argues that psychological continuity theories of personal identity are in tension with the idea that human persons are material objects. The arguments van Inwagen gives would also undermine the idea that mind uploading would preserve personal identity, given the assumption that we are material objects.

may have inchoate dualist sympathies. For example, in both philosophical and nonphilosophical contexts, mind uploading is very often described as uploading "a consciousness" to a computer. This use of "consciousness" as a count noun sure sounds like talk of an immaterial soul.

That being said, I don't think that mind uploading *requires* substance dualism. Suppose, for simplicity, that we are our bodies (what I say will be applicable if we are other sorts of composite physical objects, e.g., brains). Supposing we are bodies, we certainly cannot "leave" our biological bodies in the sense that we cease to be *identical* with our bodies, since nothing can cease being identical with itself without ceasing to exist. But there are other ways we might "leave" our biological bodies. For example, we may cease to be composed of any biological parts and come to be composed of synthetic parts (e.g., some synthetic parts arranged computer-wise). Whether it is *plausible* that this would happen if we tried to upload ourselves is another matter, to which I will return in §9.3.

9.2.3 Computers

One materialist-friendly account of what we would be if we were to upload ourselves is that we would be computers, or networks of computers, or parts of computers, or physical objects constituted by, but not identical with, computers, computer networks, or parts of computers.[13] Here, I have in mind physical hardware-based computers rather than virtual machines.

This proposal raises a number of difficult questions, questions we will need to answer in order to know whether uploading would preserve personal identity. For simplicity, I will confine my attention to the view that if we were uploaded, then we would be computers – rather than networks of computers, or parts of computers, or physical objects constituted by computers, etc. – although what I have to say will apply to those other possibilities as well.

If a single computer runs multiple whole-brain emulations simultaneously, do we end up with more than one conscious person, or one conscious person with an oddly dissociated or disunified mental life? If we should say of some simulated person that they *are* a computer, and a computer simulates two or more persons simultaneously, in that case would there be two colocated computers where we pretheoretically think there is just one computer (i.e., one computer for each simulated person)? How do you ensure that you simulate two persons (and so have two

---

[13] The constitution proposal is endorsed by Wellington 2014.

colocated computers) and not just one person with the mental life as of two persons? It's not clear how we should answer these questions. This is a problem as, should mind uploading become technologically feasible, individual computers might very well run multiple whole-brain emulations simultaneously.

Or suppose that we have a computer which is not simulating a person, and then we "upload" a person into it. What happens to the computer? The uploaded person cannot become identical with that computer, since distinct objects cannot become identical. So, the computer must either cease to exist, simply because information regarding someone's mental or physical traits was transferred into it, or after the upload we now have two colocated computers (i.e., the original computer, and the computer which is identical with the uploaded person). Neither option seems very plausible. We normally don't think that the persistence conditions of computers are so closely related to what programs they run (e.g., what objects they simulate). We don't normally think that simply by simulating a particular object a computer will either go out of existence or come to be colocated with a second computer. We also don't tend to think that the persistence conditions of computers are psychological – in other words, we don't tend to think that the persistence conditions of any computers have anything to do with what psychological states they instantiate. And more generally we do not tend to think that the persistence conditions of any computers have anything to do with the data they store or process.

Or suppose that we have a computer into which someone has been uploaded. If the person could be uploaded into that computer, then presumably they could subsequently be uploaded into a different computer. Supposing that uploaded persons are computers, then if we move someone from one computer to another, what happens? It seems very implausible that the first computer has become the second computer – two nonidentical things cannot become identical. And it also seems implausible that the first computer has moved to the location of the second computer. This is because you cannot move physical objects like computers just by moving information (I will return to this point in §9.3).[14] It is also because if we thought that the first computer *had* moved to the location of the second computer, then we would be faced with awkward questions regarding what happens to the second computer: Does it cease to exist, or is it now colocated with the first computer, or what? All in all, the most sensible thing

---

[14] Cf. Olson 2019: 71, who also notes that while it is often thought that simulated or virtual persons (if there could be such things) could be moved by transferring data from one location to another, this seems implausible if the virtual or artificial thinkers are computers.

9.2 Obscure and Problematic Ontology

to think is simply that the mental states in the first computer come to be instantiated in the second computer, and no person has been moved from one location to the other. But if that's what we should say about *computers*, then we should probably say the same thing about uploading from a *brain* to a computer. If the first sort of "mind uploading" does not move the first computer to the location of the second computer, then presumably attempting to upload a biological person into a computer would not move that person to where the computer is located, and by extension would not transform that person into a computer occupying that location.

Admittedly, the points I have just made all concern *fast* uploading rather than gradual uploading. It is more plausible to suppose that personal identity would be preserved were the parts of one's body or brain or whatever gradually replaced by artificial parts, until all of one's parts have been replaced, and one ends up being a robot (a type of computer). Or, if one is an immaterial soul, and the parts of one's body or brain or whatever are gradually replaced with artificial parts, one would end up as an immaterial soul paired with an artificial body. Or, at any rate, nothing I have said here has been intended to undermine either of these possibilities.

Suppose that, despite the concerns I have been discussing, the best ontology of uploaded persons, and simulated persons more generally, is that they would be computers (or parts of computers, etc.). It's interesting to note that this would have implications for how we evaluate Nick Bostrom's influential "simulation argument."[15] Bostrom argues that at least one of the following three propositions is true: "(1) the fraction of human-level civilizations that reach a posthuman stage is very close to zero; (2) the fraction of posthuman civilizations that are interested in running ancestor-simulations is very close to zero; (3) the fraction of all people with our kind of experiences who are living in a simulation is very close to one."[16] What's more, Bostrom argues that if (3) is true, then we are probably among the simulated persons, as there are many more simulated persons with our kind of experiences than there are nonsimulated persons with our kind of experiences.[17] One prominent way to challenge the simulation argument is to contend that there could not be conscious simulated persons, since consciousness is not substrate independent, and in particular because the computers running simulations could never be conscious, or could never produce conscious simulated persons. This objection in effect claims that

---

[15] Bostrom 2003.
[16] Bostrom 2003: 255.
[17] Incidentally, elsewhere Bostrom says that he thinks we are probably not simulated. See Bostrom 2009: 458. Presumably, then, he thinks that (3) is probably false.

(3) might be false, even if both (1) and (2) are false. But there is a different, and less widely appreciated, objection to the effect that (3) might be false, even if both (1) and (2) are false. The objection is that even if (1) and (2) are false, the correct ontology of simulated persons may make it unlikely that the proportion of persons with our kind of experiences which are simulated is large relative to the total population of persons with our kind of experiences. Supposing, for example, that a simulated person is just a computer, and we can't have colocated simulated persons/computers, this would severely constrain how many conscious simulated persons we can produce, since in order to produce more simulated persons we'll have to produce more computers. Some other ontologies of simulated persons would be more amenable to easily producing large numbers of simulated persons, and so it would require fewer resources to produce more simulated persons. For example, on some other ontologies of simulated persons, a single computer may be able to simultaneously implement numerous simulated persons.

9.2.4 *Patterns*

Sometimes proponents of mind uploading say that we are *patterns*, and that uploaded persons would be patterns, and that mind uploading will preserve personal identity so long as it preserves the patterns with which we are identical. Ray Kurzweil, one of the most famous proponents of mind uploading, endorses just this sort of view.[18] Kurzweil notes that our bodies change their parts all the time, but that we nevertheless persist across those changes because, he claims, the *pattern* remains the same. But there are a number of problems with the idea that we are patterns.

First, just because, as Kurzweil notes, we persist across changes in our bodies, it does not follow that we persist because some particular pattern persists across those changes. It also does not follow that the persistence of any such pattern is a sufficient condition for the persistence of any of us. I have always followed a very regular pattern of motion around the Sun, one so regular that an alien on another planet could in principle predict or retrodict with great accuracy (relative to astronomical scales) my location at any point over the course of my life.[19] But it doesn't follow that I persist *because* I have followed this pattern of motion, and it certainly doesn't follow that my continuing to follow this pattern is sufficient for my

---

[18] Kurzweil 2005: Ch. 7. See also Moravec 1988: 117–119 and Walker 2011 for similar views.
[19] Thanks to Peter Finocchiaro for this example.

continuing to exist. Nor, of course, does it follow that I somehow *am* the pattern.

Even if the persistence of some pattern is sufficient for the persistence of some person, it is very difficult to tell *which* pattern is the pattern sufficient for personal identity, and so difficult to know which pattern we should preserve in order to preserve the person in mind uploading. What's more, if we do not know which pattern we need to preserve, then we will not know whether that pattern is even the sort of pattern which can be instantiated in a computer. In a similar vein, Olson gives the following objection to the pattern view:

> Suppose we ask which pattern a given person might be. If there are such things as patterns, this human organism now instantiates many of them. There is, for instance, the pattern consisting of the current orientation of my limbs, and the pattern formed by the flow of material through my gut. Which pattern am I? Since I am conscious and thinking, I must be the one that instantiates those mental properties. The pattern view presupposes that of all the patterns instantiated here, one of them, and only one, can think. That's because there is just one thinking being here, namely me. But which of those patterns is the one that thinks? Of all the patterns the organism instantiates, what could make just one of them conscious? I have no idea how to answer this question.[20]

But a more basic problem with the view that we are patterns is that there just aren't any such things as patterns. There are patterned objects – or, as Olson puts it, "instances of patterns"[21] – but no reason at all to think that, in addition to the patterned objects, there is some *additional* object, the pattern. If you have a chessboard, for example, that chessboard will be patterned in a certain way – the pieces will be in some locations rather than others. But there is no reason to think that, *in addition* to the chessboard and the pieces on the chessboard, there is this *other* thing, the pattern. So, the notion that we are patterns strikes me as dubious, in part because it requires a more general ontology which is dubious, namely an ontology according to which there are such things as patterns.

9.2.5 Simulations

The most straightforward account of what we would be if we were uploaded persons is that we would be *virtual* or *simulated* objects. Here, what I have

---

[20] Olson 2017: 48–49; cf. 2022: 398–399.
[21] Olson 2017: 49.

in mind is a *sui generis* sort of object, distinct from a computer or network of computers, which nevertheless depends on a computer or network of computers for its existence. David Chalmers has recently defended this sort of view regarding virtual objects in general – that is, that there are or could be purely virtual objects simulated in a computer.[22] Similarly, Eric Steinhart argues that after "uploading" ourselves to computers, we will become virtual objects (objects which he claims are nevertheless physical because they supervene on computers, which are physical things).[23] While virtual objects are not all simulated objects, and perhaps simulated objects are not all virtual objects, in this case I will use "virtual" and "simulated" more or less interchangeably. This is because an uploaded person, conceived as a virtual object, will also be a simulated object (namely, a simulation of the flesh-and-blood human being who is purportedly uploaded), and conversely an uploaded person, conceived as a simulated object, will also be a virtual object.

It's difficult to give a fuller positive characterization of what these simulated objects are supposed to be. But I will charitably assume that Chalmers and other proponents of these objects have a positive conception of what these objects are supposed to be. For my part, I have enough to go on to discuss the proposal, and in particular to present what I take to be severe difficulties for the proposal.

Here is an initial question we can ask about this proposal: Are we now the sorts of things which could become simulated objects? Well, presumably if we are *now* simulated objects (if, say, we are now living in a computer simulation), then we would not have a problem. But what if we are immaterial souls, or composite physical objects? Suppose, for example, that we are organisms. Are organisms the sorts of things that could become simulated objects? I don't know how to answer this sort of question. A simulated object certainly seems to be a very different sort of thing than an organism (organisms, e.g., don't depend on computers for their existence). But I don't have clear intuitions about whether that would prevent an organism from becoming a simulated object, and nor am I sure my intuition on that matter would be reliable.

---

[22] Chalmers 2005, 2017, 2022. I'm not sure whether Chalmers would endorse the view that *we* would be these sorts of simulated objects if we were to upload ourselves. But given his general view about the ontology of simulated objects, it is natural to wonder whether *we* could be included among those simulated objects, were we to upload ourselves.

[23] Steinhart 2014. Cf. Pollock (2008: 276), who claims that virtual objects implemented on physical systems would be physical objects.

I do, however, have the following two objections to this proposed ontology of uploaded persons.

Objection 1: Gratuitous Ontology

First, there are no such things as simulated objects. On the current proposal, remember, simulated objects are not computers or networks of computers, but are rather *sui generis* entities (although they are presumably causally produced by, or grounded in, the activities of computers). And it is hard to see why we should believe in such things. Simply because a computer simulates, say, an apple, it does not follow that it would thereby create a *new* object, a simulated apple. When a computer simulates an apple, we are only tempted to think there exists a simulated apple because in simulating the apple the computer creates visual outputs resembling an apple: We are presented with a screen, the pixels of which are configured to look like an apple. But it would be naive to think that because the pixels are configured in that manner, there therefore really does exist some object which is the referent of the phrase "the virtual apple." I am not suggesting that there is some object, a virtual apple, which isn't a *real* apple. Rather, I am suggesting that there just isn't any such object there. There's just a computer keeping track of what pixels to light up in what way so that viewers of those pixels are presented with the image of an apple. And we should say the same thing if the image of the apple is *very* detailed, or if the simulation of the apple comes to include other sense modalities (e.g., taste, touch, smell), or if the apple-ish sensations are produced by direct neural stimulation, rather than pixels on a screen.

In short: Simulations are *ontologically gratuitous*. This point is reinforced by the fact that, as Neil McDonnell and Nathan Wildman note, nonsimulated objects are causally sufficient to cause all of our experiences (e.g., our visual impressions of a simulated apple). It follows that if simulated objects (e.g., a simulated apple) cause our experiences, then those experiences will be causally overdetermined. But this is an indication that we simply don't need to postulate simulated objected in order to explain our experiences.[24] The point here is not that an object *must* be causally nonredundant in order to exist. It's that if an object *is* causally redundant, then we will, accordingly, have fewer grounds for thinking it exists. For example, we will not need to postulate the object in order to causally explain any observable phenomena, such as our experiences of simulations.[25]

[24] McDonnell and Wildman 2019.
[25] This undermines one of Chalmers's arguments for the existence of simulated objects, from the alleged fact that those objects exercise causal powers. See Chalmers 2017: 317–318, 2022: Ch. 10.

Objection 2: Objectionable Antirealism

My second concern with the view that uploaded persons would be virtual or simulated objects is that there is an objectionable sort of antirealism or response-dependence involved in something simulating something else. Whether something is a simulation of something else seems to be mainly a matter of whether its structure is isomorphic to the structure of the thing simulated in a way that *we* recognize to be isomorphic, since, broadly interpreted, it is easy to find ways in which things' structures are isomorphic to other things' structures in *some* way or other. Here is a simple example which illustrates this point. One way to simulate a battle is to have a complex visual simulation of the battle on a computer. Yet another way to simulate the battle is to have little plastic figurine soldiers on a table. And yet another way to simulate the battle would be to pretend that some raisins on the ground are soldiers. These three different simulations are vastly different in terms of their physical constitution – one involves a visual pattern produced on the pixels of a computer screen, one involves plastic figurines on a table, and one involves dried fruit sitting on the ground. And yet they all count as simulations of the battle, primarily because *we* recognize them to be simulations of the battle. There seems to be no response-independent fact of the matter about what is "really" a simulation of the battle. There may be a fact of the matter regarding which system better or more accurately simulates the battle, given our cognitive architecture, background beliefs, goals in constructing the simulation, and so on. But, again, these are response-dependent properties of the systems in question. So, the element of antirealism here seems inescapable. It is something like this point which is recognized in the following passage from Greg Egan's novel *Permutation City*:

> Human beings were embodied, ultimately, in fields of fundamental particles – incapable, surely, of being anything other than themselves. Copies were embodied in computer memories as vast sets of *numbers*. Numbers which certainly *could be* interpreted as describing a human body sitting in a room ... but it was hard to see that meaning as intrinsic, as *necessary*, when tens of thousands of arbitrary choices had been made about the way in which the model had been coded. *Is this my blood sugar here ... or my testosterone level? Is this the firing rate of a motor neuron as I raise my right hand ... or a signal coming in from my retina as I watch myself doing it?* Anybody given access to the raw data, but unaware of the conventions, could spend a lifetime sifting through the numbers without deciphering what any of it meant.

In response to Chalmers (2017), Claus Beisbart (2019: 311–312) also argues that simulated objects are ontologically gratuitous and conflict with the constraint on theory choice that we should not multiply entities beyond necessity.

9.2 Obscure and Problematic Ontology

But surely we should not endorse this sort of antirealism with respect to simulated *persons*. Whether I continue to exist after being "uploaded" is not response-dependent – after the "uploading" process, I either exist or I don't, and it doesn't seem to be a response-dependent matter whether I exist. But if I were a simulated or virtual object after the uploading process, then presumably it *would* be a response-dependent matter whether I exist, since it would be a response-dependent matter whether the processes running on the computer into which I have allegedly been uploaded simulated me or simulated me with sufficient accuracy. So, we could not be simulated or virtual objects.[26]

Is there any way out of this objection for those who think that we *could* be simulated or virtual objects? My own solution to the antirealism concern regarding simulations is to reject belief in simulated persons, conceived as *sui generis* simulated objects (rather than, say, computers, or networks of computers). Another solution to the problem forms the basis for the plot of *Permutation City*, the novel quoted above. The solution is extreme: simulated persons are ubiquitous, and implemented in far more systems than we normally think, including systems whose components are spatially and temporally scattered. Egan calls the theory that simulated persons are ubiquitous in this way the "dust theory," because even a cloud of dust could implement any arbitrary simulation, since the particles of dust could be mapped onto the components of the thing being simulated (e.g., the particles composing the object being simulated).

An initial worry for the dust theory is given by Chalmers: If there were so many simulated persons, implemented in so many varied physical systems (physical systems whose components can occur in pretty much any temporal or spatial permutation), then we should not expect to find ourselves with the sorts of coherent and long-lived conscious experiences we actually find ourselves with.[27] This is because, given how ubiquitous simulated persons are, and how easily any such person is implemented (there being few if any requirements on the spatial or temporal configuration of the components of the system implementing that simulated person), then most such persons would not have the sorts of coherent and long-lived experiences which we have. Since the persons with noncoherent and short-lived experiences

---

[26] The argument given in this paragraph assumes that we should reject conventionalism with respect to personal identity over time, according to which whether we persist in any given scenario is largely a matter of whether human agents judge (or would judge) that we persist in that scenario (see, e.g., Braddon-Mitchell and Miller 2004; Longenecker 2022). Conventionalism regarding personal identity over time strikes me as very implausible, but it would be too much of a digression to discuss the matter in detail here.

[27] Chalmers 2022: Ch. 21.

greatly outnumber the persons with coherent and long-lived experiences, any given person should expect to find themself among the persons with noncoherent and short-lived experiences. The fact, then, that we each find ourselves with relatively coherent and long-lived experiences indicates that the persons with noncoherent and short-lived experiences don't after all greatly outnumber the persons with coherent and long-lived experiences, and so the dust theory is plausibly false.

Unfortunately, this objection to the dust theory does not work. Even if most persons simulated in the "dust" do not have coherent and long-lived experiences, it may nevertheless be true that, of the persons which have the sorts of coherent and long-lived experiences we do, most such persons are simulated.[28] So, the fact that we have these coherent and long-lived mental lives does not obviously show that we are not among the simulated persons implemented in the dust.

Here is a better reason not to believe the "dust theory." Given the dust theory we should conclude on statistical grounds that we are simulations implemented in the "dust" – that is, in an arbitrary scattered physical system – rather than the nonsimulated persons we generally think we are. But if we are simulations randomly implemented in the dust, then all of our experiences and thought processes are also randomly implemented in the dust. Once we recognize this, we lose whatever grounds we had for thinking that the dust theory is true in the first place – we no longer should trust our empirical evidence, and we no longer should trust the lines of reasoning which led us to endorse the dust theory. If this is right, then the dust theory is epistemically unstable: If you believe the theory, then you undermine your grounds for believing in the theory.[29]

There is another more promising response to the antirealism concern regarding simulations, one which can maintain belief in simulated persons whose existence is not mind- or response-dependent, but which does not, like the dust theory, go so far as to say that simulated persons are implemented in more or less any complex physical system. To understand the response, we should first note that the dust theory is a variant or relative of pancomputationalism: If all it takes for a physical system to implement a given computation is for there to be a mapping between components of the

---

[28] Cf. A similar point made by Dogramaci 2020 regarding Boltzmann brains, brains formed through the chance coalescence of particles.

[29] An argument similar to this one is sometimes given for why we should not believe that we are Boltzmann brains, even if, in sufficiently large regions of space or periods of time, most persons with experiences like ours are Boltzmann brains. See Carroll 2016: 92, 2021; Chalmers 2018: footnote 14, 2022: Ch. 24; Dogramaci 2020.

physical system and the state transitions of the computation, then, if we are creative enough, we can come up with mappings between the components of almost any complex physical system and the state transitions of all sorts of computations, and so almost any complex physical system will implement all sorts of computations.[30] How this is relevant to simulated persons: If all it takes to simulate a person is to implement the right computations, and computations are ubiquitous in the way that pancomputationalism says it is, then simulated persons will be ubiquitous as well.

Chalmers offers the following response to the dust theory, as well as to pancomputationalism:[31] Some particular computation will be implemented in some particular physical system only if the right sort of causal connections hold between the components of that physical system. In the case of simulations specifically: In order for some physical system (such as a computer) to implement some particular simulation, the causal structure which obtains in the system being simulated must be replicated in the simulation. This requirement is not trivial and does not hold of arbitrary complex physical systems.

I think this may work as a response to the dust theory and as a response to pancomputationalism. But it does not resolve the concern with which we began, that there is an element of antirealism in our deciding which physical system counts as a simulation of some particular person. In the case of mind uploading, we can't use causal structure as an objective determinant of which person is being simulated, since, given the real-world computer architecture on which simulations are implemented, the causal structure in a computer simulation of a person will not match the causal structure of the flesh-and-blood person being simulated. We can't replicate the same web of causal relations in the simulation, since the simulated objects and their causal relations are implemented on an underlying hardware whose causal relations are very different from the causal relations entered into by the components of the person being simulated. Here is a simplified example which illustrates the point I'm trying to make. In the case of a flesh-and-blood human being, the firing of neuron A may directly cause neuron B to fire. But in a computer simulating neurons A and B, the simulated firing of simulated neuron A will not directly cause the simulated firing of simulated neuron B. At most the firing of simulated neuron A will *indirectly* cause the firing of simulated neuron B, by way of the computer hardware acting as a causal intermediary. I say "at most" because it is not obvious that even these

---

[30] See Putnam 1983: Appendix; Searle 1992.
[31] Chalmers 2022: Ch. 21. See also Chalmers 1994, 1996b; Chrisley 1994.

indirect causal relations will be implemented. The firing of the simulated neurons may be epiphenomena, while the underlying physical hardware implementing the simulation does all the causal work. In that case, the underlying computer hardware will cause the firings of both simulated neurons, and the simulated neurons themselves will cause nothing. This epiphenomenalist view seems plausible in light of the fact that, as I noted above, the causal activities of the computer implementing the simulation are sufficient to causally explain everything that happens in the simulation.

Whether the simulated neurons are epiphenomena or they only indirectly causally interact with other simulated neurons, in either case the causal structure implemented in the flesh-and-blood person is not replicated in the simulation.

Here is a second objection to Chalmers's causal structure approach to simulations. There is a practical difficulty: How much causal structure is enough to simulate the person? When it comes to most simulations, there need be no crucial threshold – we can simply replicate the causal structure of the system in question to greater or lesser degrees of accuracy. But in the case of mind uploading, there will presumably be some threshold necessary degree of accuracy in order to preserve the personal identity of the simulated person. So, must we replicate the causal structure implemented by every subatomic component of their body? This is the least arbitrary answer unless we implausibly accept antirealism with respect to simulated persons, or something like the dust theory (i.e., a simulation of a person to any degree of accuracy results in a simulated version of that person). But then mind uploading is much less feasible than it otherwise would be.[32]

Finally, here is a third objection to Chalmers's causal structure approach to simulations. In what is the causal structure implemented? There are a few possibilities, each of which is problematic. First, the causal structure may be implemented in the simulated person. This will not work. The simulated person's existing is a precondition for their implementing any causal structure. So, we face a bootstrapping problem: In order to bring some simulated person into existence, we must ensure that they implement the appropriate causal structure, but the causal structure can only be implemented in some preexisting medium. In other words, we can't bring the simulated person into existence by ensuring that they implement the required causal structure, since they must exist *before* any causal structure can be implemented in them. So, Chalmers should contend that something

---

[32] For a more general discussion of how we might go about determining similarity relations between causal structures, see Eva et al. 2019.

other than the simulated person implements the relevant causal structure, and this will somehow ensure that the correct person is simulated. But the "something else" in question cannot be simulated objects (e.g., simulated neurons), as we would then face an infinite regress: We will need to implement the right sort of causal structure in some *other* objects, in order to ensure that we bring these simulated objects into existence, and if those *other* objects are also simulated, then we will need yet further objects to implement the right causal structure, and so on. What Chalmers should say, then, is that the causal structure must be implemented not in the simulated person, and not in any other simulated objects, but in some *non*simulated object(s), presumably the computer or network of computers running the simulation. This way we avoid an infinite regress of simulated objects, and we avoid the bootstrapping problem, since the computer or network of computers already exists prior to our implementing a causal structure in them. But if it is the computer or network of computers implementing the relevant causal structure, then we face significant pressure to identify the simulated person with the computer or network of computers, and so abandon the ontology of simulated persons according to which they are *sui generis* simulated objects. Suppose, for example, that a computer simulates someone's brain and implements all the causal structure implemented in that brain. In this case, rather than having, say, the firing of one simulated neuron directly cause the firing of a second simulated neuron, we would instead have the firing of one physical, but nonbiological, neuron directly cause the firing of a second physical but nonbiological neuron, in precisely the manner in which the firing of some neuron of the flesh-and-blood human directly causes the firing of another one of their neurons. Perhaps we could, in principle, build a computer or network of computers of this sort. But then we would essentially have constructed a robot (or something much like a robot), and it's hard to see why we should not simply identify the "simulated" person with this robot. What reasons do we have to suppose that, in addition to the robot, there is a *sui generis* virtual person as well? Wouldn't those reasons also lead us to conclude that, in the case of a biological human organism, we also have a *sui generis* virtual person? But I'm not aware of any philosophers who think that we are at present virtual or simulated objects, paired with our biological bodies. The view seems to be unmotivated. And I suggest that it would be similarly unmotivated in the case of a robot (or something much like a robot) whose components replicate the causal structure in the components of my brain or body.

Those were some difficulties with the causal structure approach to simulations. Here is another, similar, approach. Chalmers might claim that what matters is not that the causal structure of some simulated person matches the causal structure of the flesh-and-blood person being simulated, but rather that the *structure of counterfactual relations* in the simulated person matches the structure of counterfactual relations in the flesh-and-blood person being simulated.[33] What I have in mind is something like this. Suppose that some flesh-and-blood person's brain is such that if neuron A fires, then neuron B fires, and if neuron A does not fire, then neuron B does not fire. The structure of counterfactual relations will be implemented in our simulation of the person in question if simulated neurons A and B are such that if simulated neuron A fires, then simulated neuron B fires, and if simulated neuron A does not fire, then simulated neuron B does not fire. This structure of counterfactual relations can obtain even if the *causal* structure of the nonsimulated neurons does not match the causal structure of the simulated neurons – even if, for example, the firing of nonsimulated neuron A directly causes the firing of nonsimulated neuron B, while the firing of simulated neuron A does not directly cause the firing of simulated neuron B (and perhaps does not even indirectly cause the firing of simulated neuron B).

This counterfactual structure view seems to resolve the first concern I had with the causal structure view, that in the case of a simulated person the causal structure of the components of the simulation would not match the causal structure of the components of the flesh-and-blood person being simulated. But the counterfactual structure view still faces the other concerns I had regarding the causal structure view. First, there is the concern that, barring antirealism and the dust theory, the least arbitrary degree of precision with which the counterfactual structure in some person must be replicated in a simulation is perfect precision, or at least a precise replication of the counterfactual structure implemented in all of one's atomic components. And this makes constructing simulated persons far less feasible than it otherwise would be. Second, there is the bootstrapping concern. In what is the counterfactual structure implemented? If it is implemented in the simulated person themself, then it is hard to see how they could be bootstrapped into existence: In order to exist, they must implement the right counterfactual structure, but in order to implement that counterfactual structure they must already exist. We cannot say that the counterfactual structure is implemented in some other simulated objects (e.g., simulated neurons), or we face an infinite regress, as the existence of

---

[33] In response to the "dust theory," Chalmers (2022: Ch. 21) sometimes focuses on the structure of counterfactual relations implemented in a simulation, rather than the causal structure.

those simulated objects will in turn depend on some relevant counterfactual structure being implemented in some *other* simulated objects. And, finally, if the counterfactual structure is implemented in some preexisting physical system, presumably a computer or network of computers, then we will face considerable pressure to abandon the ontology of *sui generis* simulated objects and simply identify the "simulated" person with the physical system implementing the counterfactual structure.

The counterfactual structure view faces an additional problem as well, a problem which was not faced by the causal structure view. As Klein notes,[34] whether some counterfactual holds true in the case of a computation (and, we might add, in the case of a simulation) can depend on factors that don't seem relevant to whether the computation is implemented. For example, suppose that, simply given the physical computer implementing a simulation, there would be some true counterfactual to the effect that were simulated neuron A to fire then simulated neuron B would fire. But I am standing by with a hammer, and I will smash and destroy the computer should simulated neuron A fire, before simulated neuron B would have a chance to fire. So, simply because I am standing by with that hammer, it is not true that were simulated neuron A to fire then simulated neuron B would fire. And this is the case even if as a matter of fact simulated neuron A never *does* fire, and so even if I never use my hammer. It seems, then, that whether the structure of counterfactual relations entered into by the simulation matches the structure of counterfactual relations entered into by the thing being simulated can depend on external factors of this sort (e.g., my standing by with the hammer). But those external factors seem to be irrelevant to whether some computer implements a given simulation, and by the same token seem to be irrelevant to whether some simulated person exists.

I conclude that the antirealism concern regarding simulated persons persists. One straightforward response to the concern, the dust theory, is unacceptable. And appealing to causal or counterfactual structure as a mind-independent ground for some simulation's being a simulation of one particular person rather than another also does not seem to work.

9.3 How Do You Move Someone into a Computer?

Above I wrote that the ontology of uploaded persons is obscure and that various proposed ontologies of uploaded persons are problematic. Here is

---

[34] Klein 2008: 145.

an additional worry for the notion that uploading ourselves to computers is a feasible strategy for thwarting death. The problem lies with the idea that we can move a person into a computer by way of the processes involved in fast mind uploading, namely by way of a transfer of information regarding the body, brain, or mind of a person. Note that the problem I have in mind does not obviously affect *gradual* uploading, where the parts of our bodies or brains are gradually replaced until they are entirely artificial. I will return to this point below, after I describe the problem with fast uploading. The sort of "fast" uploading I have in mind is the uploading which would occur in a whole sale transfer or simulation or emulation of our mental states, or of the physical states of our bodies or brains (in, e.g., the sort of "mind uploading" which would occur in whole-brain emulation). This sort of uploading is "fast," not in the sense that the entire process must occur very quickly (after all, scanning my brain in detail may in principle be a slow process). Rather, it is "fast" in the sense that, once a computer has whatever information is required in order to simulate or emulate my mental and/or physical states, the simulation or emulation can be turned on rather quickly, at which point, it is alleged, I myself will be transferred into the computer in some sense. Gradual uploading, by contrast, has no such definitive moment at which, it is alleged, I am transferred into a computer, since gradual uploading involves only the gradual replacement of my parts with artificial parts.

So, with those preliminary points out of the way, here is my concern with fast uploading. For fast uploading to work, it would have to be the case that a mere transfer of information into a computer (i.e., information regarding our mental and/or physical states) would move *us* into the computer. But it seems implausible that we could move someone into a computer simply by transferring information regarding that person into the computer. Normally, when we move someone from one location to another, we do so by moving some particular physical object, their body. (Even if we are unlocated immaterial souls, there is a *sense* in which we move from one location to another by moving our bodies. After all, even if I am an unlocated immaterial soul, there is something right about the statement "I have been to the United States" and something wrong about the statement "I have been to Mars," and what's right about the former statement seems to be that my body has been in the United States, while what's wrong about the latter statement is that my body has never been on Mars.) But in fast mind uploading, you simply move some information from one place to another – for example, from a brain, by way of a scanning device, to a computer. Why, then, would that cause the *person* to move from one location to another? This does not strike me as something which simply *couldn't* happen, in the sense that it is metaphysically impossible. Rather, it just strikes me as something which is very unlikely to *actually* happen. The transfer of information, all by itself, should not have any tendency to move a person *described* by that information. To suppose otherwise, we will require some gratuitous addition to our total theory, to account for the link between the information and the person. For example, we may need some metaphysical law which says that the person goes where the information goes. Or we may need a God who is, for some reason, willing to move the person to where the information goes.[35]

Here is another way of seeing the worry I have. The process of mind uploading involves a transfer of information into a computer, and in particular a transfer of information regarding the psychological and/or physical properties of the person who we are attempting to upload. *Why* would the person follow the information into the computer? How do they even know where to go? Suppose the information is broadcast into space in all directions, and only at one particular point in space, several light-years away, is the information used to construct a simulation or a robot with your psychological traits. Since it takes so long for signals to pass between here and there, your simulation or robot is constructed years before anyone here knows that it has been constructed. How could what happens to you possibly track what happens several light-years away, especially if there is, for several years, no causal signal sent back to where you are on Earth? How does the composite object you are, or the soul you are, "know" to travel all the way to that extremely distant destination in order to inhabit that computer or robot? What is needed here is some mechanism which links you with the information transferred, even at vast distances, and even when the current location of the information (e.g., the robot on Alpha Centauri with your psychological states) has not yet sent any causal signal to your

---

[35] The objection to fast uploading given in this paragraph is similar to an objection to mind uploading given in Corabi and Schneider 2014, except that they lay more stress on the fact that an uploaded person's location would be discontinuous with their location prior to uploading, something they regard as implausible. Van Inwagen (1996, 2002) gives a similar objection to psychological continuity theories of personal identity. Van Inwagen's concern is that materialism is in tension with the idea that personal identity over time tracks psychological continuity. This is because if personal identity over time tracked psychological continuity, then we would be able to move a physical object (e.g., you or me) just by transferring information regarding our psychological states. But it is implausible that we could move a physical object simply by this sort of transfer of information. Olson (2017, 2022: 392–395) gives a similar objection to mind uploading, except that what we thinks is problematic about moving a person merely by way of a transfer of information is that this does not involve any physical continuity between the preupload person and the postupload person. Finally, Hauskeller (2012: 199) and Goldwater (2021) also raise a similar objection to mind uploading.

current or former location (e.g., Earth). And that there is a mechanism of this sort just seems wildly implausible, whether we are composite objects or souls. The only mechanism I can think of which might possibly work is God's moving you to where the information is, but then, in order to make it probable that the transfer of information would move *you*, we'd need some reason to think that God would care to move you several light-years just because information regarding your psychological and/or physical states has moved that distance.

Note that the problem I am pressing is applicable regardless of which of the accounts of personal ontology discussed in this book we endorse (other than the nonself thesis, which is incompatible with any movement of a person from one place to another, since it is incompatible with the existence of people). The problem is to provide some mechanism to account for the fact that in mind uploading a person is moved simply by way of a transfer of information. And this problem applies whether one thinks that we are immaterial souls or whether one instead thinks that we are composite physical objects.[36]

Why then do proponents of mind uploading think that moving information regarding my psychological or physical properties would move *me*? One sometimes gets the impression that proponents of mind uploading seem to think that simply by making someone who is alot like me in various respects (e.g., psychologically) we will thereby ensure that that person is *me*.[37] But there is no good reason to think that someone alot like me will automatically *be* me.[38] That being said, however, Michael Huemer has recently argued for something like this theory of personal identity, although not in the context of a discussion of mind uploading, and his argument is worth addressing.[39] The thought is this. Suppose that time is infinite into the past and the future. If you exist for only a finite period of time, what is the probability that the time at which you would exist would overlap with *this* time, right now? The probability would be 0, given that time is infinite. But if you exist for an *infinite* period of time (if, say, you keep coming back in an eternal recurrence-type situation), then it would be much less improbable that you exist now. So, your existence now is evidence for the view you will exist for an infinite period of time. And one natural way for us

---

[36] Corabi and Schneider (2014: 135–137) make the same point regarding their similar objection to mind uploading.
[37] Presumably, an antibranching clause will need to be included here, however, since two or more individuals who are each simultaneously "alot like me in various respects" could not all be numerically identical with me, since they are not numerically identical with each other.
[38] Cf. Hopkins 2012: 235; Olson 2022: 390–392.
[39] See Huemer 2021.

to exist for an infinite period of time is for there to be an infinite number of qualitative duplicates of ourselves in the past and future, and for the nature of personal identity to be such that we are each identical with any of our qualitative duplicates in the past or future. This argument is very intriguing, but it does not show that mind uploading preserves personal identity, for three reasons. First: I do not think that we can take it for granted that time is infinite in the past, and while Huemer gives arguments for the thesis that past time is infinite, I do not think that these arguments are convincing. Second: Even if it's probability 0 that you only exist for a finite stretch of time which overlaps with the present time, it simply does not follow that you are identical with your qualitative duplicates in the past or future. You might exist for an infinite number of years, but not be identical with just any qualitative duplicate in the past or future. This shows that Huemer's argument does not demonstrate that the nature of personal identity is such that we are each identical with any of our qualitative duplicates in the past or future, even if we accept his view that time stretches infinitely into the past and future. Third: In fast mind uploading as it is generally conceived there is mental similarity but little physical similarity. After all, computers generally do not have much physical resemblance to human beings. So, even if we endorse a theory of personal identity according to which someone in the future sufficiently qualitatively like you is thereby numerically identical to you, mind uploading may not involve the right sort of similarity, or the right degree of similarity, to preserve personal identity.

The concerns I have presented in this section have been directed specifically against fast uploading. In gradual uploading, it seems less mysterious that you would "move" into the computer or robot. Recall that in gradual uploading the parts of one's body or brain are gradually replaced by synthetic parts, so that at the end of the process one's body or brain is composed entirely of synthetic parts. If each step of the process preserves personal identity, then presumably one would exist at the end of the process as well, and presumably one would be entirely synthetic (i.e., a robot, or a computer, or something like that), or related to a synthetic body in whatever way one was originally related to one's biological body (e.g., a soul paired with a computer, which was previously paired with a biological body).

Chalmers presents a sorites argument for the conclusion that just this sort of gradual replacement of one's parts would preserve personal identity: If each step of the process (i.e., each part replacement) preserves personal identity, then the whole process will preserve personal identity.[40] But he

---

[40] Chalmers 2010: 52–55. Cf. Walker 2008.

goes on to present a sorites argument regarding the *speed* with which one's parts are replaced: If a gradual replacement of parts preserves personal identity, then progressively faster replacements of one's parts should also preserve personal identity. In the limiting case, all of one's parts are replaced instantaneously. So, we are led from thinking that gradual uploading preserves personal identity to the conclusion that fast uploading preserves personal identity as well. If that's right, then my argument against fast uploading might after all show that gradual uploading does not preserve personal identity. Alternatively, if we accept Chalmers's argument for the conditional claim that fast uploading preserves personal identity if gradual uploading does, and if we think that gradual uploading does preserve personal identity, then we should conclude that fast uploading preserves personal identity, and any argument I give to the contrary fails.

But I think that we should be suspicious of these sorts of sorites arguments regarding personal identity. Consider a sorites argument exactly analogous to Chalmers's argument, where my parts are gradually removed or destroyed but not replaced. Some philosophers think that this sort of argument shows that I do not exist, since I do not exist after all of my parts are destroyed, and there is no point in the process of having my parts destroyed where it seems plausible that I would cease to exist.[41] And if I don't exist, then I can't be uploaded. So, if a sorites argument of this sort should lead me to think that I do not exist, then presumably Chalmers's exactly analogous sorites argument should not lead me to think that I could survive uploading, since we can't endorse both arguments. The point I am gesturing toward is one which I think that many philosophers would endorse, that we should be suspicious of sorites arguments in general. Even if you encounter one sorites argument which seems to you to be plausible, there is likely an analogous sorites argument for an incompatible, or at any rate unacceptable, conclusion.

One way out of the sorites argument against my own existence would be to endorse the view that I am simple, or composed of so few parts that the removal of one of them really would cause me to go out of existence. But if this response to the sorites argument against my own existence works, then we could give a similar response to Chalmers's sorites argument for uploading – for example, we could say that the replacement of one of my parts with a synthetic part *would* cause me to go out of existence, since I'm a simple, and so to replace that one part means that you would replace *me*, and I can't survive *that*.

---

[41] Unger 1979a gives this sort of argument for the view that he does not exist.

Alternatively, perhaps what the sorites argument where my parts are gradually destroyed or replaced shows is that I can exist without any parts, even if I am currently a composite object, or, if I am an immaterial soul, that I can exist in a disembodied state, without any body parts. If this is our reaction to a sorites argument where my parts are destroyed and not replaced, then the lesson to draw from these sorts of arguments may just be that we are very modally flexible, since we can exist in such a wide variety of conditions, including conditions in which we have no parts (despite the fact that we are currently composite objects) or no body parts (despite the fact that we are currently embodied). And if that's right, then perhaps mind uploading really would preserve personal identity, although not for any special reason having to do with the processes involved in mind uploading – for example, not because those processes preserve psychological continuity. Rather, sorites arguments of the sort presented by Chalmers may just lead us to think that we can survive almost any sort of change, or at any rate any sort of change which can be partitioned out gradually, instead of merely all at once.

9.4 Practical Lessons

Are there any practical lessons we might draw from the forgoing discussion of mind uploading and personal identity? There are two questions in particular which interest me here: (1) How should we behave toward (apparent) simulated persons? (2) Should we try to upload ourselves in order to thwart death?

Start with the first question. While we currently do not have any conscious simulated persons, scientists are actively working to build computer simulations of various human and animal brain structures, with the eventual goal for some researchers being the simulation of an entire human brain.[42] So, it makes sense to begin trying to answer the question of what sorts of ethical guidelines we should follow when we think we might have created a conscious simulated person, perhaps by way of a whole-brain emulation.[43] Of course, there is the preliminary question of whether we should try to create simulated persons in the first place. These questions are

---

[42] See, e.g., Markram et al. 2015; Amunts et al. 2016; Einevoll et al. 2019.
[43] Some recent work on this issue includes Sparrow 2004; Bancroft 2013; Bostrom and Yudkowsky 2014; Sandberg 2014a, 2014b; Schwitzgebel and Garza 2015, 2020; Mishra 2018; Agar 2020; Liao 2020; Schuklenk 2021; Sinnott-Armstrong and Conitzer 2021; Lawrence and Harris 2021; Shulman and Bostrom 2021.

related. For example, if we are sure that we cannot harm or violate the rights of simulated persons, this would reduce the moral risk in creating them in the first place. On the other hand, if we think that we could harm or violate the rights of simulated persons, or if we are not sure what to think about that, then this would count against trying to create a simulated person. Whether we should attempt to create a simulated person despite these risks will depend on the degree of risk involved, as well as the potential benefits of creating simulated persons (in, e.g., understanding the human brain or reducing the need for animal experimentation).

Despite the moral risks involved, it seems likely that we will eventually create detailed simulations of human persons, although it is unclear whether we will simulate a human brain or mind in exacting detail, or whether we will create a simulated person that we should regard as a conscious subject. It seems advisable that we should exercise caution and try not to do anything that might harm or violate the rights of a simulated person, even if it's unclear whether, on some particular occasion, we really have a simulated person, or rather just a nonconscious computer that behaves alot like a simulated person.[44] Eric Schwitzgebel and Mara Garza[45] suggest, in response to the uncertainty surrounding the moral status of artificial persons, that we should only try to create artificial persons whose moral status is clear. This may be overly cautious. In other contexts, we do not necessarily refrain from creating something whose moral status is unclear to us (perhaps, e.g., fetuses, or certain nonhuman animals). Extra caution in our treatment of the beings whose moral status is unclear may be enough.

In the case of simulated persons, this caution seems advisable regardless of which ontology of simulated persons turns out to be correct. But what other guidelines we should follow in our interactions with simulated persons may depend on which account of the ontology of simulated persons turns out to be correct. For example, if a simulated person is just a computer, then turning off the simulation will presumably not end the existence of the simulated person, since the computer is still there. By contrast, if a simulated person is constituted by, but not identical with,

---

[44] Cf. Sandberg 2014a; Schwitzgebel and Garza 2015, 2020; Agar 2020; Schneider 2020: 453–455. Agar also suggests that you don't date a simulated person, since you might become emotionally attached to something which isn't really conscious. This is good advice. The suggestion that we should exercise caution in our treatment of simulated persons, given our uncertainty regarding their moral status, resembles widely discussed suggestions regarding our treatment of other beings whose moral status is unclear or controversial: e.g., fetuses (Lockhart 2000: Ch. 3; Moller 2011), nonhuman animals (Guerrero 2007; Huemer 2019: 17–21).
[45] Schwitzgebel and Garza 2015, 2020: 465.

the computer(s) on which it is run, and if the computer(s) constitutes the person only when the simulation is run, then if the computer(s) is shut off, or it stops running the simulation, then this may cause the simulated person to go out of existence. Perhaps it will be brought back into existence when the simulation is turned back on. But then again, maybe not. It's not at all clear what to say about this.

Here is a further concern: A computer can easily be taken apart and put back together again. If that happens, is the simulated person run on that computer after the reassembly going to be identical with any simulated person run on the computer before the reassembly? Maybe, maybe not. We don't normally face a similar problem with human beings. In fact, whether a reassembly of the parts of a human body would preserve personal identity is generally only discussed in the context of discussions of the general resurrection. As we have seen in Chapter 8, §8.2, it is controversial whether the sort of reassembly involved in resurrection (assuming the resurrection *would* involve reassembly) would preserve personal identity. I suggested, however, that personal identity could be preserved in a case of resurrection by reassembly with God's help. But when we reassemble a computer, we can't count on God to help us out. So, if we have a simulated person run on a computer, we should be hesitant to take the computer apart, or even to replace any of its parts. (Are some parts more important for the preservation of personal identity? Who knows?) This will create obvious obstacles to our repairing or upgrading these computers.

Yet another concern: Humans are generally located in one fairly well-circumscribed location, namely wherever our brains or bodies are located. But any simulated persons we create are likely to be run on distributed networks of computers or supercomputers with spatially distributed nodes. This may affect the way we treat the computers running the simulations. For simplicity, assume that a simulated person is run on a network of computers, rather than a supercomputer with spatially distributed nodes. If we are concerned that replacing or removing the parts of a computer might not preserve the personal identity of the simulated person run on that computer, we should also be concerned that replacing or removing one or more of the computers on the network of computers running the simulation would similarly fail to preserve the personal identity of that simulated person. We may also worry about the *way* in which the information regarding the simulation is stored among the computers running the simulation. For example, if a large chunk of the stored information regarding the simulated person is transferred from computer A to a geographically distant computer B, this may not change the behavior of the simulation, but it is a significantly different physical configuration than if the information was kept on computer A, especially if computer B was not previously involved in running the simulation. This significant change in the physical configuration of the network of computers may be so large as to destroy the simulated person and replace it with a very similar, but numerically distinct, simulated person. Compare: Normally when we have a macroscopic physical object (and a simulated person might very well be a macroscopic physical object), we worry that that object may not be able to survive fast and large-scale changes in its physical configuration. This is why, for example, we wonder if the Ship of Theseus can survive large changes in its parts. While the story of the Ship of Theseus normally involves a gradual replacement of its parts, our concerns about the identity of the ship would be compounded if the Ship of Theseus changed its parts very quickly. Similarly, a *rapid* change in the physical medium storing information about a simulated person might also result in that simulated person's ceasing to exist. Or, at any rate, this is something we would have to worry about if we create simulated persons.

We mostly don't face these sort of problems when it comes to biological human bodies. This is true even if some sort of "extended mind" thesis is true with respect to human beings, so that our cognitive processes are distributed in some sense beyond the confines of the human body, just as the simulated person's cognitive processes are distributed across a network of computers.[46] If I perform some calculations on a sheet of paper, then my cognitive processes might extend to the sheet of paper. But it does not automatically follow that *I* extend to the sheet of paper, in the sense that I have that sheet of paper as a part, or in the sense that I am "paired" with the sheet of paper in the same way in which I am paired with my body. But it also certainly does not follow that destroying the sheet of paper would risk my destruction.[47]

I've just been discussing the question of how we should behave toward (apparent) simulated persons. Here is the second question I said I would address in this section: Should we try to upload ourselves in order to thwart death? This is not a purely hypothetical question, or something we will only have to figure out at some point in the distant future, since today some people undergo cryonic preservation of their bodies after death, and they must decide whether to leave instructions to the effect that they be "uploaded" rather than resuscitated.[48] Of course, that raises the question of

---

[46] See Clark and Chalmers 1998.
[47] Although see Heersmink 2017 for the contrary view.
[48] Chalmers 2010 also makes this point in his discussion of mind uploading.

9.4 Practical Lessons

whether *cryonics* can be expected to preserve personal identity, and whether it would be a good idea for any of us to try to thwart death via cryonics. Cryonics involves freezing one's body (or part of one's body, such as the head) at death, with the hope that future medical technology will allow the resuscitation of one's frozen corpse. Cryonics strikes me as a much safer bet than mind uploading. The problems noted above for mind uploading do not seem to affect cryonics. The ontology of a resuscitated corpse is no more obscure than personal ontology in general – for example, if we are immaterial souls prior to death, then we would presumably be immaterial souls postresuscitation, and we could say something similar about any other account of personal ontology. This assumes that cryonics involves the preservation of the entire human body. Sometimes cryonics merely involves the preservation of one's head, because this is cheaper and easier. Some accounts of personal ontology may not be compatible with one's continued existence if only one's head is preserved. For example, on some ways of thinking of animalism, you could not survive as a mere head, nor could you survive if your head is attached to a new body, and your original body is destroyed. Perhaps some versions of animalism would also be incompatible with cryonics preserving personal identity, even where the entire body is preserved. This may be the case for versions of animalism which require for persistence over time that the biological processes involved in the maintenance of a life not be halted, or halted in the way in which they would be halted were our bodies to be frozen. But simply from the bare thesis of animalism – that is, from the bare thesis that we are animals – I do not think that it follows that cryonics would not preserve personal identity.

Cryonics also seems to avoid the second worry I raised for mind uploading, that it is problematic to think that we could move into a computer merely by virtue of a transfer of information regarding our mental or physical states into that computer. Cryonics simply requires that you move where your body (or head) moves, and this is compatible with virtually every account of personal ontology other than the nonself thesis. (Again, barring concerns about whether given some versions of animalism you could survive if only your head is preserved.)

Of course, just because cryonics is a *safer* bet than mind uploading, that does not mean that it is a safe bet. There are serious technical hurdles to our resuscitating a frozen corpse, and it is unclear if these technical hurdles can be overcome. What's more, cryonics may not be a prudent or morally permissible bet simply because one's organs, and the large amount of money required to freeze and preserve your body, could be put to much better use elsewhere.[49]

But let's return to the subject of mind uploading. Since scanning a human brain or body at the level of detail required for mind uploading is currently not technically feasible, we don't need to worry about its current monetary cost, since it has none. What's more, it is unclear how expensive this sort of scanning will be in the distant future, when it becomes widely available (if it ever does). So, let's ignore the financial cost of mind uploading. Ignoring financial concerns and assuming we had the technology required to scan the human brain or body in sufficient detail, would it be prudent to try to upload oneself in order to thwart death?

The answer to this question presumably depends on what nonfinancial costs are associated with mind uploading, including opportunity costs. One concern for whole-body cryonics is that the frozen person hogs their organs, which could be used to help other people. This is a cost of cryonics that does not affect mind uploading.

What other nonfinancial costs might be associated with mind uploading primarily depends upon whether the uploading process is destructive or not. Suppose that in order to scan my brain or body in sufficient detail I would have to be alive and healthy before the scanning process begins, and the scanning process will kill me. Note that, at least at first, the most feasible way of scanning the brain or body in sufficient detail probably *would* be fatal – for example, it might very well involve slicing the brain into thousands of slices and scanning the individual slices. Given that it is not clear which account of personal ontology we should adopt, it's not clear that we are the sorts of things which could survive mind uploading, and earlier in this chapter I raised additional concerns for the idea that mind uploading would preserve personal identity. So, this sort of destructive uploading strikes me as being pretty reckless.[50] This point is strengthened when we recognize that mind uploading will probably happen only after considerable technological and medical advances have been made, so that the choice faced by many of those considering uploading will be between uploading on the one hand and living a long and healthy biological life

---

[49] For a discussion of these concerns regarding cryonics, see Minerva 2018: Ch. 2. Note that as of September 2023, Alcor, a leading organization providing cryonic services, charges USD 200,000 for whole-body preservation, and USD 80,000 to preserve just one's head (www.alcor.org/membership/). Other fees apply as well, including annual membership fees which run into hundreds of dollars.

[50] Schneider 2019 also suggests we be very cautious in making use of mind uploading technologies, given the uncertainty surrounding whether mind uploading would preserve personal identity.

on the other hand, rather than uploading on the one hand and imminent death on the other hand.[51]

Still, if the benefits of mind uploading are sufficiently great, perhaps uploading will maximize expected utility, and so, at least from the perspective of expected utility, destructive mind uploading will be prudentially rational, even if we should not assign a high probability to destructive mind uploading preserving personal identity. It is hard to know what to think here, since it is hard to predict in advance what sort of utility we should expect to derive from a successful upload. Uploaded persons could in principle have all sorts of great experiences, but they could have all sorts of terrible experiences as well, and they may be at the mercy of whoever controls the hardware on which the uploaded person is being run. And there are some positive reasons to think that uploaded persons would not have a very high quality of life. As Robin Hanson notes, in a world of easily copied digital persons (including uploaded persons), computational resources will be finite and in high demand. The ability to interact with the physical nonsimulated world in real or faster than real time will require particularly large computational resources. But since uploaded persons are easily copied, it will be difficult to earn one's keep, and so difficult to get one's desired computational resources. Whatever the demand for skilled simulated workers, the demand can easily be met by simply copying the most skilled workers an indefinite number of times. Skilled workers will be far too plentiful. So, one's standard of living as a simulated person may suffer as a result.[52] This assumes, of course, that simulated persons (whether uploaded or not) *could* easily be copied. Whether that's true might depend on which personal ontology of simulated persons is correct. If, for example, simulated persons would be computers, or parts of computers, then it would be much more difficult to copy them, as this would require producing new physical hardware.

The most optimistic proponents of mind uploading predict that mind uploading can give us a form of eternal life, and so, over the long term, *infinite* positive expected utility. Even if it is very unlikely that they are right about that, as long as there is a nonzero probability that they are correct, then mind uploading really would end up having infinite positive expected utility. In that case, it's hard to know what to think about the prudential rationality of destructive mind uploading. After all, if there is a nonzero probability that mind uploading will result in infinite positive

---

[51] This point is made in Agar 2013: Ch. 4, which contains an extended argument for the conclusion that destructive mind uploading is prudentially irrational.
[52] For this and other predictions regarding the lives of simulated persons, see Hanson 2016.

utility over the long term, there is also a nonzero probability that mind uploading will result in infinite *negative* utility over the long term, as there is a nonzero probability that after you are uploaded you will be tortured for all eternity. These same considerations crop up in discussions of Pascal's wager. The debate over Pascal's wager is complex and ongoing. I don't feel qualified to write at length on either Pascal's wager or the analogous issues raised in debates over potentially infinite lifespans in the case of mind uploading. But here is one important consideration which seems to me to be plausible. Perhaps, following a line of thought from some defenders of Pascal's wager,[53] we should say that, when faced with multiple incompatible courses of action, each of which has infinite positive or negative expected utility, our decisions about which actions to choose should be guided by the probabilities of the outcomes of those actions. So, for example, assume that if you were to upload, then there is a .999999 probability that you will experience eternal bliss, and a .000001 probability that you will experience eternal torment. Suppose also that if you choose not to upload yourself, then there is a .000001 probability that you will experience eternal bliss, and a .000001 probability that you will experience eternal torment. Leaving aside other considerations that might factor into your decision, uploading seems to be clearly preferable to refraining from uploading, despite the fact that uploading does not have greater expected utility than refraining from uploading.

So far I have mainly focused on the prudential rationality of destructive uploading. Nondestructive uploading is less risky, at least in one respect: There is less opportunity cost if uploading does not manage to preserve personal identity. Given nondestructive uploading, we might reason that uploading yourself is worth a shot, since at best you become immortal, and at worst you don't lose much of value.[54] Here I assume that your brain or body is scanned prior to death, and the uploaded person is only constructed or activated after you die. After all, if it is constructed or activated prior to your death, then the uploaded person would presumably not be you. Of course, if there is an afterlife, then you very well may exist after your death – say, as a corpse, or a disembodied soul, or a body in some sort of intermediate state – in which case your upload would also presumably not be you. This concern just points toward the fact

---

[53] Jackson and Rogers 2019: §3.2. Jackson and Rogers also note the similarity between debates over Pascal's wager and debates over the prudential rationality of mind uploading (2019: 78).

[54] A similar thought process is employed by the main character in Neal Stephenson's science fiction novel *Fall; or, Dodge in Hell*. Some proponents of cryonics have employed similar reasoning, explicitly modeled after Pascal's wager. See Shaw 2009: 519–521.

that there are various obstacles toward our reasonably thinking that the uploaded person really *would* be you. And these obstacles are pretty large. Nevertheless, if uploading is nondestructive, then you might think that it's worth a shot, even if there is no very good reason to think that it will succeed. But it is important to keep in mind an additional risk, alluded to above, beside the risk that the uploaded person will not be you: even if the uploaded person *will* be you, and even if it is conscious, you still might worry that after you are uploaded you would not have a life worth living. It is hard to know how worried we should be about that possibility.

One more point to note, and then I'll end my discussion of mind uploading. In any discussion of the prudential rationality of mind uploading, we must keep in mind that uploading is likely to be a *transformative experience*. The topic of transformative experience has recently received a great deal of attention.[55] As mind uploading is likely to be a transformative experience, this introduces complications of the sort discussed in the transformative experience literature for what we should say about the prudential rationality of mind uploading. In particular, your desires and preferences can be expected to change dramatically as a result of your radically new mode of life postupload, but it is difficult to predict prior to the upload *how* those desires and preferences will change. When you're trying to figure out whether mind uploading is prudentially rational, you should take into consideration your present desires and preferences, but you should presumably also take into consideration those desires and preferences you can be expected to have postupload. But since uploading would be a transformative experience, you can't take into account those postupload desires and preferences, or at least you will have great difficulty doing so.[56]

---

[55] Much of it in conversation with Paul 2014.
[56] Earlier, I noted that debates over the prudential rationality of mind uploading are similar to debates over Pascal's wager. Chan 2019 notes that religious conversions are often transformative experiences and argues that this observation creates new challenges for those wishing to defend the prudential rationality of religious conversion on the basis of Pascal's wager. Given the similarities between debates over Pascal's wager and debates over the prudential rationality of mind uploading, and given the plausible observation that mind uploading is a transformative experience, Chan's arguments should presumably be taken into consideration by those wondering about the prudential rationality of mind uploading. For a response to Chan, see Jackson and Rogers 2019: §5.7.

References

Adam, M. T. (2010). No self, no free will, no problem: Implications of the *Anattalakkhaṇa Sutta* for a perennial philosophical issue. *Journal of the International Association of Buddhist Studies*, 33(1–2):239–265.

Agar, N. (2013). *Humanity's End: Why We Should Reject Radical Enhancement*. MIT Press, Cambridge, MA.

(2020). How to treat machines that might have minds. *Philosophy and Technology*, 33:269–282.

Albahari, M. (2002). Against no-Ātman theories of anattā. *Asian Philosophy*, 12(1):5–20.

(2006). *Analytical Buddhism: The Two-Tiered Illusion of Self*. Palgrave Macmillan, London.

Al-Ghazālī (2000). *The Incoherence of the Philosophers*. Brigham Young University Press, Provo, second edition. Translated by Michael E. Marmura.

Almeder, R. F. (1992). *Death and Personal Survival: The Evidence for Life after Death*. Rowman and Littlefield, Lanham.

Amunts, K., Ebell, C., Muller, J., Telefont, M., Knoll, A., and Lipper, T. (2016). The human brain project: Creating a European research infrastructure to decode the human brain. *Neuron*, 92(3):574–581.

Anālayo, B. (2018). *Rebirth in Early Buddhism and Current Research*. Wisdom Publications, Somerville.

Anselm (1995). *Monologion and Proslogion: With the Replies of Gaunilo and Anselm*. Hackett, Indianapolis. Translated by Thomas Williams.

Aquinas, T. (1947). *Summa Theologica*. Benziger Bros., New York.

(1975). *Summa Contra Gentiles*. University of Notre Dame Press, Notre Dame.

Armstrong, D. M. (1978). Naturalism, materialism and first philosophy. *Philosophia*, 8:261–276.

(1993). *A Materialist Theory of the Mind*. Routledge, London, revised edition.

(1997). *A World of States of Affairs*. Cambridge University Press, Cambridge.

Audi, P. (2011). Primitive causal relations and the pairing problem. *Ratio*, 24(1):1–16.

Augustine (1991). *The Trinity*. New City Press, Brooklyn.

(1998). *The City of God against the Pagans*. Cambridge University Press, Cambridge.

Averill, E. and Keating, B. F. (1981). Does interactionism violate a law of classical physics? *Mind*, 90(357):102–107.

Avicenna (1959). *Avicenna's De Anima: Being the Psychological Part of Kitāb al-Shifā*, chapter On the Soul. Oxford University Press, London.

Bailey, A. M. (2015). Animalism. *Philosophy Compass*, 10(12):867–883.

(2016). Composition and the cases. *Inquiry*, 59(5):453–470.

(2020a). Magical thinking. *Faith and Philosophy*, 37(2):181–201.

(2020b). Material through and through. *Philosophical Studies*, 177:2431–2450.

(2021). *Monotheism and Human Nature*. Cambridge University Press, Cambridge.

Bailey, A. M. and Brenner, A. (2020). Why composition matters. *Canadian Journal of Philosophy*, 50(8):934–949.

Bailey, A. M., Rasmussen, J., and Horn, L. V. (2011). No pairing problem. *Philosophical Studies*, 154:349–360.

Bailey, A. M. and van Elswyk, P. (2021). Generic animalism. *The Journal of Philosophy*, 118(8):405–429.

Baker, L. R. (1995). Need a Christian be a mind/body dualist? *Faith and Philosophy*, 12(4):489–504.

(2000). *Persons and Bodies: A Constitution View*. Cambridge University Press, Cambridge.

(2001). Material persons and the doctrine of resurrection. *Faith and Philosophy*, 18(2):151–167.

(2005). Death and the afterlife. In Wainwright, W. J., editor, *The Oxford Handbook of Philosophy of Religion*, pages 366–391. Oxford University Press, Oxford.

(2007). Persons and the metaphysics of resurrection. *Religious Studies*, 43(3):333–348.

(2011a). Christian materialism in a scientific age. *International Journal for Philosophy of Religion*, 70(1):47–59.

(2011b). Brains and souls: Grammar and speaking. In Baker, M. C. and Goetz, S., editors, *The Soul Hypothesis: Investigations into the Existence of the Soul*, pages 73–93. Continuum, New York.

Bamford, S. and Danaher, J. (2017). Transfer of personality to a synthetic human ("mind uploading") and the social construction of identity. *Journal of Consciousness Studies*, 24(11–12):6–30.

Bancroft, T. D. (2013). Ethical aspects of computational neuroscience. *Neuroethics*, 6:415–418.

Barker, J. (2020). Debunking arguments and metaphysical laws. *Philosophical Studies*, 177:1829–1855.

Baxter, D. (1988). Many-one identity. *Philosophical Papers*, 17:193–216.

(2014). Identity, discernibility, and composition. In Baxter, D. and Cotnoir, A., editors, *Composition as Identity*, pages 244–253. Oxford University Press, Oxford.

Bayne, T. (2018). Problems with unity of consciousness arguments for substance dualism. In Loose, J. J., Menuge, A. J. L., and Moreland, J. P., editors, *The Blackwell Companion to Substance Dualism*, pages 208–225. Wiley-Blackwell, Hoboken.

Beauregard, M. (2007). Mind does really matter: Evidence from neuroimaging studies of emotional self-regulation, psychotherapy and placebo effect. *Progress in Neurobiology*, 81(4):218–236.

Beauregard, M. and O'Leary, D. (2009). *The Spiritual Brain: A Neuroscientist's Case for the Existence of the Soul*. HarperCollins, New York.

Beebee, H. (2018). Philosophical scepticism and the aims of philosophy. *Proceedings of the Aristotelian Society*, 118(1):1–24.

Beisbart, C. (2019). Virtual realism: Really realism or only virtually so? A comment on D. J. Chalmers's Petrus Hispanus lectures. *Disputatio*, 11(55):297–331.

Bennett, K. (2007). Mental causation. *Philosophy Compass*, 2(2):316–337.

(2008). Exclusion again. In Hohwy, J. and Kallestrup, J., editors, *Being Reduced: New Essays on Reduction, Explanation, and Causation*, pages 280–307. Oxford University Press, Oxford.

(2011). By our bootstraps. *Philosophical Perspectives*, 25:27–41.

(2017). *Making Things Up*. Oxford University Press, Oxford.

Benovsky, J. (2018). *Eliminativism, Objects, and Persons: The Virtues of Non-existence*. Routledge, New York.

Billon, A. (2015). Why are we certain that we exist? *Philosophy and Phenomenological Research*, 91(3):723–759.

(2023). The sense of existence. *Ergo*, 9(68):1806–1848.

Black, D. L. (2008). Avicenna on self-awareness and knowing that one knows. In Rahman, S., Street, T., and Tahiri, H., editors, *The Unity of Science in the Arabic Tradition*, pages 63–87. Springer, Dordrecht.

Blatti, S. (2012). A new argument for animalism. *Analysis*, 72(4):685–690.

Bodhi, B. (2000). *The Connected Discourses of the Buddha: A Translation of the Saṃyutta Nikāya*. Wisdom Publications, Boston.

Bohn, E. D. (2012). Monism, emergence, and plural logic. *Erkenntnis*, 76:211–223.

Bostrom, N. (2003). Are we living in a computer simulation? *The Philosophical Quarterly*, 53(211):243–255.

(2009). The simulation argument: Some explanations. *Analysis*, 69(3):458–461.

Bostrom, N. and Yudkowsky, E. (2014). The ethics of artificial intelligence. In Frankish, K. and Ramsey, W. M., editors, *The Cambridge Handbook of Artificial Intelligence*, pages 316–334. Cambridge University Press, Cambridge.

Braddon-Mitchell, D. and Miller, K. (2004). How to be a conventional person. *The Monist*, 87(4):457–474.

Bradley, D. (2018). Philosophers should prefer simpler theories. *Philosophical Studies*, 175(12):3049–3067.

Brenner, A. (2015a). Mereological nihilism and the special arrangement question. *Synthese*, 192(5):1295–1314.

(2015b). Mereological nihilism and theoretical unification. *Analytic Philosophy*, 56(4):318–337.

(2017a). Mereological nihilism and personal ontology. *The Philosophical Quarterly*, 67(268):464–485.

(2017b). Simplicity as a criterion of theory choice in metaphysics. *Philosophical Studies*, 174(11):2687–2707.

(2018). Science and the special composition question. *Synthese*, 195(2):657–678.

(2020a). Ontological pluralism, Abhidharma metaphysics, and the two truths: A response to Kris McDaniel. *Philosophy East and West*, 70(2):543–557.

(2020b). Rejoinder to Kris McDaniel. *Philosophy East and West*, 70(2):565–569.

(2021). Mereology and ideology. *Synthese*, 198(8):7431–7448.

(2022). How to be a mereological anti-realist. In Buchak, L. and Zimmerman, D. W., editors, *Oxford Studies in Philosophy of Religion*, volume 10, pages 83–119. Oxford University Press, Oxford.

(forthcoming-a). Sense perception and mereological nihilism. *The Philosophical Quarterly*.

(forthcoming-b). Theoretical virtues and the methodological analogy between science and metaphysics. *Synthese*.

(MS-a). Against dismissivism.

(MS-b). Metaphysical laws, ontological innocence, and theory choice.

(MS-c). Personal identity, fission, and arbitrariness.

(MS-d). Presupposition failure and compatibilist semantics in ontology.

Brower, J. E. (2014). *Aquinas's Ontology of the Material World: Change, Hylomorphism, and Material Objects*. Oxford University Press, Oxford.

Brown, W. S. and Strawn, B. D. (2012). *The Physical Nature of Christian Life: Neuroscience, Psychology, and the Church*. Cambridge University Press, Cambridge.

Bryant, A. (2020). Keep the chickens cooped: The epistemic inadequacy of free range metaphysics. *Synthese*, 197(5):1867–1887.

Buddhaghosa, B. (2010). *The Path of Purification: Visuddhimagga*. Buddhist Publication Society, Kandy, fourth edition.

Butler, A. (2015). The problem of believing in yourself: Hume's doubts about personal identity. In Ainslie, D. C. and Butler, A., editors, *The Cambridge Companion to Hume's Treatise*, pages 165–187. Cambridge University Press, New York.

Bynoe, W. and Jones, N. K. (2013). Solitude without souls: Why Peter Unger hasn't established substance dualism. *Philosophia*, 41(1):109–125.

Bynum, C. W. (1995). *The Resurrection of the Body in Western Christianity, 200–1336*. Columbia University Press, New York.

Calosi, C. (2016). Composition is identity and mereological nihilism. *The Philosophical Quarterly*, 66(263):219–235.

Cameron, R. P. (2007). The contingency of composition. *Philosophical Studies*, 136:99–121.

(2012). Composition as identity doesn't settle the special composition question. *Philosophy and Phenomenological Research*, 84:531–554.

(2014). Parts generate the whole, but they are not identical to it. In Baxter, D. and Cotnoir, A., editors, *Composition As Identity*, pages 90–107. Oxford University Press, Oxford.

Carmichael, C. (2011). Vague composition without vague existence. *Noûs*, 45(2):315–327.

Carroll, S. M. (2016). *The Big Picture: On the Origins of Life, Meaning, and the Universe Itself*. Dutton, Boston.

(2021). Why Boltzmann brains are bad. In Dasgupta, S., Dotan, R., and Weslake, B., editors, *Current Controversies in Philosophy of Science*, pages 7–20. Routledge, New York.

Carter, W. R. (1999). Will I be a dead person? *Philosophy and Phenomenological Research*, 59(1):167–171.

Caves, R. L. J. (2018). Emergence for nihilists. *Pacific Philosophical Quarterly*, 99(1):2–28.

Cerullo, M. A. (2015). Uploading and branching identity. *Minds and Machines*, 25:17–36.

Chadha, M. (2021a). Eliminating selves and persons. *Journal of the American Philosophical Association*, 7(3):273–294.

(2021b). Reference, representation, and the meaning of the first-person singular pronoun. *Philosophy East and West*, 71(1):38–56.

Chakrabarti, A. (1982). The Nyāya proofs for the existence of the soul. *Journal of Indian Philosophy*, 10:211–238.

(1992). I touch what I saw. *Philosophy and Phenomenological Research*, 52(1):103–116.

Chalmers, D. J. (1994). On implementing a computation. *Minds and Machines*, 4:391–402.

(1996a). *The Conscious Mind*. Oxford University Press, Oxford.

(1996b). Does a rock implement every finite-state automaton? *Synthese*, 108:309–333.

(2005). The matrix as metaphysics. In Grau, C., editor, *Philosophers Explore the Matrix*, pages 132–176. Oxford University Press, New York.

(2010). The singularity: A philosophical analysis. *Journal of Consciousness Studies*, 17(9–10):7–65.

(2017). The virtual and the real. *Disputatio*, 9(46):309–352.

(2018). Structuralism as a response to skepticism. *The Journal of Philosophy*, 115(12):625–660.

(2022). *Reality+: Virtual Worlds and the Problems of Philosophy*. W. W. Norton, New York.

Chan, R. (2019). Transformed by faith. *Faith and Philosophy*, 36(1):4–32.

Chisholm, R. (1978). Is there a mind-body problem? *Philosophical Exchange*, 2:25–34.

(1994). On the observability of the self. In Cassam, Q., editor, *Self-Knowledge*, pages 94–108. Oxford University Press, Oxford.

Chrisley, R. L. (1994). Why everything doesn't realize every computation. *Minds and Machines*, 4:403–420.

Christensen, D. and Lackey, J., editors (2013). *The Epistemology of Disagreement: New Essays*. Oxford University Press, Oxford.

Churchland, P. (1984). *Matter and Consciousness*. MIT Press, Cambridge, MA.

Clark, A. (2010). There is no non-materialist neuroscience. *Cortex*, 46(2):147–149.

Clark, A. and Chalmers, D. (1998). The extended mind. *Analysis*, 58(1):7–19.

Clayton, P. (2004). *Mind and Emergence: From Quantum to Consciousness*. Oxford University Press, Oxford.

Collins, R. (2008). Modern physics and the energy-conservation objection to mind-body dualism. *American Philosophical Quarterly*, 45(1):31–42.

— (2011). The energy of the soul. In Baker, M. C. and Goetz, S., editors, *The Soul Hypothesis: Investigations into the Existence of the Soul*, pages 123–133. Continuum, New York.

Collins, S. (1982). *Selfless Persons: Imagery and Thought in Theravāda Buddhism*. Cambridge University Press, Cambridge.

Cooper, J. W. (1989). *Body, Soul, and Life Everlasting: Biblical Anthropology and the Monism-Dualism Debate*. Eerdmans, Grand Rapids.

— (2018). "absent from the body ... present with the lord" is the intermediate state fatal to physicalism? In Loftin, R. K. and Farris, J. R., editors, *Christian Physicalism? Philosophical Theological Criticisms*, pages 319–339. Lexington Books, Lanham.

Corabi, J. and Schneider, S. (2014). If you upload, will you survive? In Blackford, R. and Broderick, D., editors, *Intelligence Unbound: The Future of Uploaded and Machine Minds*, pages 131–145. Wiley-Blackwell, Chichester.

Corcoran, K. (1998). Persons and bodies. *Faith and Philosophy*, 15(3):324–340.

— (2001). Physical persons and postmortem survival without temporal gaps. In Corcoran, K., editor, *Soul, Body, and Survival: Essays on the Metaphysics of Human Persons*. Cornell University Press, Ithaca.

— (2006). *Rethinking Human Nature: A Christian Materialist Alternative to the Soul*. Baker Academic, Grand Rapids.

— (2016). Constitution, resurrection, and relationality. In Gasser, G., editor, *Personal Identity and Resurrection: How Do We Survive Our Death?*, pages 191–205. Routledge, London.

Cornell, D. (2017). Mereological nihilism and the problem of emergence. *American Philosophical Quarterly*, 54(1):77–87.

Cotnoir, A. (2013). Composition as general identity. In Bennett, K. and Zimmerman, D. W., editors, *Oxford Studies in Metaphysics*, volume 8, pages 295–322. Oxford University Press, Oxford.

— (2014). Composition as identity. In Baxter, D. and Cotnoir, A., editors, *Composition As Identity*, pages 3–23. Oxford University Press, Oxford.

Craig, W. L. and Moreland, J. P., editors (2009). *The Blackwell Companion to Natural Theology*. Wiley-Blackwell, Chichester.

Cucu, A. C. and Pitts, J. B. (2019). How dualists should (not) respond to the objection from energy conservation. *Mind and Matter*, 17(1):95–121.

Dasgupta, S. (2014). The possibility of physicalism. *The Journal of Philosophy*, 111(9/10):557–592.

Davids, T. W. R., editor (1890). *The Questions of King Milinda*. Clarendon Press, Oxford.
Davis, S. T. (2016). Resurrection, personal identity, and the will of god. In Gasser, G., editor, *Personal Identity and Resurrection: How Do We Survive Our Death?*, pages 19–31. Routledge, London.
DeGrazia, D. (2005). *Human Identity and Bioethics*. Cambridge University Press, Cambridge.
Dennett, D. C. (1991). *Consciousness Explained*. Back Bay Books, Boston.
deRosset, L. (2013). Grounding explanations. *Philosophers' Imprint*, 13(7):1–26.
Descartes, R. (1991). *The Philosophical Writings of Descartes*, volume III: The Correspondence. Cambridge University Press, Cambridge.
 (1996). *Meditations on First Philosophy*. Cambridge University Press, Cambridge.
 (2006). *A Discourse on the Method of Correctly Conducting One's Reason and Seeking Truth in the Sciences*. Oxford University Press, Oxford.
Dogramaci, S. (2020). Does my total evidence support that I'm a Boltzmann Brain? *Philosophical Studies*, 177:3717–3723.
Dorr, C. (2002). *The Simplicity of Everything*. PhD thesis, Princeton University.
Dowland, S. C. (2016). Embodied mind sparsism. *Philosophical Studies*, 173(7):1853–1872.
Duncan, M. (2019). The self shows up in experience. *Review of Philosophy and Psychology*, 10(2):299–318.
Duncan, S. (2012). Leibniz's mill arguments against materialism. *The Philosophical Quarterly*, 62(247):250–272.
Eccles, J. C. (1994). *How the Self Controls Its Brain*. Springer-Verlag, Berlin.
Egan, G. (2013). *Permutation City*. Self published, second edition.
Einevoll, G. T., Destexhe, A., Diesmann, M., et al. (2019). The scientific case for brain simulations. *Neuron*, 102(4):735–744.
Eva, B., Stern, R., and Hartmann, S. (2019). The similarity of causal structure. *Philosophy of Science*, 86(5):821–835.
Fales, E. (2007). Naturalism and physicalism. In Martin, M., editor, *The Cambridge Companion to Atheism*, pages 118–134. Cambridge University Press, Cambridge.
Farah, M. J. (2005). Neuroethics: The practical and the philosophical. *Trends in Cognitive Sciences*, 9(1):34–40.
Feigl, H. (1958). *The "Mental" and the "Physical": The Essay and a Postscript*. University of Minnesota Press, Minneapolis.
Feldman, F. (1992). *Confrontations with the Reaper*. Oxford University Press, New York.
Feldman, R. and Warfield, T. A., editors (2010). *Disagreement*. Oxford University Press, Oxford.
Fine, K. (2001). The question of realism. *Philosophers' Imprint*, 1:1–30.
Flanagan, O. (1991). *The Science of the Mind*. MIT Press, Cambridge, MA, second edition.
 (2011). *The Bodhisattva's Brain: Buddhism Naturalized*. MIT Press, Cambridge, MA.

Ford, N. M. (1991). *When Did I Begin? Conception of the Human Individual in History, Philosophy and Science.* Cambridge University Press, Cambridge.

Foster, J. (1968). Psychophysical causal relations. *American Philosophical Quarterly*, 5:64–70.

— (1991). *The Immaterial Self.* Routledge, London.

— (2001). A brief defense of the Cartesian view. In *Soul, Body, and Survival: Essays on the Metaphysics of Human Persons*, pages 15–29. Cornell University Press, Ithaca, NY.

Francescotti, R. (2017). Surviving death: How to refute termination theses. *Inquiry*, 61(2):178–197.

French, R. (2016). An argument for the ontological innocence of mereology. *Erkenntnis*, 81(4):683–704.

Friedman, M. (1974). Explanation and scientific understanding. *The Journal of Philosophy*, 71(1):5–19.

Ganeri, J. (2012). *The Self: Naturalism, Consciousness, and the First-Person Stance.* Oxford University Press, Oxford.

Garfield, J. L. (2022). *Losing Ourselves: Learning to Live without a Self.* Princeton University Press, Princeton.

Gasparov, I. (2015). Emergent dualism and the challenge of vagueness. *Faith and Philosophy*, 32(4):432–438.

Gaunilo (1995). Reply on behalf of the fool. In *Monologion and Proslogion: With the Replies of Gaunilo and Anselm*, pages 121–126. Hackett, Indianapolis. Translated by Thomas Williams.

Gendler, T. S. (2000). *Thought Experiment: On the Powers and Limits of Imaginary Cases.* Garland Press, New York. Garland Dissertations in Philosophy.

— (2002). Personal identity and thought-experiments. *Philosophical Quarterly*, 52(206):34–54.

Gert, J. (2021). Information-theoretic adverbialism. *Australasian Journal of Philosophy*, 99(4):696–715.

Gethin, R. (1986). The five khandhas: Their treatment in the Nikāyas and early Abhidhamma. *Journal of Indian Philosophy*, 14:35–53.

— (1998). *The Foundations of Buddhism.* Oxford University Press, Oxford.

Glazier, M. (2016). Laws and the completeness of the fundamental. In Jago, M., editor, *Reality Making*, pages 11–37. Oxford University Press, Oxford.

— (2023). Is the macro grounded in the micro? *The Philosophical Quarterly*, 73(1):105–116.

Goetz, S. and Taliaferro, C. (2011). *A Brief History of the Soul.* Wiley-Blackwell, Chichester.

Goff, P. (2017). *Consciousness and Fundamental Reality.* Oxford University Press, Oxford.

Goldwater, J. (2021). Uploads, faxes, and you: Can personal identity be transmitted? *American Philosophical Quarterly*, 58(3):233–250.

Gombrich, R. (2009). *What the Buddha Thought.* Equinox, London.

Gombrich, R. F. (2006). *How Buddhism Began: The Conditioned Genesis of the Early Teachings.* Routledge, London, second edition.

Goodman, C. (2009). *Consequences of Compassion: An Interpretation and Defense of Buddhist Ethics*. Oxford University Press, Oxford.

Gowans, C. W. (2003). *Philosophy of the Buddha*. Routledge, London.

Grajner, M. (2021). Grounding, metaphysical laws, and structure. *Analytic Philosophy*, 62(4):376–395.

Guerrero, A. A. (2007). Don't know, don't kill: Moral ignorance, culpability, and caution. *Philosophical Studies*, 136(1):59–97.

Haleem, M. A. S. A., editor (2005). *The Qur'an*. Oxford University Press, Oxford.

Hales, S. D. (2001). Evidence and the afterlife. *Philosophia*, 28:335–346.

Hanson, R. (2016). *The Age of Em: Work, Love, and Life When Robots Rule the Earth*. Oxford University Press, Oxford.

Harvey, P. (1995). *The Selfless Mind: Personality, Consciousness and Nirvāṇa in Early Buddhism*. Routledge, London.

Hasker, W. (1999). *The Emergent Self*. Cornell University Press, Ithaca, NY.

(2010). Persons and the unity of consciousness. In Koons, R. C. and Bealer, G., editors, *The Waning of Materialism*, pages 175–190. Oxford University Press, Oxford.

(2011). Materialism and the resurrection: Are the prospects improving? *European Journal for Philosophy of Religion*, 3(1):83–103.

(2016). Do my quarks enjoy Beethoven? In Crisp, T. M., Porter, S. L., and Elshof, G. T., editors, *Neuroscience and the Soul: The Human Person in Philosophy, Science, and Theology*, pages 13–40. Eerdmans, Grand Rapids.

(2018). The case for emergent dualism. In Loose, J. J., Menuge, A. J. L., and Moreland, J. P., editors, *The Blackwell Companion to Substance Dualism*, pages 62–72. Wiley-Blackwell, Hoboken.

Hauskeller, M. (2012). My brain, my mind, and I: Some philosophical assumptions of mind-uploading. *International Journal of Machine Consciousness*, 4(1):187–200.

Hawley, K. (2014). Ontological innocence. In Baxter, D. and Cotnoir, A., editors, *Composition As Identity*, pages 70–89. Oxford University Press, Oxford.

Heersmink, R. (2017). Distributed selves: Personal identity and extended memory systems. *Synthese*, 194:3135–3151.

Hershenov, D. B. (2001). The thesis of vague objects and Unger's problem of the many. *Philosophical Papers*, 30(1):57–67.

(2002). Van Inwagen, Zimmerman, and the materialist conception of resurrection. *Religious Studies*, 38(4):451–469.

(2005). Do dead bodies pose a problem for biological approaches to personal identity? *Mind*, 114(453):31–59.

Himma, K. E. (2005). What is a problem for all is a problem for none: Substance dualism, physicalism, and the mind-body problem. *American Philosophical Quarterly*, 42(2):81–92.

(2011). Explaining why this body gives rise to me qua subject instead of someone else: An argument for classical substance dualism. *Religious Studies*, 47(4):431–448.

Hooker, M. (1978). Descartes' denial of mind-body identity. In Hooker, M., editor, *Descartes: Critical and Interpretive Essays*. Johns Hopkins University Press, Baltimore.

Hopkins, P. D. (2012). Why uploading will not work, or, the ghosts haunting transhumanism. *International Journal of Machine Consciousness*, 4(1):229–243.

Horgan, T. and Potrč, M. (2008). *Austere Realism: Contextual Semantics Meets Minimal Ontology*. MIT Press, Cambridge, MA.

Hudson, H. (2001). *A Materialist Metaphysics of the Human Person*. Cornell University Press, Ithaca.

— (2016). Multiple location and single location resurrection. In Gasser, G., editor, *Personal Identity and Resurrection: How Do We Survive Our Death?*, pages 87–101. Routledge, London.

Huemer, M. (2019). *Dialogues on Ethical Vegetarianism*. Routledge, New York.

— (2021). Existence is evidence of immortality. *Noûs*, 55(1):128–151.

Hughes, J. (2013). Transhumanism and personal identity. In More, M. and Vita-More, N., editors, *The Transhumanist Reader: Classical and Contemporary Essays on the Science, Technology, and Philosophy of the Human Future*, pages 227–233. Wiley-Blackwell, Chichester.

Hume, D. (2000). *A Treatise of Human Nature*. Oxford University Press, Oxford, second edition. First edition by Selby-Bigge published in 1888.

Ichigo, M. (1985). *Madhyamakālaṃkāra of Śāntarakṣita with His Own Commentary or Vṛtti and with the Subcommentary or Pañjikā of Kamalaśīla*. Buneido, Kyoto.

Ismael, J. T. (2007). *The Situated Self*. Oxford University Press, Oxford.

Jackson, E. and Rogers, A. (2019). Salvaging Pascal's wager. *Philosophia Christi*, 21(1):59–84.

Jackson, F. (1982). Epiphenomenal qualia. *Philosophical Quarterly*, 32:127–136.

Jacobs, J. D. and O'Connor, T. (2010). Emergent individuals and the resurrection. *European Journal for Philosophy of Religion*, 2(2):69 88.

James, W. (1890). *The Principles of Psychology*. Dover, New York.

— (1898). *Human Immortality: Two Supposed Objections to the Doctrine*. Houghton, Mifflin and Company, Boston.

Johnston, M. (1987). Human beings. *Journal of Philosophy*, 84:59–83.

— (2007). "Human beings" revisited: My body is not an animal. In Zimmerman, D. W., editor, *Oxford Studies in Metaphysics*, volume 3, pages 33–74. Oxford University Press, Oxford.

— (2010). *Surviving Death*. Princeton University Press, Princeton.

Kant, I. (1998). *Critique of Pure Reason*. Cambridge University Press, Cambridge.

Kaplan, D. (1989). Demonstratives. In Almog, J., Perry, J., and Wettstein, H., editors, *Themes from Kaplan*, pages 481–563. Oxford University Press, New York.

Kaukua, J. (2015). *Self-Awareness in Islamic Philosophy: Avicenna and Beyond*. Cambridge University Press, Cambridge.

Kenny, A. (1968). *Descartes*. Random House, New York.

Kim, J. (1998). *Mind in a Physical World: An Essay on the Mind-Body Problem and Mental Causation*. MIT Press, Cambridge, MA.

(2005). *Physicalism, or Something near Enough*. Princeton University Press, Princeton.

(2011). *Philosophy of Mind*. Westview Press, Boulder, third edition.

Klein, C. (2008). Dispositional implementation solves the superfluous structure problem. *Synthese*, 165:141–153.

Klein, S. B. (2014). *The Two Selves: Their Metaphysical Commitments and Functional Interdependence*. Oxford University Press, Oxford.

Klein, S. B. and Nichols, S. (2012). Memory and the sense of personal identity. *Mind*, 121(483):677–702.

Kment, B. (2014). *Modality and Explanatory Reasoning*. Oxford University Press, Oxford.

Koch, C. (2012). *Consciousness: Confessions of a Romantic Reductionist*. MIT Press, Cambridge, MA.

Koene, R. A. (2013). Uploading to substrate-independent minds. In More, M. and Vita-More, N., editors, *The Transhumanist Reader: Classical and Contemporary Essays on the Science, Technology, and Philosophy of the Human Future*, pages 146–156. Wiley-Blackwell, Chichester.

(2014). Feasible mind uploading. In Blackford, R. and Broderick, D., editors, *Intelligence Unbound: The Future of Uploaded and Machine Minds*, pages 90–101. Wiley-Blackwell, Chichester.

Koksvik, O. (2007). Conservation of energy is relevant to physicalism. *Dialectica*, 61(4):573–582.

Kriegel, U. (2008). Composition as a secondary quality. *Pacific Philosophical Quarterly*, 89:359–383.

(2012). Kantian monism. *Philosophical Papers*, 41(1):23–56.

(2013). The epistemological challenge of revisionary metaphysics. *Philosophers' Imprint*, 13(12):1–30.

Kripke, S. (1980). *Naming and Necessity*. Blackwell, Malden.

Kuhse, H. and Singer, P. (1990). Individuals, humans, and persons: The issue of moral status. In Singer, P., Kuhse, H., Buckle, S., Dawson, K., and Kasimba, P., editors, *Embryo Experimentation: Ethical, Legal and Social Issues*, pages 65–75. Cambridge University Press, Cambridge.

Kurzweil, R. (2005). *The Singularity Is Near: When Humans Transcend Biology*. Penguin Books, New York.

Ladyman, J., Ross, D., Spurrett, D., and Collier, J. (2007). *Every Thing Must Go: Metaphysics Naturalized*. Oxford University Press, Oxford.

Langford, S. (2017). A defence of anti-criterialism. *Canadian Journal of Philosophy*, 47(5):613–630.

Lawrence, D. R. and Harris, J. (2021). Monkeys, moral machines, and persons. In Clarke, S., Zohny, H., and Savulescu, J., editors, *Rethinking Moral Status*, pages 290–305. Oxford University Press, Oxford.

Leibniz, G. W. (1989). The principles of philosophy, or, the monadology. In Ariew, R. and Garber, D., editors, *Philosophical Essays*, pages 213–225. Hackett, Indianapolis.

(2001). *Theodicy: Essays on the Goodness of God, the Freedom of Man and the Origin of Evil*. Wipf and Stock, Eugene. Translated by E. M. Huggard.

Lester, D. (2005). *Is There Life after Death? An Examination of the Empirical Evidence*. McFarland and Company, Jefferson.

Levy, N. (2007). *Neuroethics*. Cambridge University Press, Cambridge.

Lewis, D. (1971). Counterparts of persons and their bodies. *Journal of Philosophy*, 68:203–211.

— (1976). Survival and identity. In Rorty, A. O., editor, *The Identities of Persons*, pages 17–40. University of California Press, Berkeley.

— (1986). *On the Plurality of Worlds*. Blackwell, Oxford.

— (1991). *Parts of Classes*. Blackwell, Oxford.

— (1993). Many, but almost one. In Bacon, J., Campbell, K., and Reinhardt, L., editors, *Ontology, Causality, and Mind: Essays on the Philosophy of D. M. Armstrong*, pages 23–42. Cambridge University Press, Cambridge.

Liao, S. M. (2020). The moral status and rights of artificial intelligence. In Liao, S. M., editor, *Ethics of Artificial Intelligence*, pages 480–503. Oxford University Press, Oxford.

Lichtenberg, G. (1971). *Schriften und Briefe*, volume 2. Carl Hanser Verlag, Munich.

Locke, J. (1997). *An Essay concerning Human Understanding*. Penguin Books, London.

Lockhart, T. (2000). *Moral Uncertainty and Its Consequences*. Oxford University Press, Oxford.

Longenecker, M. T.-S. (2022). Community-made selves. *Australasian Journal of Philosophy*, 100(3):459–470.

Loss, R. (2018). A sudden collapse to nihilism. *The Philosophical Quarterly*, 68(271):370–375.

Lowe, E. J. (1996). *Subjects of Experience*. Cambridge University Press, New York.

— (2001). Identity, composition, and the simplicity of the self. In Corcoran, K., editor, *Soul, Body, and Survival*. Cornell University Press, Ithaca.

— (2006). Non-Cartesian substance dualism and the problem of mental causation. *Erkenntnis*, 65(1):5–23.

— (2008). A defence of non-Cartesian substance dualism. In Antonietti, A., Corradini, A., and Lowe, J., editors, *Psycho-Physical Dualism Today: An Interdisciplinary Approach*, pages 167–183. Lexington Books, Lanham.

— (2010). Substance dualism: A non-Cartesian approach. In Koons, R. C. and Bealer, G., editors, *The Waning of Materialism*, pages 439–461. Oxford University Press, Oxford.

— (2014). Why my body is not me : The unity argument for emergentist self-body dualism. In Lavazza, A. and Robinson, H., editors, *Contemporary Dualism: A Defense*, pages 245–265. Routledge, New York.

Lund, D. (2014). Materialism, dualism, and the conscious self. In Lavazza, A. and Robinson, H., editors, *Contemporary Dualism: A Defense*, pages 56–78. Routledge, New York.

Lusthaus, D. (2009). Pudgalavāda doctrines of the person. In Edelglass, W. and Garfield, J., editors, *Buddhist Philosophy: Essential Readings*, pages 275–285. Oxford University Press, Oxford.

Lycan, W. (2009). Giving dualism its due. *Australasian Journal of Philosophy*, 87(4):551–563.

(1995). Introduction. In Lyons, W., editor, *Modern Philosophy of Mind*. Everyman, London.

Machery, E. (2017). *Philosophy within Its Proper Bounds*. Oxford University Press, Oxford.

Machuca, D. E., editor (2013). *Disagreement and Skepticism*. Routledge, New York.

Mackie, P. (2006). *How Things Might Have Been: Individuals, Kinds, and Essential Properties*. Oxford University Press, Oxford.

Madden, R. (2015). The naive topology of the conscious subject. *Noûs*, 49(1):55–70.

Madell, G. (2015). *The Essence of the Self: In Defense of the Simple View of Personal Identity*. Routledge, New York.

Mandelbaum, E. (2022). Everything and more: The prospects of whole brain emulation. *Journal of Philosophy*, 119(8):444–459.

Mandik, P. (2015). Metaphysical daring as a posthuman survival strategy. *Midwest Studies in Philosophy*, 39(1):144–157.

Markosian, N. (1998). Brutal composition. *Philosophical Studies*, 92:211–249.

(2014). A spatial approach to mereology. In Kleinschmidt, S., editor, *Mereology and Location*, pages 69–90. Oxford University Press, Oxford.

Markram, H., Muller, E., Ramaswamy, S., et al. (2015). Reconstruction and simulation of neocortical microcircuitry. *Cell*, 163(2):456–492.

Marmura, M. (1986). Avicenna's "flying man" in context. *The Monist*, 69(3):383–395.

Martin, M. and Augustine, K., editors (2015). *The Myth of an Afterlife: The Case against Life after Death*. Rowman and Littlefield, Lanham.

Matheson, J. (2015). *The Epistemic Significance of Disagreement*. Palgrave Macmillan, Basingstoke.

Matthews, S. (2010). Personal identity, the causal condition, and the simple view. *Philosophical Papers*, 39(2):183–208.

Mavrodes, G. I. (1977). The life everlasting and the bodily criterion of identity. *Noûs*, 11(1):27–39.

McDaniel, K. (2010). Composition as identity does not entail universalism. *Erkenntnis*, 73(1):97–100.

(2019). Abhidharma metaphysics and the two truths. *Philosophy East and West*, 69(2):439–463.

McDonnell, N. and Wildman, N. (2019). Virtual reality: Digital or fictional? *Disputatio*, 11(55):371–397.

McGinn, C. (1993). *Problems in Philosophy: The Limits of Inquiry*. Blackwell, Oxford.

(1999). *The Mysterious Flame: Conscious Minds in a Material World*. Basic Books, New York.

McMahan, J. (2002). *The Ethics of Killing: Problems at the Margins of Life*. Oxford University Press, Oxford.

(2007). Killing embryos for stem cell research. *Metaphilosophy*, 38(2–3):170–189.

Meixner, U. (2010). Materialism does not save the phenomena – and the alternative which does. In Koons, R. C. and Bealer, G., editors, *The Waning of Materialism*, pages 417–437. Oxford University Press, Oxford.

(2014). Against physicalism. In Lavazza, A. and Robinson, H., editors, *Contemporary Dualism: A Defense*, pages 17–34. Routledge, New York.

Melnyk, A. (2003). *A Physicalist Manifesto: Thoroughly Modern Materialism*. Cambridge University Press, Cambridge.

Mercer, C. (2015). Whole brain emulation requires enhanced theology, and a "handmaiden". *Theology and Science*, 13(2):175–186.

Merricks, T. (1994). A new objection to a priori arguments for dualism. *American Philosophical Quarterly*, 31(1):81–85.

(1998). There are no criteria of identity over time. *Noûs*, 32:106–124.

(1999a). Composition as identity, mereological essentialism, and counterpart theory. *Australasian Journal of Philosophy*, 77:192–195.

(1999b). The resurrection of the body and the life everlasting. In Murray, M. J., editor, *Reason for the Hope Within*, pages 261–286. Eerdmans, Grand Rapids.

(2001). How to live forever without saving your soul: Physicalism and immortality. In *Soul, Body, and Survival: Essays on the Metaphysics of Human Persons*. Cornell University Press, Ithaca.

(2003). *Objects and Persons*. Clarendon Press, Oxford.

(2009). The resurrection of the body. In Flint, T. P. and Rea, M. C., editors, *The Oxford Handbook of Philosophical Theology*, pages 476–490. Oxford University Press, Oxford.

Metzinger, T. (2009). *The Ego Tunnel: The Science of the Mind and the Myth of the Self*. Basic Books, New York.

Miller, K. (2010). The existential quantifier, composition and contingency. *Erkenntnis*, 73(2):211–235.

Millière, R. and Newen, A. (in press). Selfless memories. *Erkenntnis*.

Minerva, F. (2018). *The Ethics of Cryonics: Is It Immoral to Be Immortal?* Palgrave Macmillan, Cham.

Mishra, A. (2018). Moral status of digital agents: Acting under uncertainty. In Müller, V. C., editor, *Philosophy and Theory of Artificial Intelligence 2017*, pages 273–287. Springer International Publishing, Cham.

Moller, D. (2011). Abortion and moral risk. *Philosophy*, 86(3):425–443.

Montero, B. (1999). The body problem. *Noûs*, 33(2):183–200.

(2006). What does the conservation of energy have to do with physicalism? *Dialectica*, 60(4):383–396.

Mooney, J. (2018). The possibility of resurrection by reassembly. *International Journal for Philosophy of Religion*, 84:273–288.

Moravec, H. (1988). *Mind Children: The Future of Robot and Human Intelligence*. Harvard University Press, Cambridge, MA.

Moreland, J. P. (2008). *Consciousness and the Existence of God: A Theistic Argument*. Routledge, New York.
  (2018a). In defense of a Thomistic-like dualism. In Loose, J. J., Menuge, A. J. L., and Moreland, J. P., editors, *The Blackwell Companion to Substance Dualism*, pages 102–122. Wiley-Blackwell, Hoboken.
  (2018b). Substance dualism and the diachronic/synchronic unity of consciousness. In Loftin, R. K. and Farris, J. R., editors, *Christian Physicalism? Philosophical and Theological Criticisms*, pages 43–73. Lexington Books, Lanham.
  (2018c). Substance dualism and the unity of consciousness. In Loose, J. J., Menuge, A. J. L., and Moreland, J. P., editors, *The Blackwell Companion to Substance Dualism*, pages 184–207. Wiley-Blackwell, Hoboken.
Murphy, N. (1998). Human nature: Historical, scientific, and religious issues. In Brown, W. S., Murphy, N., and Malony, H. N., editors, *Whatever Happened to the Soul? Scientific and Theological Portraits of Human Nature*, pages 1–31. Fortress Press, Minneapolis.
  (2006). *Bodies and Souls, or Spirited Bodies?* Cambridge University Press, Cambridge.
Ñāṇamoli, B. and Bodhi, B. (1995). *The Middle Length Discourses of the Buddha: A Translation of the Majjhima Nikāya*. Wisdom Publications, Boston.
Nagel, T. (1974). What is it like to be a bat? *The Philosophical Review*, 83(4):435–450.
  (1986). *The View from Nowhere*. Oxford University Press, New York.
Newland, G. and Tillemans, T. J. F. (2011). An introduction to conventional truth. In *Moonshadows: Conventional Truth in Buddhist Philosophy*, pages 3–22. Oxford University Press, Oxford.
Nichols, S. and Bruno, M. (2010). Intuitions about personal identity: An empirical study. *Philosophical Psychology*, 23(3):293–312.
Nida-Rümelin, M. (2006). *Der Blick von innen: zur transtemporalen Identität bewusstseinsfähiger Wesen*. Suhrkamp, Frankfurt.
  (2007). Dualist emergentism. In McLaughlin, B. P. and Cohen, J., editors, *Contemporary Debates in Philosophy of Mind*, pages 269–286. Blackwell, Malden.
  (2010). An argument from transtemporal identity for subject–body dualism. In Koons, R. C. and Bealer, G., editors, *The Waning of Materialism*, pages 191–211. Oxford University Press, Oxford.
  (2013). The argument for subject body dualism from transtemporal identity defended. *Philosophy and Phenomenological Research*, 86(3):702–714.
Ninan, D. (2009). Persistence and the first-person perspective. *The Philosophical Review*, 118(4):425–464.
Noonan, H. W. (2003). *Personal Identity*. Routledge, London, second edition.
Nozick, R. (1981). *Philosophical Explanations*. Belknap Press, Cambridge, MA.
Olson, E. T. (1997). *The Human Animal: Personal Identity without Psychology*. Oxford University Press, Oxford.

(1998). There is no problem of the self. *Journal of Consciousness Studies*, 5(5–6):645–657.

(2007). *What Are We? A Study in Personal Ontology*. Oxford University Press, Oxford.

(2013). The person and the corpse. In Bradley, B., Feldman, F., and Johansson, J., editors, *The Oxford Handbook of Philosophy of Death*, pages 80–96. Oxford University Press, Oxford.

(2015). Life after death and the devastation of the grave. In Martin, M. and Augustine, K., editors, *The Myth of an Afterlife: The Case against Life after Death*, pages 409–423. Rowman and Littlefield, Lanham.

(2016). Immanent causation and life after death. In Gasser, G., editor, *Personal Identity and Resurrection: How Do We Survive Our Death?*, pages 51–66. Routledge, London.

(2017). The central dogma of transhumanism. In Berčić, B., editor, *Perspectives on the Self*, pages 35–58. University of Rijeka, Rijeka.

(2019). The metaphysics of artificial intelligence. In Guta, M. P., editor, *Consciousness and the Ontology of Properties*, pages 67–84. Routledge, London.

(2022). The metaphysics of transhumanism. In Hübner, K., editor, *Human: A History*, pages 381–403. Oxford University Press, Oxford.

Oppy, G. (1995). *Ontological Arguments and Belief in God*. Cambridge University Press, Cambridge.

Osborne, R. C. (2016). Debunking rationalist defenses of common-sense ontology: An empirical approach. *Review of Philosophy and Psychology*, 7(1):197–221.

Owen, M. (2021). *Measuring the Immeasurable Mind: Where Contemporary Neuroscience Meets the Aristotelian Tradition*. Rowman and Littlefield, London.

Papineau, D. (2001). The rise of physicalism. In Gillett, C. and Loewer, B., editors, *Physicalism and Its Discontents*, pages 3–36. Cambridge University Press, Cambridge.

(2002). *Thinking about Consciousness*. Oxford University Press, Oxford.

Parfit, D. (1984). *Reasons and Persons*. Clarendon Press, Oxford.

(2012). We are not human beings. *Philosophy*, 87(1):5–28.

Paul, L. A. (2012). Metaphysics as modeling: The handmaiden's tale. *Philosophical Studies*, 160:1–29.

Paul, L. A. (2014). *Transformative Experience*. Oxford University Press, Oxford.

Pearce, K. L. (2017). Mereological idealism. In Goldschmidt, T. and Pearce, K. L., editors, *Idealism: New Essays in Metaphysics*, pages 200–216. Oxford University Press, Oxford.

Perry, J. (1978). *A Dialogue on Personal Identity and Immortality*. Hackett, Indianapolis.

Persson, I. (1995). Genetic therapy, identity and the person-regarding reasons. *Bioethics*, 9(1):16–31.

Piccinini, G. and Bahar, S. (2015). No mental life after brain death: The argument from the neural localization of mental functions. In Martin, M. and Augustine, K., editors, *The Myth of an Afterlife: The Case against Life after Death*, pages 135–170. Rowman and Littlefield, Lanham.

Pigliucci, M. (2014). Mind uploading: A philosophical counter-analysis. In Blackford, R. and Broderick, D., editors, *Intelligence Unbound: The Future of Uploaded and Machine Minds*, pages 119–130. Wiley-Blackwell, Chichester.

Pitts, J. B. (2020). Conservation laws and the philosophy of mind: Opening the black box, finding a mirror. *Philosophia*, 48:673–707.

(2021). Conservation of energy: Missing features in its nature and justification and why they matter. *Foundations of Science*, 26:559–584.

(2022). General relativity, mental causation, and energy conservation. *Erkenntnis*, 87:1931–1973.

Plantinga, A. (2006). Against materialism. *Faith and Philosophy*, 23(1):3–32.

(2007). Materialism and Christian belief. In van Inwagen, P. and Zimmerman, D., editors, *Persons: Human and Divine*, pages 99–141. Oxford University Press, Oxford.

(2008). *Knowledge of God*, chapter Against Naturalism, pages 1–69. Blackwell, Malden.

Pollock, J. L. (2008). What am I? Virtual machines and the mind/body problem. *Philosophy and Phenomenological Research*, 76(2):237–309.

Pope Pius XII (1950). *Humani Generis*. The Catholic Church.

Popper, K. R. and Eccles, J. C. (1977). *The Self and Its Brain*. Springer International, Berlin.

Price, A. F. and Mou-Lam, W., editors (2012). *The Diamond Sūtra and the Sūtra of Hui-Neng*. Shambhala Publications, Boston.

Princess Elisabeth of Bohemia and Descartes, R. (2007). *The Correspondence between Princess Elisabeth of Bohemia and René Descartes*. The University of Chicago Press, Chicago.

Puccetti, R. (1973). Brain bisection and personal identity. *British Journal for the Philosophy of Science*, 24(4):339–355.

Putnam, H. (1983). *Realism and Reason: Philosophical Papers,* volume 3. Cambridge University Press, Cambridge.

Quinn, P. L. (1997). Tiny selves: Chisholm on the simplicity of the soul. In Hahn, L. E., editor, *The Philosophy of Roderick M. Chisholm*, pages 55–67. Open Court, Chicago.

Quinton, A. (1962). The soul. *Journal of Philosophy*, 59(15):393–409.

Ratzinger, J. (1988). *Eschatology: Death and Eternal Life*. The Catholic University of America Press, Washington, DC.

Reichenbach, B. R. (1990). *The Law of Karma: A Philosophical Study*. Macmillan, Houndmills.

Rice, R. L. H. (2022). *Death and Persistence*. Cambridge University Press, Cambridge.

Rickabaugh, B. L. (2018). Against emergent dualism. In Loose, J. J., Menuge, A. J. L., and Moreland, J. P., editors, *The Blackwell Companion to Substance Dualism*, pages 73–86. Wiley-Blackwell, Hoboken.

Rickabaugh, B. L. and Evans, C. S. (2018). Neuroscience, spiritual formation, and bodily souls: A critique of Christian physicalism. In Loftin, R. K. and Farris,

J. R., editors, *Christian Physicalism? Philosophical and Theological Criticisms*, pages 231–256. Lexington Books, Lanham.

Robinson, H. (2016). *From the Knowledge Argument to Mental Substance: Resurrecting the Mind*. Cambridge University Press, Cambridge.

Roebuck, V. J., editor (2003). *The Upaniṣads*. Penguin Books, London.

Roelofs, L. (2019). *Combining Minds: How to Think About Composite Subjectivity*. Oxford University Press, Oxford.

Rosen, G. (2006). The limits of contingency. In MacBride, F., editor, *Identity and Modality*, pages 13–39. Oxford University Press, Oxford.

— (2010). Metaphysical dependence: Grounding and reduction. In Hale, B. and Hoffmann, A., editors, *Modality: Metaphysics, Logic, and Epistemology*, pages 109–136. Oxford University Press, Oxford.

— (2017). Ground by law. *Philosophical Issues*, 27:279–301.

Rosen, G. and Dorr, C. (2002). Composition as a fiction. In Gale, R., editor, *The Blackwell Guide to Metaphysics*, pages 151–174. Blackwell, Oxford.

Ryle, G. (2009). *The Concept of Mind*. Routledge, London.

Salje, L. (2020). Lit from within: First-person thought and illusions of transcendence. *Canadian Journal of Philosophy*, 50(6):735–749.

Sandberg, A. (2013). Feasibility of whole brain emulation. In Müller, V. C., editor, *Philosophy and Theory of Artificial Intelligence*, pages 251–264. Springer, Berlin.

— (2014a). Being nice to software animals and babies. In Blackford, R. and Broderick, D., editors, *Intelligence Unbound: The Future of Uploaded and Machine Minds*, pages 279–297. Wiley-Blackwell, Chichester.

— (2014b). Ethics of brain emulations. *Journal of Experimental & Theoretical Artificial Intelligence*, 26(3):439–457.

Śāntideva (1995). *The Bodhicaryāvatāra*. Oxford University Press, Oxford.

Saucedo, R. (2011). Parthood and location. In Bennett, K. and Zimmerman, D. W., editors, *Oxford Studies in Metaphysics*, volume 6, pages 225–284. Oxford University Press, Oxford.

Sauchelli, A. (2016). Buddhist reductionism, fictionalism about the self, and buddhist fictionalism. *Philosophy East and West*, 66(4):1273–1291.

Schaffer, J. (2009). On what grounds what. In Chalmers, D. J., Manley, D., and Wasserman, R., editors, *Metametaphysics*, pages 347–383. Oxford University Press, Oxford.

— (2015). What not to multiply without necessity. *Australasian Journal of Philosophy*, 93(4):644–664.

— (2016). Grounding in the image of causation. *Philosophical Studies*, 173(1):49–100.

— (2017a). The ground between the gaps. *Philosophers' Imprint*, 17(11):1–26.

— (2017b). Laws for metaphysical explanation. *Philosophical Issues*, 27:302–321.

Schindler, S. (2018). *Theoretical Virtues in Science: Uncovering Reality through Theory*. Cambridge University Press, Cambridge.

— (2019). *Artificial You: AI and the Future of Your Mind*. Princeton University Press, Princeton.

(2020). How to catch an AI zombie: Testing for consciousness in machines. In Liao, S. M., editor, *Ethics of Artificial Intelligence*, pages 439–458. Oxford University Press, Oxford.

Schuklenk, U. (2021). Moral recognition and the limits of impartialist ethics: On androids, sentience, and personhood. In Clarke, S., Zohny, H., and Savulescu, J., editors, *Rethinking Moral Status*, pages 123–138. Oxford University Press, Oxford.

Schwitzgebel, E. and Garza, M. (2015). A defense of the rights of artificial intelligences. *Midwest Studies in Philosophy*, 39(1):98–119.

(2020). Designing AI with rights, consciousness, self-respect, and freedom. In Liao, S. M., editor, *Ethics of Artificial Intelligence*, pages 459–479. Oxford University Press, Oxford.

Seacord, B. (2021). The evidential value of out-of-body near-death experiences. In Byerly, T. R., editor, *Death, Immortality and Eternal Life*, pages 51–61. Routledge, London.

Searle, J. R. (1992). *The Rediscovery of the Mind*. MIT Press, Cambridge, MA.

(2004). *Mind: A Brief Introduction*. Oxford University Press, Oxford.

Shaw, D. (2009). Cryoethics: Seeking life after death. *Bioethics*, 23(9):515–521.

Shoemaker, D. (2008a). *Personal Identity and Ethics: A Brief Introduction*. Broadview Press, Peterborough.

Shoemaker, S. (1984). *Personal Identity*, chapter Personal Identity: A Materialist's Account, pages 67–132. Blackwell, Oxford.

(1996). Introspection and the self. In *The First-Person Perspective and Other Essays*. Cambridge University Press, Cambridge.

(1999). Self, body and coincidence. *Aristotelian Society, Supplementary Volume*, 73:287–306.

(2008b). Persons, animals, and identity. *Synthese*, 162:313–324.

Shrader, W. (2006). The unity of consciousness: Trouble for the materialist or the emergent dualist? *Faith and Philosophy*, 23(1):33–44.

Shulman, C. and Bostrom, N. (2021). Sharing the world with digital minds. In Clarke, S., Zohny, H., and Savulescu, J., editors, *Rethinking Moral Status*, pages 306–326. Oxford University Press, Oxford.

Sider, T. (2013). Against parthood. In Bennett, K. and Zimmerman, D. W., editors, *Oxford Studies in Metaphysics*, volume 8. Oxford University Press, Oxford.

Siderits, M. (2007). *Buddhism as Philosophy: An Introduction*. Ashgate, Aldershot.

(2015). *Personal Identity and Buddhist Philosophy: Empty Persons*. Ashgate, New York, second edition.

(2022). *How Things Are: An Introduction to Buddhist Metaphysics*. Oxford University Press, Oxford.

Siderits, M. and Katsura, S. (2013). *Nāgārjuna's Middle Way: Mūlamadhyamakakārikā*. Wisdom Publications, Somerville.

Singer, P. (1993). *Practical Ethics*. Cambridge University Press, Cambridge, second edition.

Sinnott-Armstrong, W. and Conitzer, V. (2021). How much moral status could artificial intelligence ever achieve? In Clarke, S., Zohny, H., and Savulescu, J., editors, *Rethinking Moral Status*, pages 269–289. Oxford University Press, Oxford.
Smart, J. J. C. (1959). Sensations and brain processes. *Philosophical Review*, 68: 141–156.
Smid, J. (2015). The ontological parsimony of mereology. *Philosophical Studies*, 172(12):3253–3271.
— (2017). What does "nothing over and above its parts" actually mean? *Philosophy Compass*, 12(1):1–13.
Smith, B. and Brogaard, B. (2003). Sixteen days. *The Journal of Medicine and Philosophy*, 28(1):45–78.
Smith, P. and Jones, O. R. (1986). *The Philosophy of Mind: An Introduction*. Cambridge University Press, Cambridge.
Smith, S. M. (2021). The negation of self in Indian Buddhist philosophy. *Philosophers' Imprint*, 21(13):1–23.
Snowdon, P. F. (2014). *Persons, Animals, Ourselves*. Oxford University Press, Oxford.
Sober, E. (2000). *Philosophy of Biology*. Westview Press, Boulder, second edition.
Sorabji, R. (2006). *Self: Ancient and Modern Insights About Individuality, Life, and Death*. The University of Chicago Press, Chicago.
Sosa, E. (1984). Mind-body interaction and supervenient causation. In French, Jr., P. A., Uehling, T. E., and Wettstein, H., editors, *Midwest Studies in Philosophy*, volume 9, pages 271–281. University of Minnesota Press, Minneapolis.
Spackman, J. (2013). Consciousness and the prospects for substance dualism. *Philosophy Compass*, 8(11):1054–1065.
Sparrow, R. (2004). The Turing triage test. *Ethics and Information Technology*, 6:203–213.
Steinhart, E. C. (2014). *Your Digital Afterlives: Computational Theories of Life after Death*. Palgrave Macmillan, New York.
Stephenson, N. (2019). *Fall; or, Dodge in Hell*. William Morrow, New York.
Stevenson, I. (1974). *Twenty Cases Suggestive of Reincarnation*. University Press of Virginia, Charlottesville.
Strawson, G. (2009). *Selves: An Essay in Revisionary Metaphysics*. Oxford University Press, Oxford.
— (2017). *The Subject of Experience*. Oxford University Press, Oxford.
Strawson, P. F. (1966). *The Bounds of Sense: An Essay on Kant's Critique of Pure Reason*. Routledge, Abingdon.
Stump, E. (1995). Non-Cartesian substance dualism and materialism without reductionism. *Faith and Philosophy*, 12(4):505–531.
Sullivan, M. (2012). The minimal A-theory. *Philosophical Studies*, 158(2):149–174.
— (2017). Are there essential properties? No. In Barnes, E., editor, *Current Controversies in Metaphysics*, pages 45–61. Routledge, New York.
Swinburne, R. (1984). *Personal Identity*, chapter Personal Identity: The Dualist Theory, pages 1–66. Blackwell, Oxford.

(1986). *The Evolution of the Soul*. Oxford University Press, Oxford.
(2004). *The Existence of God*. Clarendon Press, Oxford, second edition.
(2012). How to determine which is the true theory of personal identity. In Gasser, G. and Stefan, M., editors, *Personal Identity: Complex or Simple?*, pages 105–122. Cambridge University Press, Cambridge.
(2013). *Mind, Brain, and Free Will*. Oxford University Press, Oxford.
(2014). What makes me me? A defense of substance dualism. In Lavazza, A. and Robinson, H., editors, *Contemporary Dualism: A Defense*, pages 139–153. Routledge, New York.
(2019). *Are We Bodies or Souls?* Oxford University Press, Oxford.
Taliaferro, C. (1994). *Consciousness and the Mind of God*. Cambridge University Press, Cambridge.
Taliaferro, C. and Goetz, S. (2008). The prospect of Christian materialism. *Christian Scholar's Review*, 37(3):303–321.
Thompson, E. (2020). *Why I Am Not a Buddhist*. Yale University Press, New Haven.
Thornton, A. (2019). Disembodied animals. *American Philosophical Quarterly*, 56(2):203–217.
Turner, Jr., J. T. (2019). *On the Resurrection of the Dead: A New Metaphysics of Afterlife for Christian Thought*. Routledge, Abingdon.
Unger, P. (1979a). I do not exist. In Macdonald, G. F., editor, *Perception and Identity: Essays Presented to A. J. Ayer with His Replies to Them*, pages 235–251. Macmillan, New York.
   (1979b). Why there are no people. In French, P., Uehling, Jr., T. E., and Wettstein, H. K., editors, *Midwest Studies in Philosophy IV*, pages 177–222. University of Minnesota Press, Minneapolis.
   (1980). The problem of the many. In French, P., Uehling, Jr., T. E., and Wettstein, H. K., editors, *Midwest Studies in Philosophy V: Studies in Epistemology*, pages 411–467. University of Minnesota Press, Minneapolis, MN.
   (2006). *All the Power in the World*. Oxford University Press, Oxford.
van Inwagen, P. (1978). The possibility of resurrection. *International Journal for Philosophy of Religion*, 9(2):114–121.
   (1990). *Material Beings*. Cornell University Press, Ithaca.
   (1994). Composition as identity. *Philosophical Perspectives*, 8:207–220.
   (1995). Dualism and materialism: Athens and Jerusalem? *Faith and Philosophy*, 12(4):475–488.
   (1996). Materialism and the psychological continuity account of personal identity. In Tomberlin, J., editor, *Philosophical Perspectives 10: Metaphysics*, pages 305–319. Blackwell, Cambridge, MA.
   (1998). Modal epistemology. *Philosophical Studies*, 92:67–84.
   (2002). What do we refer to when we say "I"? In Gale, R. M., editor, *The Blackwell Guide to Metaphysics*, pages 175–189. Blackwell, Oxford.
   (2014). Introduction: Inside and outside the ontology room. In *Existence: Essays in Ontology*, pages 1–14. Cambridge University Press, Cambridge.
   (2015). *Metaphysics*. Westview Press, Boulder, fourth edition.

Vasubandhu (2003). *Indian Buddhist Theories of Persons: Vasubandhu's "Refutation of the Theory of a Self"*. Routledge, London.
— (2009). Vasubandhu's Abhidharmakośa: The critique of the soul. In Edelglass, W. and Garfield, J., editors, *Buddhist Philosophy: Essential Readings*, pages 297–308. Oxford University Press, Oxford. Translated by Charles Goodman.
Vicente, A. (2006). On the causal completeness of physics. *International Studies in the Philosophy of Science*, 20(2):149–171.
Walker, M. (2008). Cognitive enhancement and the identity objection. *Journal of Evolution and Technology*, 18(1):108–115.
— (2011). Personal identity and uploading. *Journal of Evolution and Technology*, 22(1):37–51.
Walker, R. C. (2014). On what we must think. In Lavazza, A. and Robinson, H., editors, *Contemporary Dualism: A Defense*, pages 171–187. Routledge, New York.
Wallace, M. (2011). Composition as identity: Part 1. *Philosophy Compass*, 6: 804–816.
— (2014). Composition as identity, modal parts, and mereological essentialism. In Baxter, D. and Cotnoir, A., editors, *Composition As Identity*, pages 111–129. Oxford University Press, Oxford.
Walls, J. L. and Dougherty, T., editors (2018). *Two Dozen (or so) Arguments for God: The Plantinga Project*. Oxford University Press, Oxford.
Wasserman, R. (2002). The standard objection to the standard account. *Philosophical Studies*, 111:197–216.
Wellington, N. (2014). Whole brain emulation: Invasive vs. non-invasive methods. In Blackford, R. and Broderick, D., editors, *Intelligence Unbound: The Future of Uploaded and Machine Minds*, pages 178–192. Wiley-Blackwell, Chichester.
Westerhoff, J. (2016). On the nihilist interpretation of Madhyamaka. *Journal of Indian Philosophy*, 44:337–376.
— (2020). *The Non-existence of the Real World*. Oxford University Press, Oxford.
Westphal, J. (2016). *The Mind-Body Problem*. MIT Press, Cambridge, MA.
White, C., Kelly, R. M., and Nichols, S. (2016). Remembering past lives. In Cruz, H. D. and Nichols, R., editors, *Advances in Religion, Cognitive Science, and Experimental Philosophy*, pages 169–196. Bloomsbury, New York.
Wilkes, K. (1988). *Real People: Personal Identity without Thought Experiments*. Clarendon Press, Oxford.
Willard, M. B. (2013). Game called on account of fog: Metametaphysics and epistemic dismissivism. *Philosophical Studies*, 164(1):1–14.
— (2014). Against simplicity. *Philosophical Studies*, 167:165–181.
Williams, B. (1970). The self and the future. *Philosophical Review*, 79:161–180.
— (2005). *Descartes: The Project of Pure Enquiry*. Routledge, London.
Williams, P. (2009). *Mahāyāna Buddhism: The Doctrinal Foundations*. Routledge, London, second edition.
Wilsch, T. (2015). The nomological account of ground. *Philosophical Studies*, 172(12):3293–3312.

Wilson, D. L. (2015). Nonphysical souls would violate physical laws. In Martin, M. and Augustine, K., editors, *The Myth of an Afterlife: The Case against Life after Death*, pages 349–367. Rowman and Littlefield, Lanham.

Wilson, J. (2006). On characterizing the physical. *Philosophical Studies*, 131:61–99.

Wright, N. T. (2003). *The Resurrection of the Son of God*. Fortress Press, Minneapolis.

Yang, E. T. and Davis, S. T. (2017). Composition and the will of god: Reconsidering resurrection by reassembly. In *Paradise Understood: New Philosophical Essays About Heaven*, pages 213–227. Oxford University Press, Oxford.

Yi, B. (1999). Is mereology ontologically innocent? *Philosophical Studies*, 93: 141–160.

(2002). *Understanding the Many*. Routledge, New York.

Zahavi, D. (2005). *Subjectivity and Selfhood: Investigating the First-Person Perspective*. MIT Press, Cambridge, MA.

Zahn, R., Talazko, J. and Ebert, D. (2008). Loss of the sense of self-ownership for perceptions of objects in a case of right inferior temporal, parieto-occipital and precentral hypometabolism. *Psychopathology*, 41(6):397–402.

Zimmerman, D. W. (1991). Two Cartesian arguments for the simplicity of the soul. *American Philosophical Quarterly*, 28(3):217–226.

(1999). The compatibility of materialism and survival: The "falling elevator" model. *Faith and Philosophy*, 16(2):194–212.

(2010). From property dualism to substance dualism. *Aristotelian Society Supplementary Volume*, 84(1):119–150.

(2011). From experience to experiencer. In Baker, M. C. and Goetz, S., editors, *The Soul Hypothesis: Investigations into the Existence of the Soul*, pages 168–196. Continuum, New York.

(2012). Materialism, dualism, and "simple" theories of personal identity. In Gasser, G. and Stefan, M., editors, *Personal Identity: Complex or Simple?*, pages 206–235. Cambridge University Press, Cambridge.

(2013). Personal identity and the survival of death. In Bradley, B., Feldman, F., and Johansson J., editor, *The Oxford Handbook of Philosophy of Death*, chapter 4, pages 97–154. Oxford University Press, Oxford.

(2016). Bodily resurrection: The falling elevator model revisited. In Gasser, G., editor, *Personal Identity and Resurrection: How Do We Survive Our Death?*, pages 33–50. Routledge, London.

Index

aggregates, 113–115, 132
Al-Ghazālī, 163, 167
Albahari, 127, 139, 144, 147, 148, 151
animalism, 2, 75, 150, 211
Anselm, 14–15
anti realism, mereological, 68–69, 100, 162–163, 184
antireflexivity principle, 134–138, 148
Aquinas, 3, 161, 167
arguments against substance dualism
    causal closure/exclusion, 27–29
    conservation laws, 29–33
    correlation between mental states and brain states, 33–37
    duplication argument, 37–38
    how do we reidentify immaterial souls over time?, 42–44
    parsimony, 20–27
        nomic parsimony, 23–27
        ontological parsimony, 20–23
    where do souls come from?, 38–42
arguments against the existence of the self
    impermanence, 113–132
    lack of control, 132–138
    neither one nor many, 138–139
    simplicity or parsimony, 139–142
arguments for substance dualism
    epistemic, 78–80
    facts regarding personal identity outstrip the physical facts, 80–82
    Lowe's argument from unity, 92–96
    modal, 70–78
    phenomenology and intentionality, 82–87
    problem of the many, 96–101
    replacement, 76–78
    unity of consciousness, 87–92
arguments for theism, ontological, 14–15, 102
Armstrong, 22, 27, 40
Augustine, 3, 163–165, 167, 168
Avicenna, 79

Bailey, 2, 6, 48, 63, 68, 74, 75, 87, 100, 105, 155, 161, 162, 174
Baker, 3, 48, 161, 162, 168, 174
Bennett, 22, 27, 48, 65
Benovsky, 139, 141, 154
Bible, 160
Bodhi, 3, 112, 114, 116, 129, 132, 134
Boltzmann brains, 196
Brenner, 6–8, 10, 20, 24, 28, 29, 47, 53, 55, 68, 69, 91, 92, 100, 110, 126, 142, 147, 161, 162, 176, 184
Brower, 13
Buddha, 3, 113–117, 128, 129, 132–134
Buddhaghosa, 112, 129, 175

Cameron, 8, 9, 25, 26
cannibalism, 167–168
causation, immanent, 165–167
Chalmers, 82, 185, 192, 194–200, 205–207, 210, 211
Chisholm, 11, 76, 144, 158
Churchland, 21, 33, 40
Collins, 31, 113, 114, 133
composition, 6–7
composition as identity, 7–11, 22, 52, 173
Cotard's syndrome, 146, 151
cryonics, 210–212

Davids, 112, 129
Davis, 68, 100, 161, 162
DeGrazia, 2, 13, 42, 54
Dennett, 30, 45, 144
Descartes, 3, 39, 70, 79, 149
Diamond Sutra, 130
Dorr, 3, 28, 126, 147, 154
dust theory, 195–197, 200

Eccles, 69, 87, 100
Egan, 195
essentialism, mereological, 9–10, 76

Index

existence
　conventional, 109–111
　ultimate, 109–111

fission, 52–55, 80
Flanagan, 21, 30, 118
Foster, 3, 43, 46, 57, 69, 100, 151

Gaunilo, 14–15
God, 37–38, 161–174, 176–177, 184, 203, 209
Goetz, 34, 39, 44, 61, 73–74, 76
Goodman, 112, 139, 154
Gowans, 114, 115, 120–122
Gregory of Nyssa, 167

Harvey, 127, 128, 131
Hasker, 23, 61, 87–92, 165
Hershenov, 98, 167, 171
Horgan, 21, 91, 111
Hudson, 98, 101, 161
Huemer, 204–205, 208
Hume, 3, 144

innocence, ontological, 22–23
intermediate state, 174

James, 153, 159–160
Jerome, 167
Johnston, 3, 13, 33, 42, 161

Kant, 42, 87, 154
karma, 176–177
Kim, 21, 24, 27, 45–47, 51
Kripke, 109

laws
　mereological, 24–27, 36–38, 41–42, 89, 104
　psycho-physical, 24, 36–38, 41–42, 87, 89, 104
Leibniz, 3, 82–84, 86, 171
　Leibniz's mill, 82–83, 86
Lewis, 2, 8, 22, 41, 75, 98, 99
Lichtenberg, 149
Locke, 2, 42
Lowe, 2, 42, 61, 71, 76, 92–96

Markosian, 47, 52, 58–59
McGinn, 14, 27, 30, 33, 45
Meixner, 71, 76, 93
Melnyk, 21, 24, 27, 33
mereology, 6–7
Merricks, 2, 7–9, 28–29, 74, 106, 111, 147, 161, 167, 172, 174
mind uploading, gradual vs. fast, 182, 202
Mooney, 161, 166, 168

Moreland, 12, 76, 87
Murphy, 33, 34, 161

Nāṇamoli, 116, 129, 134
Nāgārjuna, 129–130
Nida-Rümelin, 39, 80, 81
nihilism, mereological, 6–7, 111, 126, 142, 154
nonself thesis, 3, 108–158, 175–176, 186
nothing over and above, 23

occasionalism, 19
Olson, 2, 5, 6, 11, 12, 33, 37, 47, 109, 111, 150, 156, 159–161, 165–167, 171, 183, 186, 188, 191, 203, 204

Pāli Canon, 112, 113, 129
　Anattalakkhaṇa Sutta, 3
　Anattalakkhaṇa Sutta, 113, 114, 132
　Bhikkhunīsaṃyutta, 112
pancomputationalism, 197
panpsychism, 155
Parfit, 2, 42, 43, 53, 180–181
parodies, 14–15, 20–101
parsimony, 20–27, 43–44, 55–57, 139–142, 152
　nomic, 23–27
　ontological, 20–23
Pascal's wager, 213–215
Paul, L. A., 20, 55, 176, 215
Paul, the Apostle, 160
personal identity over time, theories of, 1–2
personal ontology, theories of, 2–3
"physical," definition of, 105
Plantinga, 3, 69, 71, 76, 83–87, 100
Pope Pius XII, 69, 100
Potrč, 21, 91, 111
Princess Elisabeth of Bohemia, 46
Pudgalavādins, 131

Qur'an, 160, 163, 170

reincarnation, 174–181
　evidence for, 177–178
resurrection, 160–174
Rosen, 3, 25, 126, 147, 154

Śāntarakṣita, 138
Śāntideva, 130
Schaffer, 22, 25–26, 90
Schneider, 183, 203, 204, 208, 212
Searle, 30, 33, 197
"self," definition of, 108–109
Ship of Theseus, 49–51, 82, 210
Shoemaker, 2, 3, 42, 54, 150

Sider, 3, 24, 91, 112, 126, 147, 154
Siderits, 53, 110, 112, 114, 117–119, 134–139, 148, 152
simulation argument, 189–190
Skywalker, 172
sorites argument, 205–207
Strawson, 42, 122–127, 136, 150, 157
"substance dualism," definition of, 3
substance dualism, interactionist, 19
Swinburne, 2, 3, 39, 43, 53–54, 61, 67, 69, 70, 75–76, 80–82, 100, 145, 151, 177

Taliaferro, 34, 39, 44, 61, 73–74, 76
Tertullian, 167
The Questions of King Milinda, 112, 129
thought insertion, 145
transformative experience, 215
trialism, 13
trilemma, 5, 11–13

truth
 conventional, 109–111
 ultimate, 109–111

Unger, 3, 96–98, 138, 206
Upaniṣads, 115–116, 127, 133

vagueness, 39–40, 99–100
van Inwagen, 2, 5, 6, 8, 30, 33, 37–38, 71–72, 85–86, 98, 99, 109, 111, 155–156, 161–165, 168, 169, 172, 175, 186, 203
Vasubandhu, 46, 111, 139–140, 143, 154

Walker, 44, 71, 185, 190, 206
Westerhoff, 109, 138, 150

Yang, 68, 100, 161, 162
Yoda, 172

Zimmerman, 71–72, 80, 96, 99, 100, 161, 166, 169–170

For EU product safety concerns, contact us at Calle de José Abascal, 56–1º,
28003 Madrid, Spain or eugpsr@cambridge.org.

www.ingramcontent.com/pod-product-compliance
Lightning Source LLC
LaVergne TN
LVHW020343260326
834688LV00045B/1510